DICK CAVETT AND C

ISTOPHER PORTERFIELD

HARCOURT BRACE JOVANOVICH

New York and London

To C. N. and S.

Printed in the United States of America

The lines from T. S. Eliot's *The Waste Land* are used by permission of Harcourt Brace Jovanovich, Inc. The excerpts from the article by John J. O'Connor in *The New York Times* of January 20, 1973, and from Dick Cavett's letter of reply in the issue of February 11, 1973, are copyright © 1973 by The New York Times Company and are reprinted by permission.

Library of Congress Cataloging in Publication Data

Cavett, Dick.
  Cavett.

  1. Cavett, Dick.   I. Porterfield, Christopher,
joint author.   II. Title.
PN1992.4.C33A32     791.45′092′4   [B]     74-8492
ISBN 0-15-116130-5

First edition

B C D E

# CONTENTS

For much of this book the authors have followed the format in which Dick Cavett is most at home and in which he is familiar to millions of television viewers—that of conversation. But conversation in which the tables or, rather, the chairs, are turned: with Christopher Porterfield acting as the host of a sort of talk show in prose and Cavett as the sole guest. The two sections that depart from this format—"Fitzgeraldian Fantasies" and the first part of "Inside the Monster"—were written by Porterfield, with, of course, the advice and consent of Cavett.

# PART ONE
# IDYLLIC IMAGES

CHRISTOPHER PORTERFIELD: I was with you once when you were introduced to a rather precious easterner who said, when he learned where you were from, "But surely there's no such *place* as Nebraska." The stories you've told me about growing up in Nebraska tend to evoke broad elm-shaded streets, tall old white frame houses, firm but kindly Leon Ames-type elders with big round watches in their vests, and smudge-faced, innocently prankish kids. Is there such a place? Was there ever?

DICK CAVETT: I do remember Nebraska in idyllic images. Playing guns with my friends, or kick-the-can, or ditch, watching airplanes drone overhead on lazy Sunday afternoons, collecting June bugs in a jar on summer nights, playing statues, making mud slippers. Joan Darling, the actress, once said to me, "I hate you. You're the only person I ever met who had a happy childhood." I guess I did. I know there are people who can't dredge up a single pleasant memory of their childhood, and I can come up with a hundred from mine, some of them right off a calendar or out of *Tom Sawyer:* exploring an old cave outside of town, skinny-dipping in the Platte River, lying on the bank of a lake on a lazy summer day with my friend Hugh

McKnight waiting for bullheads to bite . . . I could go on and on.

Some of the pranks were not so innocent, though. Like blowing up people's mailboxes with cherry bombs, or throwing bags of water at moving cars in the dark. The one I remember most vividly was being taken along with three older guys to light a sack of shit on an old lady's porch, and ringing the bell so she'd come out and try to stamp it out. Real Swiftian satire. One of those guys is now an oil executive in Texas, one works in a mill, and I've lost track of the other one. I heard a rumor that he works for the Mafia lighting sacks of shit on old ladies' porches.

Then there were the movies. I used to go every Saturday afternoon with my best friend, Mary Huston. Usually it was Hopalong Cassidy—and a serial. The serials were the most important thing in my life for a while. One week my parents punished me for something by not letting me go to the serial. I was stunned. It was the week we were to learn the identity of the masked Black Hangman, and I couldn't conceive how anyone could be so cruel as to make me miss it. I plotted horrible revenge against my parents, except I couldn't think of anything equally bad to do back to them. I'm still sore about it, as you can see.

Eventually I became disillusioned with the serials, when I caught on to the fact that they were cheating. Jack Armstrong would be knocked out of an airplane door at the end of one episode, and you'd see him actually falling for a few feet before they cut. Then when the next episode opened he would have caught himself by his knees! It made me furious.

Mary and I were often sat next to at these shows by lascivious old men who would put a hand on our knees. We knew enough to tell an usher or change seats, and we also knew enough *not* to tell our parents, who would have quickly ended our Saturday afternoons at the flicks. One week, when for some reason I went alone, I encountered my first full-out pervert, and I guess I mean literally full-out. I had a feeling that the man next to me was doing something nasty under the coat on his lap. Then he leaned toward me and said, "Put your hand under here and squeeze." I was embarrassed and scared, and said I didn't want to. He took my hand and held it where he wanted it. I was so humiliated that I pretended nothing was happening and tried to take a redoubled interest in the movie while working out a plan of escape. Luckily the movie was ending, and when the lights went on I shot up the aisle, ducked out the front door, and worked my way home deviously. I knew if I told *anyone* about this it would be the end of Jack Armstrong, Hoppy, and the rest of the gang.

CP: Ah, the fatal attraction you exert on homosexuals.

DC: It started early. I was getting my fanny caressed in the men's rooms of bus depots or libraries for as far back as I can remember. Forlorn and desperate-looking old sods would follow me around. Many of them were exhibitionists. Reminds me of the line in Nabokov's *Pale Fire* about the old college porter who one day "showed a squeamish coed something of which she had no doubt seen better samples." I remember using some boyhood version of "knock it off" at about age seven to an old goat who offered me candy corn in the movie-theater john. There was quite an incongruity in our voices. His was high and mine was deep, even as a small child. He said, "Don't you have a big voice for such a little thing?" I should have said, "Don't you have a big thing for such a little voice?" and really floored him, but I hadn't yet been influenced by Groucho Marx and didn't think of it.

CP: Your childhood is sounding less and less idyllic.

DC: Well, I'll try to shift to more pleasant things, like World War II. Really—I remember it clearly. Mary and I used to scratch Hitler's face in the dirt and chalk it on the sidewalk, then stomp on it. I remember ration stickers on windshields, war-stamp booths at school, the jaunty voice on the radio identifying itself as Bob "Fourth War Loan" Hope, and, best of all, the German prison camp in Grand Island, which was my home at that time. The town, I mean, not the prison camp.

The camp was actually an old brick schoolhouse right in the middle of town—of German architecture, ironically; a lot of the original settlers of Grand Island had been *Deutscher*. The prisoners seemed to have been stamped from a pattern. They were all tall and enormously handsome, and, as I recall, they were even all blond. They were from an elite troop of some kind that had been captured at the Battle of the Bulge, and they really looked like pure Aryan supermen, which presumably they were. They built their own camp, driving stakes and putting up barbed wire, and they worked on local farms, all under the supervision of armed American guards who were noticeably inferior to them physically. At night they were allowed to sit in the windows of the schoolhouse, drink beer, and sing lieder like *"Du Liegst Mir im Herzen."* A lot of the local people resented that. They said, "You can imagine how they're treating *our* guys." A hell of a lot of the prisoners didn't go back after the war. They married local girls and are still there. Only now they're singing American songs on Saturday nights. "Don't Fence Me In," perhaps.

To me there was a feeling of awe and romance about it all. Here were the same Germans I was seeing in the movies, two blocks away! Still, I envied some relatives of ours on the West Coast because they had actually seen the flames of a Japanese plane that was shot down over the Pacific. I assumed that the war was a constant condition and that I and everyone around me would eventually grow up and go off to fight on Iwo Jima. Sometimes I fantasized Grand Island being occupied by the enemy and me sniping at them from a tree with my father's twenty-two. Or I imagined working for the underground, which I pictured as a network of tunnels, literally underground. There were a few gaps in my knowledge, then as now.

CP: Do you realize that we're the last generation that can remember World War II—"the war" to us? People just five years younger than we are don't even know what a victory garden was.

DC: Listen, a kid *one* year behind me in high school once asked me whether Pearl Harbor was World War I or II. I was five when Pearl Harbor was bombed. When I started hosting talk shows I made a mental note to myself that if the talk ever came to a halt and the guests were over thirty I would ask, "Where were you when Pearl Harbor was bombed?"

CP: Surely the talk did come to a halt a few times?

DC: Yes, but I panicked and forgot what it was I was supposed to remember. Anyway, Pearl Harbor was Sunday afternoon, and Mary and I were playing in the back yard. Someone called us inside and said, "You'd better hear this, and someday you'll understand it." Something extremely solemn was being said on the radio, and we knew from the attitude of the adults that it was important. I asked what was happening, and my mother said, "The Japs have gotten us into the war." Maybe because my parents were teachers, I remember someone saying, prophetically, "The kids who are in high school right now are going to get the worst of this."

I asked my father if he would have to go, and I was kind of hurt that he wanted to. I had no idea what the war was about, or if it was being fought in America or somewhere else. I was immediately attracted to it. I loved the war movies, loved to play "Germans and Japs," and wanted a Luger pistol and samurai sword more than anything. The enemy or enemies had peculiar attractions for me. The Germans had better-looking uniforms, better-looking arms, and were much more glamorous than the gung-ho Yanks, who struck me as somewhat silly. And the Japanese had some sort of esthetic appeal for me that was deep and lasting. I got every book on Japan from the library. (I was constantly being told that I had wandered into the adult part of the library and that "the little folks' room" was downstairs. I would furiously explain that I didn't like the little folks' books, or little folks, for that matter, and that I had a special arrangement allowing me to check out adult books on my parents' card.)

I remember blackouts, which I thought were great fun, and my father being an air-raid warden, which pleased me. I also remember the tasteful propaganda posters that began to appear, showing Japanese with rat bodies and fangs crawling out of a sewer to infest the globe. The lurid posters showing a dead GI with his brains blown out and the caption "Somebody Talked!" The "Don't Discuss Troop Movements! They May Not Get There!" posters made me suspicious of everybody who looked strange. I had fantasies of being whisked into a house on the way home from school and being forced to discuss troop movements, then having to fight my way out.

It was a while before I could sort out the fact that my grandmother and her relatives were German, which in turn meant that I was part enemy. Once I saw my grandmother and her sister weeping bitterly over the news of the bombing of Aachen, where they had relatives, and wailing, "That beautiful city!" My aunt Hedwig's husband, Robert, shot himself dead when the war began going disastrously for Germany. (He was also ill.) He had served under the Kaiser, and I'd been told that he had gotten his house in Grand Island splashed with yellow paint for making injudicious remarks about his sympathies within earshot of some patriotic Grand Islanders.

Everybody in our neighborhood had a victory garden. Once a cop came to our door to complain that our dog was off its leash and running through people's victory gardens, and he implied that this was not only illegal, but unpatriotic as well. My father admitted the illegality, but told the cop that they were even on the unpatriotic part: the cop, in parking his car out front, had come slightly over the curb, and one of his wheels was resting in *our* victory garden. The funniest part—assuming that any of this is funny—is that the blushing cop's name was Officer Crapp. My father, with a very badly concealed smirk, said, "I promise to do better, Officer Crapp."

I know that sounds like something from an application form to the Famous Writers School, but it's a true story. My conversation sometimes sounds so much like something you'd make up that it scares me.

CP: How does Nebraska look nowadays when you revisit it?

DC: The elm-shaded streets and the Leon Ameses are still there in many places, although my old block in Grand Island is now mostly a parking lot. The first time I went back there I turned the corner breathlessly, expecting to see the old playhouse, swing on the old swing, and so on, and suddenly everything was out of proportion. There was all this asphalt, and a big supermarket. It was like seeing the aftermath of a bombing. I felt that they'd wiped out my past without asking my permission.

The people out there still feel they're leading a healthy, wholesome life, and every once in a while a hideous murder shatters the illusion.

I wonder whether anybody has ever done a study of midwestern murders—something that goes beyond a book like Truman Capote's *In Cold Blood*, fine as that was. Either midwestern murders are more hideous than those in other regions or else they just seem so because of the contrast between them and the homey atmosphere of the little towns where they happen. Charlie Starkweather, the guy who went on a killing spree with his girl friend in the late fifties, was my family's garbage man in Lincoln. My father, who has always attracted forlorn types that feel overlooked by everybody else, passed the time of day with him a few times. And, as in so many of these cases, there didn't seem to be anything peculiar or ominous about him at all.

The disturbing element that all these crimes seem to have in common is the murderer's desire to "be somebody"—or, in the words of the girl who shot Eddie Waitkus, the baseball player, "to be in the limelight." What a crushing disappointment these poor devils must feel after the first rush of celebrity subsides, when the limelight turns out to feel no different from the garage light or the refrigerator light. It's sad. There is a premium in the Midwest on "going places," rising above the folks at home, making a splash in the Big Pond, that seems to make some people commit murders and prompts others to go into show business—to make a killing, as it were.

Another frequently quoted comment from the guy who suddenly drives across the state shooting innocent hitchhikers or killing gas-station attendants is "I got tired of being pushed around." If being pushed around is an incitement to murder, it seems odd that there aren't ten thousand homicides a day in the city of New York alone, considering that it is possible for someone to feel pushed around in, say, Central City, Nebraska. But then, maybe an overdose of tranquillity can trigger violent passion—a desire to shatter the numbing sameness of a life in which "nothing happens." In *Old Jules* Mari Sandoz talks about the homesteaders out in the sand hills who would succumb to despair during the winter and kill themselves and/or someone else in the family out of what seemed no more than a profound boredom. In one remote county of Nebraska, the mothers of two out of the five families who lived there hanged themselves and their children in a single winter, leaving notes to their husbands saying that they just couldn't take it any more.

CP: But is it entirely an illusion, that healthy, wholesome midwestern life? Many people who see you on television feel that beneath the varnish of Yale and show biz there is some kind of sturdy midwestern grain. What is that, exactly?

DC: Varicose grain, I guess. Seriously, folks, down deep I think I do have a prejudice in favor of the Midwest, murders notwithstanding. It's sort of the norm from which you depart when you experience the world. It's closer to nature. Is this too profound?

CP: Not so far.

DC: Thanks. I needed that. I do think you're better off if

you start life more simply, without all the complexities of the big city, the East, the urban jumble, and all that. Getting used to being alive is hard enough when you're young, but having to do it in the jangling, nerve-racking metropolis can't be good for you. Just look at your typical midwesterners: me, Marlon Brando, Orson Welles, T. S. Eliot . . .

CP: Tell me, how *did* you get used to being alive?

DC: I never have. I could easily be convinced that life is a dream, or at least that mine is. My mind still wanders so easily that it can take me a month to read a book, and I constantly have to remind myself what it is I do that causes people to recognize me on the street. That's strange, and when I was a kid this strangeness took the form of my feeling that I was different from the other kids. Not only that, I felt that *they* knew I was different. I was aware, for example, that I talked differently. Without trying to, I talked more like an adult. They sounded their age, and I sounded like the fine print in an insurance policy.

CP: Was this because you were smarter than they were? Or did you feel chosen, in some non-Jewish sense? Was it your shortness that set you apart? Select the best answer and briefly state your reasons. Take your time, and good luck.

DC: I did feel smarter than the other kids, because teachers tactlessly announced in front of everybody that I was, with the result that I nearly needed a bodyguard to get home safely.

CP: You were beaten up?

DC: Several times. Once a guy named Gordon Fink told me he was going to beat me up someday after school—this was second grade, I think—and just about the time that I had forgotten the threat, he did. At that time I used to react half-passively. I remember thinking, "Here we are rolling around in the leaves and dirt, and I'm getting beaten up, and, like going to the dentist, it'll be over after a while and I'll go home."

It seemed pointless to fight back, because if I really hit the guy he might get mad and beat me up even longer. My formula was to resist without actually fighting, submit to getting pinned and go home. I don't recall any fear of being hurt; just embarrassment about the whole thing.

Another nemesis of mine was an older bully named Elton Louis, but I had my revenge on him. A call went out at school for information leading to the vandal who had broken about thirty windows in the school building one weekend. Even though I had no idea who had done it, I went to the principal and fingered Elton Louis, making up various details of the crime. It turned out Elton *was* the one. To this day he has no idea how he was found out. If he reads this, I may get the air let out of my bicycle tires, unless he's gone on to bigger things.

CP: What else made you feel different?

DC: My shortness, which played a major part in my development—or lack of it. I suppose that during the first few years of school I was about five inches shorter than the next shortest student in my class. Later, during high school, I shot up to my present height of five feet, six and three-quarters inches. But in earlier years my size was a terrible problem. I tried to talk my parents into letting a plastic surgeon give me permanent five-inch heels, but they scoffed.

CP: Could I just take another look at those heels of yours?

DC: Keep your hands to yourself, big boy.
My shortness plus an extraordinarily deep voice made me a kind of droll gnome fitting no known category. I was born virtually sounding like an adult. When I was still being carried in my mother's arms a conductor on a train asked her, "And how old is the baby?" The baby astonished everybody by booming out, "He will be two in November." I soon got so sick of old folks bending over me with their sulphurous breath and saying "How did such a little fellow get such a big voice?" that I considered carrying a tiny Luger. I developed the strange feel-

ing that I had someone else inside me, that the voice was not my own, but some adult's—my father's, perhaps. It made me feel self-conscious as well as mysteriously possessed.

CP: It did have its advantages, though?

DC: It always got me attention. Whenever I asked a question from the back of a room everyone would turn around. Years later, when there was a celebrity I wanted to meet, my voice usually got me to him. Someone famous could be stepping out of a car, and I and four other people could all ask him a question at the same time, yet he would always come to me. My voice made me sound serious, intelligent, and concerned, which shows you how deceptive it was.

Once it saved my neck. One night, raising hell on the way home from a party, a group of us threw empty Coke bottles through a glass panel in some old folks' front door. We ran, but we must have been recognized, because the next day we were summoned to the police station. We were questioned separately, then sent home. Most of us suspected, but didn't know for sure, that one of us had squealed, and I for one was panic-stricken. The dread of a scandal, with my parents being school-teachers, images of the penitentiary, all that. For two nights I couldn't sleep a wink. I recognized that feeling years later when I had the reaction most people get from reading *Crime and Punishment:* all my own guilty secrets boiled up in my mind. Finally I had an inspiration. I remembered that people constantly took me for an adult over the phone. With my heart in my mouth, I called the police investigator, identified myself as the father of one of the guilty boys, and said that my son had confessed. My master stroke was congratulating the cop on his brilliant job of handling the whole affair, especially letting the boys stew the way he did, and telling him I was sure their guilt had taught them a far better lesson than simply arresting them would have done. I was laying it on with a garden implement. I made the call from a Walgreen's phone booth, and I remember wondering if the police were surrounding it even as

I talked. But it worked, and the cop on the line soaked up my compliments like a sponge. He thought he had talked to a man of forty-five. If only he could have seen this kid walking out of the booth, twelve years old, five foot three, in a sweat-soaked T-shirt! Later, the other guys and I scraped together about twenty dollars in cash and put it in the victims' mailbox by dark of night. I hope the statute of limitations has run out on this.

CP: Were you a good boy in school? Too good?

DC: My old report cards show two things. One is that throughout grade school, teachers were always appending the note "Dick does not work up to his ability." Since I got very good grades without working up to my ability, I could never see why I should. The other thing is that I was frequently reprimanded for "inability to control talking" or "visiting with others." This is about as seriously as I misbehaved ninety per cent of the time. But there were odd, intermittent outbursts of rebellion, when I would take on a teacher. In third grade we came to a story about kite-flying in Japan, which I'd been looking ahead at and forward to because I was going through a period of Nippophilia, despite the fact that we were then at war with Japan. When the teacher said, "I don't think we want to read a story about the Japanese; I'm certainly not fond of them," I was outraged. I steamed about it overnight, and the next day raised my hand and announced, "I've been thinking about your decision to skip the story about Japan, and think it's shortsighted of you to impose your prejudices on us." That's actually the way I talked then. The teacher was thunderstruck and asked the class to discuss the matter, or, rather, to second her own feeling, which all the finks in the class did. A few people congratulated me at recess, but I remember thinking I should have gotten more credit than I did.

A year or so later, a teacher who frequently used the expression "stubborn as a German" went too far and said "sneaky as an Indian." I loved Indians, and I erupted again. This time I said (I remember the exact words again), "I think our parents might be interested in knowing that you use class time to foist your racial prejudices on us." She nearly shat. This too resulted in a discussion, in which *all* the girls defended the teacher but several boys took my side. I was beginning to build a constituency.

Where my obsession with tolerance came from at such a tender age I'm not sure. It felt genuine, but I'm also aware of an element of wanting to pick a fight with authority and seeing an opening to do so. The same teacher, the "sneaky as an Indian" one, once brought the whole class in early from recess because of something I had done (the killing-of-hostages technique) and gave a speech about how a rat in a cargo has to be smoked out and eliminated. I can still feel the mixture of humiliation and rage with which I, the rat, sat through all this. And the contrast between these episodes and my general "good citizen" deportment in elementary school still puzzles me.

Sometimes I think some of the teachers must have been nuts. There was a terribly retarded girl named Mary Ann in my first or second-grade class—feeble-minded was the common phrase then—and one day she "soiled herself"—as the euphemism goes—while sitting at her desk. The teacher, apparently at a total loss, sent her home, then had one of the more fractious boys clean up the mess, accusing him of having made it *with crayons!*

I have two other recollections of Mary Ann. One is of her crying after some of the other kids had pasted bits of construction paper over the lenses of her glasses, and of the general amusement in the class as she went stumbling over things to the teacher. The other is of a mob clustered and yelling at recess, and in the middle of it Mary Ann getting kicked and pushed until the teacher broke it up. I'm appalled to confess that I was part of that mob and felt caught up in a strange sense of exhilaration. I suppose a psychologist would explain it as stemming from the primitive experience of the kill by the dominant group, the tribe. I don't remember any lecture or reprimand from the teacher, or any tears of shame from us. Just the viciousness of the attack. And I can still see Mary Ann's thick full-length stockings, which helped make her a figure of scorn.

A couple of years ago I visited Dachau, and as I walked around looking at the barbed wire and the ovens and having the now too usual reaction, "How could human beings . . . ?," I thought of Mary Ann. After all, British imperialists used to boast that their battles were won and lost on the playing fields of Eton. I think it's just as possible that concentration camps could be prefigured in playground cruelties like ours.

CP: A lady I know was rather surprised to read somewhere that you had spent a substantial sum of money to fix up your parents' house in Lincoln. She thought you might have been the sort of person who would leave his parents to fend for themselves.

DC: The fact is, I haven't fixed up my parents' house. I think the lady must have me confused with Muhammad Ali. My parents know that any time they want their house fixed up they can always enter into negotiations with my lawyer.

CP: I mention this because it illustrates something I'm sure you're aware of, that some people do get an impression of coldness from you. They find you both aloof and elusive. Are you hiding something?

DC: What goddam business is it of yours? Excuse me, I don't know what came over me. Hand me those salts, will you, while I fan myself?

Actually, so far as I know, I came with the full spectrum of emotions a person is supposed to be born with. I'm not aware of any benumbed areas of feeling. I'm as sentimental as the next person. I can be moved by the cruddiest sentimental junk. It has to be above the cold-cash, calculated-masturbation-of-the-tear-ducts level of a Walter Keane painting, but not much. I don't think a good cry hurts you, but it's better if it also involves the brain, if you learn something from it that you didn't know before.

cp: But irony, which is your natural mode, is, among other things, a way of skirting emotion, even emotion you may feel very deeply. Would you say that you tend to shrink at least from the *expression* of naked feeling?

dc: I suppose I do, but it depends on the circumstances and who I'm with. There are people around whom I'm totally undemonstrative, protective of my inner self, and all that; and then there are others who say they're surprised at how open I am—to them I spill my guts. Since I've become a celebrity, and therefore have had the benefit of seeing myself criticized in the public print, I've thought about this a little. Once a magazine article quoted an anonymous ABC publicity man as saying I was "a cold fish." It bothered me at first, but then I decided, why worry about it? I don't feel like a cold fish, and I'd hate to develop a sense that I have to convince every jackass I meet that I'm not. I would be interested in knowing who the publicity man was, so I could try to recall how I behaved around him that gave him this impression. There is one guy at ABC who resembles a fish, and I was probably trying to make him feel at home.

At a party recently, I realized suddenly that I had no idea what the person talking to me was saying. But my exterior self was indicating all the proper responses, and I was even making all the conventional interjections—"And then what?," and so on. I hadn't the slightest idea what was going on. There are certain people you meet—the majority, I think would be a safe estimate —who indicate in their first six words to you a total picture of their being, and you know instantly that this person is incapable of interesting you, ever, at any time, on any subject. And others who give off such rich signals quickly and surely that you kind of fall into their personality, as 'twere, and there isn't enough time for both of you to get in all the things you want to say.

cp: This protection of your inner self, as you call it, must have been conditioned to some extent by the merciless over-exposure of nightly TV shows.

DC: On the air, I've been very moved by certain things people have said to me during the show. When I watch the tape later, though, I see that I not only conceal it completely, but when I say "We'll be back in a minute" I look as if I hadn't even been listening. I do resist moments when I know I could score points as a good, warm soul by mouthing the kind of banality I have heard others make use of on the tube. Part of this, in other words, is merely a loathing of the kind of phony emotion so common on TV. But I can't deny that part of it is more deep-seated, and inaccessible to explanation.

CP: Let's talk about that part for a moment. Do you think it goes back somehow to the death of your mother—that the reaction to that pain caused a toughness to form, like scar tissue over a wound?

DC: I don't think I have ever recovered completely from my mother's death. She died of cancer when I was ten, and I still can't talk about it easily. I was in fifth grade at the time, and having a dying mother was, aside from the sadness, an acute embarrassment to me. It sounds strange to say that, I know, but any kid who has been through it at such an age would know what I mean. Or would he? Some kids might enjoy the added attention, I suppose, but it killed me. I had the bad luck to be the only kid in my class, or that I had ever heard of, it seemed, who had such a thing happen to him, and it was excruciating. I already felt conspicuous because of my voice and my shortness and the loathsome fact that I was considered a "brain," and this added burden of sympathy was just too much.

For me it was doubly hard because, unlike most kids, I couldn't get through the dying part without everybody in school knowing about it. Because the teachers knew my parents, solicitous inquiries were everywhere and everybody knew. My mother had been a very popular teacher in junior high school, and I remember asking my father what I could possibly say when the junior high kids I met walking home from school asked how she was. The true answer was "She's dying," but this was out of the question. My father suggested "About the same." It usually got the reply "That's good."

Maudlin sympathy angered and somehow shamed me, and whenever I overheard phrases like "poor little tyke" from supposedly well-meaning grownups I wished them incinerated on the spot. Then there were the well-meaning morons who would say, "Don't worry, it'll probably turn out to be just a problem coming from a bad wisdom tooth or an allergy of some sort," and I would conjure up a particularly hot corner of hell for them to roast in.

Some friends of ours, the Belknaps, whose son Rowan was in my class, would sometimes waylay me after school and suggest I come over to their house to play and have supper. I never let on that I knew this meant my mother was going through a particularly bad day at home, which probably included screaming with pain, and that they had been enlisted to keep me away. It was a charitable deception, and they did it as well as anyone could, but I think they knew I knew.

It wasn't until years later that it occurred to me what it must have been like for my father, who somehow maintained a full teaching schedule except on the worst days (although he lost about forty pounds) and saw that I was gotten through it all as well as possible. He had sweated out the earlier time, after my mother's first and only partly successful operation, when the doctors told him that sometime in the next few years the disease would undoubtedly strike again.

After my mother's death Dorcas Crawford, a next-door neighbor and a schoolteacher who'd been a good friend of ours, often took care of me. Dorcas became my stepmother when my father remarried about a year later. I now realize I went through a period of thinking he was an unfaithful swine to do such a thing. Dorcas, an incredibly accomplished and remarkable woman, who had my best interests at heart, put up with untold crap from me. I found "stepmother" hard to say in introductions, I suppose because of the stigma attached to the word in fairy tales and fiction, and I couldn't introduce Dorcas as my mother because she wasn't and to say it would have made me feel somehow unfaithful. With all the tension from this, I made life miserable for everybody concerned.

I'm sure all this affected me in a profound way, and I'd love to be able to get a look inside my psyche and see just how much damage was done. I think it accounts for my unconquerable streak of pessimism, odd in one who otherwise generally enjoys life. I am always sure that an Olivier or a Welles won't show up for the taping, that the lead actor will be sick the night I go to the performance, that the restaurant will be closed, and that all things I might be so foolish as to pin my hopes on won't work out. I suppose it's an obvious defense mechanism against my again being caught by surprise, as I was so totally and vulnerably at the age of ten.

CP: Do you have a favorite memento of your mother?

DC: For several years after I was born she kept a series of clothbound journals called "Scribble-In Books." I knew these books existed, but for a long time couldn't bring myself to read them. Finally I asked my father for them. Most of the entries are little observations of my behavior. Reading them over, I get a double *frisson* from seeing myself through her eyes and, in effect, hearing her voice again.

Here are a few typical jottings.

AT FOUR MONTHS: *Laughed out loud. Has developed recently a great aptitude for showing off . . . rears out chest and snorts then awaits laughs. . . . Shows disappointment if the proper appreciation isn't shown.*

AT EIGHTEEN MONTHS: *Talks in paragraphs rather than sentences. . . . Plays with a Jim Cavett; product of imagination. I hope nothing prophetic. Recites nursery rhymes:*

> *I am a little boy, not very big.*
> *My father's such a bore, I could have been a pig.*

*Profanity is very evident at times. Where the devil do you suppose he gets it?*

AT TWO AND A HALF: *In my bath—giggled until he could scarcely speak pointing out part of my anatomy and stammering, "That's what Dadda calls a titty."*

AT THREE: *Dick has a "wailing chair" wedged between the bookcase and the radio. He retreats there when pressure becomes great against his wishes. Since Christmas candy has been a major issue in this household I can't help ruing the day I ever started sanctioning it for Dick. His apparently unusual intelligence seems to be no assurance against overindulgence. It never seems to work that way. It takes a rustic I guess to be sane in living habits. Do you suppose it is lack of opportunity only that keeps us from harmful vices? Perhaps criminals are not after all so different, but only lack that fear of consequence which makes renunciators of us.*

AT THREE: *Dick asked, "Where are you before you are born?" Insisted with tears that he had to be someplace before we were married.*

AT THREE: *Dick: "Do you know who knows who made God?"*
*"No I don't, Dick."*
*Dick: "Nobody does but God."*

AT THREE: *We had quite a "bug" drama. In the process of cutting papers, Dick completely annihilated a box-elder bug. Remorse hit him so forcibly that he was unable to control himself in telling of his crime. An uneasy pillow was his when he tried to sleep.*

AT FOUR: *Moved to Grand Island and, evincing an innate belief in predestination, on being told he probably wouldn't have known his new friend Mary Huston if we had taken the Abbott apt. asserted, "I would have known Mary wherever I had lived."*
*Couldn't get his conscience in line for a nap because he had pushed Mary. "My head won't let me sleep because I pushed Mary. But I had to do it."*

AT FIVE: *In Dick's falling out of the back of the car I have become more and more aware of my inadequacies. I could borrow his own phrase picked up in his rapid-moving mind heaven knows where,*

*"My golly a hundred, what to do now?" It takes a jolt like that every so often to make me aware of the fact that I'm living my life now . . . and what fun and pleasure we are going to have together has to be packed in to the days that are.*

CP: Many of the people you've mentioned so far could have been created by W. C. Fields's scriptwriters—Officer Crapp, Gordon Fink, and so on—and you seem to relish the sound of their names. What others stick in your memory?

DC: Noddy Snigg is almost my favorite. I think his real first name was Norris, and no kid wants to be called that, obviously, but when your last name is Snigg there's no good way out. I was baby-sat with in Grand Island by a girl named Betty Mae Whore. She was the youngest of the Locust Street Whores, I don't know how they managed to get through life. The very tight-sweatered—and to good advantage—leading lady in one of our high school plays was a girl named Bobbi Tease. There was also an Outhouse family in our neighborhood, but I believe they pronounced it O'Thoosey.

CP: Now wait a minute.

DC: I'm not making this up. I also have, and this will test the elasticity of your credulity, some sort of distant second aunt who was born Edna Picton and married a man named Ralph Appaloff. Hence, Edna Picton Appaloff.

CP: Sherwood Anderson was right. The strictures of convention in a small midwestern town must not only mask but also in some cases actually produce a reactionary streak of the bizarre and grotesque, a substratum of wild fantasy.

DC: Hey, you talk good.

CP: Thanks. I needed that.

DC: Most of my fantasies, and I don't know what strictures caused them (perhaps too tight clothing), were produced by tales my little friends told of older girls who lured them into garages and, amidst the smell of old tires and crankcase oil, introduced them to visual and tactile treats of a mind-blowing nature.

CP: You once told me that when you were still a tyke you and a girl friend went into a playhouse in her back yard and, playing doctor or whatever, took your clothes off. But then she called for help. Would you say that episode was your introduction to the allure and perfidy of women?

DC: We weren't both naked; only she was. And that fact makes her ultimate treachery even more astounding. It was Mary Huston again. I remember that May Day was coming, and I kept promising her more May baskets if she would just take off one more item of apparel. Just what at the age of five I intended to do when she got them off, I don't know. But we never found out, because just as I ran out of hypothetical May baskets and Mary of clothes her mother happened into the yard. We would have been okay, but to my horror Mary stuck her head out the window and yelled, "Mom, Dick made me take all my clothes off!" Mary was dragged into the house and spanked, and I was sent home bearing a heavy burden of shame at my overdeveloped lust. After that I preserved my precocious sexual alacrity and determined to lay waste at least a half acre of corn-fed virgins before the advent of my eleventh year. But I still get a slight jolt of guilt whenever I see Mrs. Huston.

CP: Did you forgive Mary?

DC: I had to because—isn't life strange?—she later saved my life. Her parents had taken us swimming at the lake outside Grand Island, even though I couldn't swim at the time, only splash around. It was dusk and there was nobody else around. Mary and I were resting on the barrel that marked the boundary of the shallow area. For some reason I forgot which way I was facing and stepped into the deep side. I remember feeling the water close over my head, touching bottom, bouncing back to the surface, and realizing as I went under again that I was going to drown. In my mind's eye I saw an article in the paper about my death, with my parents reading it. As I was sinking for the second time Mary grabbed my arm and managed to pull me out. We sat there for a moment, stunned, and agreed that, like our experiences with the lechers in the movie theater, we'd better not tell this one or we'd have swimming privileges revoked. For several years I felt that any additional life lived after that moment was a bonus.

CP: What's your earliest sexual memory, if it isn't too personal?

DC: Nonsense—how could a person's sex life be personal? My earliest memory has to do with a pole that supported a kind of grape arbor in Mary's back yard. It was slightly slippery and therefore hard to climb, and I discovered that climbing to the top and holding tightly with my hands and loosely with my legs gave me a curiously gratifying sensation in the crotch. That pole is gone now, but I spent a lot of time on it, and I suppose if I could ever find it again it would be a rather sentimental reunion.

I remember identifying that mysterious feeling as an intensified version of the sensation I got when an older girl named Patty would hang by her knees from a bar, letting her dress come down over her head, and would say accusingly, "Get your eyes full!"

At Yale I took a psychology course called "Development of Personality," a shorthand for its official title, "Studies in Freudian Psychosexual Development." Curious things would float up in the memories of the students when we got into the subject of prepubescent sexual activity, the concept that practically got Freud Braunschweigered-and-feathered and ridden out of Vienna on a six-foot knackwurst. After reading case histories of children seduced by their nurses or parents, guys would remember bizarre episodes in their own lives that had been neatly repressed. One guy, writing a term paper for extra credit, got his mother to talk and discovered he had been so ardent a masturbator in the crib that he was forced to have his hands tied. That shook him up a bit. I didn't have really bizarre stuff to recall, but I found that I *could* remember being circumcised—the act itself, and the pain and the embarrassment, and being told it was good for me.

CP: How old were you?

DC: Eighteen. No, actually about six months, I guess. It should have been a preconscious experience, but somehow it has all come back with crystal clarity—I swear it. Produce a pair of scissors suddenly, and I jump.

CP: Returning to puberty, what did you go on to after your slippery pole?

DC: No particularly erotic adventures, unfortunately. As an adolescent I used to go to the movies with some guys who, when the movie got boring, would move to the back row and, to use the scientific term, jerk off. I was invited to join them, but declined, not because I exemplified a superior morality, but because, once again, my parents were schoolteachers, and I always felt that it would be twice as bad for me if I ever got caught at anything. Someone had used on me the horrible phrase "You have a reputation to uphold" to good effect.

Of course there was always Tom Craig and the vacuum cleaner. Tom and I were goofing around one day all alone in his house. We convulsed each other for a while by using the vacuum cleaner—a tank type, with a long tube and hose—to suck Kleenex out of each other's hands just as the one holding the Kleenex pretended to blow his nose. Then, when the Kleenex was all gone, Tom got a look of quizzical inspiration and announced, "I'm going to stick my dinkie in it." Tom, whose organ, incidentally, was the envy of our whole seventh-grade gym class, suited the action to the word. He turned the switch, there was a sudden sucking and jamming sound, the machine fell silent, and Tom, extricating himself therefrom, uncontrollably peed all over the living-room carpet. I sank to the floor, the dry part, helpless with laughter. The thought of how he was going to explain a peed-on carpet *and* a busted vacuum cleaner set me off again and again. I remember thinking that, of all the things our parents might have been afraid we were doing at that moment, that was probably not one of them.

CP: Aside from these substitutes, it was all fantasy, then? With real girls you were actually quite shy when you didn't have May baskets at your disposal?

DC: Paralyzed is more like it. I had absolutely no confidence with them; I blushed, felt my throat constrict, and sweated. I was the only person who ever went to the Arthur Murray dancing school who had to do book reports to graduate. That's a joke, but not far off.

My dancing could best be described as "workmanlike." I loathed dancing, or, rather, my inability to master it, which is odd, because I not only am athletically co-ordinated, but have a decent musical ear. But some internal cords of inhibition would tighten when I danced. The phrases designed to aid ("step, close, step") and the footprints glued to the floor all failed for me, partly because I could never find a physical relationship to my partner that worked. Arm's-length dancing seemed to require conversation, which caused me to lose count, and dancing close gave me an erection, which caused me and my partner to talk simultaneously, pretending not to notice. At those moments, the combined sensation of pleasure and acute embarrassment was almost too much. If I had ever chanced upon a partner who referred to the obtrusive phenomenon with a cool "Well-l-l" I would have fainted on the spot.

I'll never forget the first party I went to where I had to dance. June Stefanisin, my date, in a kind of feminine gallantry, would excuse *her*self when I lost count and stepped on her feet. My first dance of the evening traumatized me because in placing my hand on her back I could feel through her dress what I took to be the elastic on her drawers and my hand froze there, in embarrassment. Removing it would be an admission I had felt it, and leaving it there would indicate more lechery than I felt equal to. I hoped the earth would open, which it seldom does when you want it to.

When I was about ten I used to mail presents—things like boxes of candy—to girls I liked but didn't have the nerve to talk to. I also didn't have the nerve to put my name on the presents. I thought I'd reveal myself later as the anonymous donor, but I remained anonymous. This was both financially draining and emotionally unsatisfying, and led to my joining the cub scouts.

Later, the thought of an upcoming dance or sock hop was absolute agony. I knew I'd never get a date. There seemed to be only this limited number of girls I could and should be seen with, and they were all taken up by the jocks. I once tried to import one from out of town, an old girl friend from second grade. She was flattered at being invited to the metropolis of Lincoln for a weekend, but crapped out at the last minute. I had the horrific experience of appearing dateless at a major function, explaining to everyone I saw that I *had* had a date but that she had gotten sick. I probably offered to show them the long-distance phone bills to prove it.

Barbara Britten (not the actress) was the girl I wanted most of all, and the closest I ever got to her was on a double date where she was the other guy's date. We went to a high school play, and I remember sitting through the third act with a throbbing erection because my elbow was touching Barbara's. Wonderful how far a little physical contact went in those earliest postpubescent years. If she had secretly taken my hand in hers I would have exploded in a sheet of flame.

The only thing I'm proud of in this whole area is that I went to one prom with a girl who had a bad name. She was a very cute, sweet girl, but she had suffered at the hands of the gossips. At first this made me wonder whether I should reconsider my invitation—Jesus! Then I began to enjoy the hint of naughtiness. On the big night a certain number of the smart set I had always aspired to were openly appalled that I was out with this creature of shadowed reputation. Afterward we went to a dark restaurant by ourselves. After an hour or so I made a move to check the time, and she reached over to cover my watch with her hand, saying, "I don't want you to know what time it is." I said, "Why?" and she said, "Because being with you is the best thing that's ever happened to me." I melted.

CP: Where is she now?

DC: I don't know. I wish I could call her up.

CP: You're making yourself sound so forlorn. I thought you were one of the popular kids.

DC: I was, but in a peculiar way. I was elected to everything—I once won a student-council election by the highest number of votes ever—but I didn't have a lot of close friends and never seemed to be in the swing of things socially. I never quite stuck with *the* group, the big wheels, the jocks. On the other hand, I disdained the group that wanted me, on the ground that they were somehow beneath me. I was guilty of disgusting snobbery in that regard. I had neighborhood friends I used to bum around with, playing kick-the-can, fishing, prowling, and window peeking after dark. But when I encountered them in the halls at school I was vaguely embarrassed and barely acknowledged them, as if we were not on the same social level *publicly*. As a result, I was stranded betwixt the groups and ended up at home alone dreaming of a glass slipper for my little foot. Is this too heavy? Am I exaggerating? Does God love us?

CP: You even held some state-wide office in student council.

DC: President, no less. When I think of that I have to guffaw. It was one of several roles I was able to play easily, without the slightest conviction or interest. I didn't give a hoot in hell about student government, and realized that it was the aura of undefined intelligence I gave off, combined with my mature-sounding voice and my ability to make humorous self-nominating speeches, that got me elected.

CP: It sounds as though you developed an early distrust of politics.

DC: I just saw how easy it was for a totally uncommitted "personality" to give off an air of some kind that gets votes. After all the time I spent in student councildom, I don't remember what any of it was about. I only remember words like "goal" and "fulfillment" and phrases like "bridges of understanding." I spent most of my time with my jaws cramping from the constant pressure to contain a yawn, keeping myself awake mainly by trying to imagine what the girl reading the dreary report on a study of a survey would look like with her clothes off. I was just playing the game.

CP: And still envying the jocks who had the girls.

DC: I was at such a disadvantage vis-à-vis the jocks, since most of my early playmates had been girls and I had never learned any of the games that boys played. When we moved to Lincoln I remember going out to recess for something called baseball. They told me to play shortstop, and I thought they said "short stock." It was awful. Also, my size was against me, especially on the black day when I first had to play basketball. I dodged and darted around trying to look as though I were playing very hard, all the time dreading the moment when someone might throw the ball to me. I wasn't afraid of dropping it, but of not knowing what to do with it.

cp: Didn't you overhear your father saying he hoped you'd letter in something, and weren't you afraid it would have to be in debating? Yet you did acquire prowess in gymnastics.

dc: Two gold medals as state champion, which astonished my father, I think, and convinced me that, despite all those years of regarding myself as a nonathlete, I was potentially a better athlete than the guys I'd been in awe of.

This will make you laugh, but there are times now when I wish I had been an athlete or gone into some kind of outdoor life, like forest ranging. Some part of me has a voracious appetite for exercise and open spaces. I'm happy as a clam when I'm on a pack trip, diving and snorkeling, climbing, hiking. I think I still have a compulsion to prove that I can do all these athletic things, to make up for all the years I felt an inferiority about them. On my television show I've always found some excuse to throw a guest who was a wrestler, or get on the high bar with an acrobat, or whatever. One of my most gratifying moments was when George Plimpton came on to plug a special he had taped about trapeze work. We strung up a trapeze from the flies so Plimpton could use me to demonstrate how hard it is. I swung out on the thing and, partly to show off and partly to startle Plimpton, I did a pull-over in mid-swing. I was sore for a week afterward, but, God, it was worth it.

No performance nerves or stage fright of any kind has ever been as terrifying for me as the state meet in gymnastics. An entire year's work goes into your exercise, and when your name is announced and the hush falls as you walk to your equipment, you realize that the whole year can go down the drain with only one slip in a performance that will take maybe thirty seconds. The whole thing seems suddenly absurd—and exhilarating. You are going to try to be perfect during a brief space at something that is terribly difficult—and when you succeed it's as if you have defied the world and won momentarily. It turned out, after I had won my event—side horse—two years in a row, that the state meet on the third year coincided with College Board exams. Obviously gymnasts were not expected to go on to higher learning. It was a hard choice, but I decided to opt for scholarship. The team, and, I like to think, the world, lost a demon side-horse man. My triple rear dismount was a thing of beauty and a joy forever—or, more precisely, for about five seconds. But it came too late to cure my social problem in school.

CP: Was there no solution to that problem?

DC: I had a vast capacity to make myself happy with my solitary obsessions: magic, Japanese stuff, stamps, theatrical make-up, and so on. When the bug bit I would pursue these fields until I knew enough to astound the adult experts, then lose interest and start on something else. I spent endless happy hours by myself with books on magic. I discovered that the inventor of the famous Westgate Goldfish Bowl Production—in magic, "production" means a trick to make something appear, not a stage extravaganza—had once lived right across the street from me in Lincoln. I could look across to where his mother still lived and see the actual sidewalk his feet had trod. He went on to become a physicist, I believe, and moved back to Lincoln. I have a diary that I kept for a week at that time, and the first entry says: "This is probably the greatest day of my life. I met Howard Westgate!"

Later a man named Gene Gloye—now a professor of psychology—who had invented another famous trick, Watch-Out, moved to Lincoln. I wrote him a fan letter, and as a result he became a sort of tutor of magic to me. Thanks to him, I began doing magic shows, for which I earned up to thirty-five dollars a night, and did so well I was able to lend my parents seven hundred dollars with interest toward the purchase of a car. This was my first real stand-up performing experience, and I must have played every church basement and Lions Club banquet in Lincoln and environs. In 1952 I went to my first International Brotherhood of Magicians convention, in St. Louis, where I beat the president of the brotherhood in one category and won the Best New Performer trophy in another.

It was at the winners' banquet of this convention that I first was convinced of my propensity for comedy. Each winner was asked to take a bow. When my turn came I stood up, but standing up made no perceptible difference in my being visible to the crowd that was ranged around the ballroom. So I stood on my chair, which brought down the house. At that moment some instinctual thing had told me how to get that laugh.

There was a similar event when I was state president of the student council. As moderator of one of that august body's most solemn conclaves, I introduced from the lectern one of the big-cheese adults—state adviser or something. As he made his way slowly toward the stage from the back, he said to the audience, rather pompously, I felt, "I'm sorry for this long entrance. I didn't mean for it to be dramatic." I said from the stage, "Don't worry. It's not." The laugh hit like a thunderclap, and again I knew that I wanted to be a comedian.

CP: Did your performing, as Dale Carnegie would say, win you new friends and new confidence?

DC: It seemed to win me admirers more than friends. Nevertheless, the thought of my name in lights was a great solace to my social unease. I guess it's pretty clear by now that I wasn't interested in show business because I felt that it was distinguished or that it would enable me to make a contribution to our culture. It all went back somehow to those dances. When I was in ninth grade the Drama Quartet—Agnes Moorehead, Charles Laughton, Sir Cedric Hardwicke, and Charles Boyer—brought *Don Juan in Hell* to the University of Nebraska Coliseum, in Lincoln, a hall of Hitlerian proportions. I posted myself at the stage door, and when Laughton came out I remember so badly wanting to have some kind of contact with him. I said, "Hello, where are you going next?" He said, "Omaha," and I commented wittily, "Oh, then you're going east." His only other remark was the inevitable comment on what a deep voice I had. But it didn't matter; I just remember thinking, "Those people don't have to worry about things like getting a date for the prom." It was the same when Bob Hope came to town. From amidst a throng of stage-doorniks I croaked out, "Fine show, Bob," in my freakish voice, and he glanced at me and said, "Thanks, son." When I got my balance back from having spoken to Bob Hope, I thought, "Gee, if I were famous I wouldn't have to worry about being smooth like some of the jocks in my class, or about sweating when I dance with girls. If I were in the movies, they'd all be coming to me and I'd ride in limousines."

CP: Now you do ride in limousines and—

DC: —and those pretty girls I yearned for in high school are married and living on chicken farms. Well, one is. So many of my classmates mortgaged their futures by getting married right away. It strikes me as such a waste. No one should be allowed to get married until he or she has spent at least two years away from home and one year abroad, and when I'm commissar this is how it will be. Perhaps we should consider those years a sort of recess for sex, after which it can assume its proper proportion and people can feel they have a choice of lives to lead. As for too-early marriages, I feel sorriest for the women, imprisoned practically before their lives have started. The men, through the nature of their work and the fact that they can fool around more easily, have a little more freedom. But only a little more.

I know that a lot of my classmates' parents welcomed their children's marriages, partly because it removed the fear that their children would knock somebody up, or be the knockees, partly because it was a sign that their children had "settled down." And they had, in the way that a man who is thrown overboard with a stone tied to his neck settles down. I picture them one week after the honeymoon, when the novelty of bed has worn off, waking up to the realities of house, car, job, insurance, plumbing bills, and all the rest, and realizing that this is how it's going to be from here on out. If you look at the divorce, suicide, drunkenness, and nervous-breakdown rates for Middle America, this may be an enormous factor.

CP: It was the "novelty of bed," you feel, that lured most of your old classmates into these traps?

DC: A lot of them, yes: the absolutely punishing sexual frustration. I'm convinced that the combination of strong sex drive at that age, the sanctions against expressing it, the ignorance of how to express it, the fear of pregnancy, the obsession with reputation, and all the rest of it was responsible for half the problems of my generation. A well-run, legalized brothel would have been a godsend and would have prevented countless miserable marriages and miserable children. Lacking such an institution, the answer seemed to be to get married as soon as you could, assuming you hadn't already had to. I know of half a dozen girls in my high school class who were knocked up, and God knows how many more were blessed with a premature visit from the stork shortly after nuptials. When I think of the number of reasonably intelligent guys who equated marriage with "getting it every night," and who consequently found themselves selling pants to support a family that had crashed down on them before they had seen any of the outside world except Norton, Kansas, on a basketball trip, it's pathetic. One great girl whom I dated a few times—Jesus, the thought of her still gives me a charge—married an absolute nerd, and confessed to a girl friend that she did it because the thought of a two-week honeymoon in Hawaii made it all seem worth while. She is probably married to a paint-store manager somewhere in South Dakota and weaving hot pads on a loom to keep from going bananas.

CP: Speaking of bananas, could we go back to your performing?

DC: Let me just get down from this soapbox.

CP: Besides being a magician and an incipient comedian, you were a fairly experienced actor by the time you graduated from high school.

DC: It is said, though I blush at the thought of it, that at age two I used to stand on a chair and recite poetry by the yard. I have no memory of this, but when an aunt sent me my old copy of *A Child's Garden of Verses* a few years ago I had the distinct sensation of *déjà écouté*. Apparently I would recite whenever anyone suggested it, and if no one took the initiative *I* would suggest it. The thought of a towheaded two-year-old striking an oratorical pose and rendering "The Owl and the Pussycat" is a bit stomach-turning, and I'm only glad that W. C. Fields never saw it. At the end of each poem, I'm told I would ask everyone to applaud; but since at that age I interchanged my *l*'s and *r*'s the injunction would come out, "Everybody crap!" I was coaxed into this endlessly by amused adults, and I probably caught on that the mispronunciation was dynamite and, as they say, kept it in.

Later, I did the usual things in school—patriotic pageants, one-act plays in Lula B. Moore's junior high school acting class, *Arsenic and Old Lace* in high school. . . .

CP: In one of those high school productions, didn't you act with Sandy Dennis, who was a classmate of yours?

DC: That was a one-acter called *Soldadas* (*The Soldier Women*), by one of those names that sounds like Evelyn Crewes De Witt. (Is there such a person? There ought to be.) I remember standing up there, with a badly painted-on grease mustache and my hair darkened with carbon paper, delivering a line that's pretty hard to deliver with force at fourteen: "You're not going to blow me to hell with your bomb!"

Sandy played a young girl, a very melodramatic part. She actually cried onstage and was completely moving. I was taken out of myself in the way the audience was supposed to be, and I just stood there thinking, "She really has it," until I realized that I was responsible for the long silence I had become aware of onstage. Sandy's performance was all the more remarkable because in every other way I was barely aware of her at school. She was so unobtrusive that she seemed to get from one classroom to another without going through the corridors. But evidently she was already committed to acting. A friend of hers, Dottie Beindorf, later told me that she and Sandy had made a pact that if either of them became famous on Broadway the other would become her dresser, and that way both of them would get there.

CP: Did you ever feel taken out of yourself by your own performing in those days?

DC: There were maybe two or three times when I was really winging it and felt born to the stage, and those were invariably in comedies. I played the drama critic in *Arsenic and Old Lace*, and in those performances inspiration was coming from I know not where; I was getting big laughs, just killing them.

I guess I had made my own sort of pact too. Once, in junior high school, when the auditorium was empty and dark, I crept backstage and just stood there in the wings, alone, sensing the curtains and flies and footlights around me. I had a sense of this being a significant moment. I thought, "I'm going to go on the stage. This is going to be my life somehow."

CP: Music up. Montage of falling calendar leaves and roaring express trains. Cut to hero realizing youthful fantasies in triumphal opening night.

DC: Yes, my Eve Harrington syndrome. I went through it again one summer during college. I had been acting at the Oregon Shakespeare Festival, and I took a bus back home via Las Vegas. There I went into an empty lounge in one of the hotels. I went up on stage, stood behind a glistening silver microphone, and imagined a roomful of laughing people and me as the comedian in a sparkly blue suit. I thought, "I'd know how to stand here and do it."

Where were we? Sorry, these headaches . . .

CP: High school acting.

DC: My favorite acting wasn't in school at all, but on a fifteen-minute Saturday-morning radio show sponsored by the Junior League. I started acting on it in eighth grade and ended up directing it as well. It was thrilling because the show was live, and when I was directing I could cast myself in two or three parts on the same show and use different voices for each, although sometimes I would forget which voice was for which character. I had one of my triumphs on that show when, at fourteen, I played Macbeth. Our abridgment of the script must have really been something, since, thinking back on it now, I can see that a fifteen-minute show gave us hardly enough time to read the stage directions of *Macbeth*.

I can still make myself laugh over the flubs and spoonerisms of those Saturday mornings. In one of my directorial stints I cast a very ambitious but dumb girl in a one-line part. It was a Mississippi River adventure story, and all the girl had to do was hail an approaching flatboat. She worked herself into a nervous frenzy at rehearsals, and this, combined with her tendency to overact the line, worried me. But during the show itself she seemed to be under control. When her time came she approached the mike with great sweep and authority, and with perfect timing and strong feeling she sang out, *"Fat-bloat, ahoy!"* The rest of us nearly blew our eardrums out by clapping our hands over our mouths, but our unsuccessfully muffled explosions of laughter could be heard clearly by the astonished listeners, along with a feebly muttered "Excuse me" from the devastated girl.

I loved radio acting and would have been quite happy doing it as a profession. It's a shame that television killed it and that radio became mostly a purveyor of junk music and news. It was a wonderful medium, and the big network radio shows must be one of the few cases in history of a dramatic art form utterly vanishing. I hope one of the occasional experiments in bringing them back works.

CP: Johnny Carson was starting his performing career in Nebraska while you were growing up. Surely the two of you must have crossed paths.

DC: When I was fourteen he was already a Famous Man, since he was on *both* radio and TV from Omaha. I remember once waiting to go on at the Lincoln Lions Club with a magic act. From the wings I heard the announcer tell the audience, "We have a disappointment for you. We couldn't get Johnny Carson today. But we have a young man who someday is going to be just as good." I made my entrance over a noticeable but tolerant groan.

I later met Johnny when he was appearing in a church basement in Lincoln—he *was* available that time. Two friends and I, all of us magic buffs, snuck backstage and accosted him as he was setting up. He looked slightly annoyed. People are always nosing around when a magician is setting up, and the magician rightly would like to catapult them through the nearest window. When we told Johnny we were amateur magicians, however, he became quite friendly and even showed us a few card fans. Then we went back out front, aglow from our contact with a *star*. The classy thing that Johnny did that evening was to introduce us, in the middle of his act, as three young magicians and ask us to take a bow from the audience. We were thrilled. Some of the people in the audience were offended by his act, I recall. He did a cigarette trick in a church basement, and "different ones" (a favorite midwestern locution for "various people") thought that was in deplorable taste. I thought they were being unfair to my new friend. After the show my buddies and I watched him pack up and leave. How we envied him as he glamorously pulled out into the night in what looked like a '49 Chevy!

CP: When you used to do a night-club act you told a joke about your father's meager salary as a schoolteacher. You said one year he made only nine hundred dollars, and your mother had to help by taking in washing—off people's clotheslines at night. How much of that was rooted in fact? Were you poor?

DC: My parents did have some pretty hard times, but they were mostly during the Depression, before I was born. I used to hear my father reminisce about that nine-hundred-dollars-a-year teaching job, which was a fact. The thing that got me was that before he could even be confirmed in it he had to tramp out across the potato and sugar-beet fields of every literate or illiterate farmer in the district to let them all get a look at what sort of man was going to be trusted with the tender sensibilities of their adenoidal offspring.

When I was growing up we weren't really poor, but we weren't prosperous either. Before I struck it rich with my magic shows I had to go out and earn my own pocket money in the usual ways—helping my father paint houses (which was almost an avocation of his), returning pop bottles, and doing the most loathsome job in the world, caddying. Having caddied at the Lincoln Country Club, I know what it must be like to be black. The goddam golfers would call you "you" and "boy" and treat you like a dog. The game bored me to idiocy, and no matter how hard I tried to concentrate, I was invariably looking somewhere else when my player took a drive, and I'd get hell for losing the ball. You had to attend the club's golf-course-etiquette courses if you wanted to work your way up from Class C caddy, which I never did. I think they invented a D category solely for me. So help me, we were told that when we came to the ball-washing machines on the fourth and eighth holes we had to say, "Can I wash your balls, sir?" I started dreading those words the night before, and by the time I had to deliver them my throat would constrict and make my voice crack, or else I would stammer on the *b* in balls.

I finally decided it was not worth the $1.25 a day I was getting paid, having to ask total strangers if I could wash their balls. On the way from the locker room to the caddy class I cut through the parking lot and went home, and never went back.

Providence must have had a hand in my decision, because on the way home I found a five-dollar bill at the bus stop, which saw me through the rest of the summer. Five dollars went farther in those days. So did buses.

CP: You've said several times that you felt somewhat inhibited by the fact that your parents were teachers. Did that affect the atmosphere in your household?

DC: As a matter of fact, I was allowed more freedom and independence than a lot of kids my age, because of what was taken to be my unusual maturity—an illusion, as I've said, fostered by my deep voice and precocious vocabulary. The atmosphere at home was anything but pedantic. I remember it being lively, with friends coming and going, good-natured ribbing, things like that.

I relished the nights when my folks and their friends would play bridge and have coffee and cake, and I would stay up and talk with them as long as I was allowed—they never treated me as a child, which I appreciated—and when I was sent to bed I'd sit at the top of the stairs and eavesdrop on them for hours. I can still remember fragments of conversation and certain phrases. Sometimes I later passed off their remarks and opinions as my own in school and wowed my teachers. I suppose it's significant of something or other that I remember those evenings with people so much older than I as among the happiest of my life. The cozy atmosphere of the house, the easy laughter and conviviality, the good-natured and witty kidding, the funny stories—I knew that all of it was better than anything I could be doing with kids my age.

I didn't enjoy *all* adults, by any means. These friends of my parents were an attractive lot. They had all been to the Grand Island Baptist College together, got teaching degrees at Columbia together, taught together during the Depression, and thoroughly enjoyed each other's company, without competition, acrimony, or hostility. It's to be expected, but the fact that they are not all good friends today, those who are still alive, saddens me. By just repeating their names—Frank Rice, Cath Glade, the Pattersons—I can give myself a Proustian evocation of those happy times, the smell of the coffee, the cake icing, the cards being shuffled, Frank's peculiar staccato laugh, which I could still hear rising above the indistinct blur of voices when I couldn't stay awake any longer at the top of the stairs and had gotten reluctantly into bed. (I was constantly having to rush to bed whenever anyone came upstairs to pee, then return to my post when the coast was clear.)

It strikes me as odd now, as I recall those evenings, that no booze was consumed. Those people weren't teetotalers, but they didn't assume that booze was a necessary part of social fun. Perhaps this was their essential midwesternness, or simply their way of staying within schoolteachers' financial means.

The only comparably amusing and enjoyable circle of friends I've ever known is my wife's childhood friends from the Mississippi delta. When they get together I sort of fade back and just loll in the humor of their recollections, gossip, and mock disputes, their rich personalities and accents. The laughter comes as thick and fast as in those evenings in Grand Island—though here a *lot* of booze is consumed.

CP: You said your appreciation of your parents and their friends was significant of something. Of what?

DC: I guess of the fact that the discomforts I felt socially and at school were offset by the awareness that I could entertain myself in our house and be entertained by the people who came there. It had something to do with my feeling that my voice was not my own, but someone else's, someone older. I never had that feeling around my parents' friends. I felt that somehow I was their age and spoke on their level, and that it was only because of some accident of biological chronology that I had to get up and go to school the next day with little kids.

CP: And feel uneasy all over again about being the son of schoolteachers.

DC: One of the earliest prejudices I encountered firsthand had to do with that: "Naturally he got all A's. His parents are teachers." I wasn't eager for people to know I got all A's anyway, since that certainly had its price, but what I really resented was that they apparently thought I spent my time at home being taught, probably at a little desk, with my parents standing in front of it at a blackboard. Or else they may have figured that my teachers knew my parents and automatically gave A's to any teacher's kid. I resented the whole image that these people seemed to have of a strait-laced home life. I wanted them to know that my parents swore, told dirty jokes to their friends, smoked, and were not above taking a drink.

Still, I was always vaguely embarrassed about identifying my father as a schoolteacher. The very word tended to suggest a fluttery Franklin Pangborn type. When I was in elementary school all the teachers were women, and to have to tell my friends that my father was a teacher made me uneasy. Whenever I sensed that they were picturing him as a sort of male spinster, I would tell the story of what he did to the man in the bowling alley.

It took place back in Grand Island, when I was five. My father, uncle, and grandfather Cavett were bowling, and I and my four-year-old cousin were wandering around. My cousin somehow irritated one of the other bowlers, who picked him up and dumped him heavily on a bench. My cousin screamed bloody murder. My father turned, saw my cousin pointing at this guy, and started toward him with a murderous look in his eye. The guy headed for the door, thereby sealing his fate. Whatever my father imagined had taken place filled him with righteous wrath, and he took off in pursuit, followed by the entire population of the bowling alley. The culprit was larger than my father, which probably explains why my father caught up with him about half a block away, both of them out of breath. My father sent him rolling on the sidewalk with a well-placed knee to the small of the back. The guy got up and ran another half block to a diner and tore inside, apparently thinking that not even an enraged English teacher would continue a fight in a crowded diner. My uncle had been carrying me under one arm and my cousin under the other, but somehow I got loose and tore ahead to where the action was. I got inside the diner in time to see my father unleash a well-aimed right to the jaw that sent the guy about five feet backward into a stack of pop-bottle cases. Cases and bottles came crashing down around him in a spectacular cascade that was as good as anything I had seen in the movies. Just then the guy's wife, who had apparently decided somebody ought to salvage the family honor, grabbed my father's arm and ripped his shirt sleeve off. Being a gentleman, he ignored the crowd's exhortations to flatten her too and decided it was time to depart.

Later, when two cops arrived at our house to investigate the incident, they turned out to be former high school classmates of my father's. Thanks to them, the newspaper account made it appear that my grandfather had done the fighting. Even though this undoubtedly protected my father's job, I felt cheated. I guess I wanted to see a headline saying DICK CAVETT'S FATHER PULVERIZES BULLY.

CP: So you weren't always a believer in passive resistance.

DC: As I got older I became more conscious of the supposed honor at stake. You had to fight, especially if anyone was watching. Either you fought or you were one of the guys who clutched his books to his side with his arm bent instead of straight—a sure sign of being a sissy. Witness my famous bathhouse brawl, which probably never would have happened if I had been alone. It's a companion piece to the bowling alley story, not only because it involved the same cousin, but also because I was quite consciously emulating my father.

By this time I was about fourteen. My cousin and I were dressing after a swim, and the guy in the cubicle next to ours decided it would be funny to throw water over on us. I yelled, "Knock it off!" He yelled, "Knock *what* off?" I riposted, "Stick your head over the top and I'll show you," hoping to God he wouldn't. He did. So, wishing I was home in bed, I pushed my wet towel in his face. As if by magic, he appeared inside our cubicle in a split second. The wonder of what ensued was how many blows I felt myself absorbing in so short a time. It was like a hailstorm. The basket checker separated us and sent the other guy outside. I lingered inside trying to figure out some reason to stay the night. Eventually my cousin and I finished dressing and went outside to the parking lot, where the guy was waiting, as we had known he would be. I decided I had to see this thing through.

My plan was to make a brave-looking lunge at him, catching his head in my arm, then let him get me down, pretend I had hurt my back, and make like I was quitting reluctantly. I was willing to play out the sore-back imposture for days if necessary. With Errol Flynn in mind, I came flying off the steps of the bathhouse; the guy ducked, and I had the awful luck to miss his head altogether. I remember the scalding embarrassment of hitting the ground all alone, my arms forming a circle that contained no head. He instantly got me up and knocked me backward over a fallen telephone pole. As the gravel bit into my sunburned shoulder I remember hoping it would leave a permanent scar in testimony to the mayhem I had endured. At this point bystanders broke it up again.

Five minutes later, to my horror, we ran into him again, in a penny arcade. Since the previous scene had ended with me on my back, I decided to go for broke. In those days, playground fights consisted more of wrestling than of fighting—a kind of wrestling punctuated with body blows. There was an unwritten code that you didn't hit in the face. Remembering the guy in the bowling alley flying backward into the pop cases, I decided to really dazzle my cousin, and walked up to the chap to smash him in the face. It was an exciting moment. I felt as if I were going to lose my virginity. I remembered his amazed look when I walked up, stood flat-footed in front of him for a moment, and then smashed my fist into his face, just as they did in the movies. The surprising thing about hitting someone that way is how much it can hurt *you*. I felt as though I had punched a tree. And the guy didn't move. He just started to cry and said, "I know your name, and I'm going to have David Kingsbury beat the shit out of you." David Kingsbury was tough as hell; when I said, "Go ahead, see if I care," there was a flutter in my voice.

Kingsbury was never enlisted, or else he felt I was no challenge, because nothing happened. But I slept badly for a few nights, consoled only with the fact that my cousin would tell his friends that his cousin had fought like a tiger.

CP: That's a good point about what fights consisted of in the old days. Today, to talk of beating somebody up may suggest chains, pipes, bats, and the like. In your far-off Eden it hardly ever meant more than jumping a guy and wrenching him to the ground after a bit of panting and grappling.

DC: Even an attack from behind could be relatively harmless, as I inadvertently proved when I beat up a paper boy for no reason. I was walking with my new friend Tom Keene on a mild summer day and suddenly felt the urge to demonstrate that I was the John Wayne of the neighborhood. The nearest available target was an innocent paper boy making his rounds collecting. As I remember, I hit him from behind, knocked him down, pinned him, and left him stunned—not from the force of my attack, but from its lack of motivation. Tom was not so much impressed as mystified. Then I too began to wonder about the whole thing. "He'd been shooting off his mouth," I explained feebly.

CP: Fighting always seems to refer you to the movies. Did what you saw on the screen encourage you to be more—well, violent?

DC: Absolutely. There were no heroes in the movies who didn't fight. Even the pacifist or the priest, who was played by Ward Bond, would reach the last, backbreaking straw and mutter, "Forgive me, Father," while he spit on his hands and laid out the villain. I liked every violent thing I saw in the movies, and for a long time I wanted to be a stunt man. My friend Jim McConnell and I used to make ramps for our bikes so that we could fly off them and crash into piled-up cardboard boxes. We learned to fall from trees, from second-floor windows, off the tops of cars, down long flights of stairs backward—it's a wonder we didn't break our necks.

CP: The violence-appeal of movies—was it bad for you?

DC: I have no idea. I don't know whether it created an appetite for violent action in me or merely stimulated an appetite that was already there. I do know that my reason is at war with my instincts in such matters even now. If somebody is offensive in a bar, my immediate gut reaction is to hit him with a chair; but my head tells me not only that I might miss, but also that this is not the ideal way to settle things. I can't be sure my head will win out. I could easily get myself into a fight where I was outweighed or outnumbered just because of the quick flash of violent temper I'm capable of. And in the back of my mind would be images of the cowboy movies of my childhood.

Robert Mitchum once showed me how to break a man's finger in a split second. He'd been a self-defense instructor in the army. He said the finger breaking is really a peaceful move, because it gets what might otherwise be a long fight over quickly. He almost broke mine showing me. I was thinking, "Here's Mitchum in person showing me this, and he's one of the people I used to wish I could be on the screen."

CP: Too bad you didn't know the finger-breaking technique back then.

DC: I did read up on judo at the library. I practiced all the moves at home and even made a judo shirt with Japanese letters on it. When I threw the Olympic wrestling champ on my show I did it with a judo move called *yukigoshi*, and nearly broke my own back in the process.

Once my judo gave me a terrible scare. I was in another one of those playground fights, and I got the guy in a positively lethal neck hold that I'd found in an ancient judo book. He went out like a light and just lay there on the ground. His face turned gray, and a tear slowly emerged from his eyelid and rolled down his cheek. I know what it feels like to kill someone, because I thought he was dead. Finally somebody shook him and he came to, but he was sleepy for a while. I still know the hold. Here, let me show you. . . .

CP: Piss off, Mr. Moto. Or should I say, get a grip on your-self.

DC: *I'll* do the jokes.

CP: Remember how Abe Burrows proposed to rewrite the old song—"How're Ya Gonna Keep 'Em Down on the Farm After They've Seen the Farm?" Did you feel the classic yearning of the young man in the provinces—to escape, to go to the big city?

DC: Yes. When we moved from Gibbon to Grand Island I tingled with excitement at going to a big town (20,000), and the same again when we moved on to Lincoln (100,000). When I first saw Chicago I was overwhelmed, and New York was a thrilling, unattainable dream. I knew that all the excitement was there and none of it was where I was. Definitely, it was a siren call.

In Grand Island we lived by the railroad tracks, and the trains are part of my early memories. We were right on the route of the Streamliner. Standing near the tracks in the evening and watching the City of Denver or the City of San Francisco pass through used to give me goose-pimples. You could see the people inside, who were actually going to those far-off places, and I used to try to imagine what it would be like to be one of them. The giant freights, especially the double-headers, had a kind of satanic majesty at night, when you could see the fire in the engine, and the mournful whistle gave you the chills. I'm sorry those great old engines have passed into nostalgia. When I'm out in Nebraska I miss them, the way the old Indians missed the buffalo.

When my parents' friends would come over I'd revel in their exotic talk of faraway places. Like New York. I remember sitting at the top of the stairs and listening to them talking about Riverside Drive, Chinatown, double-decker buses. So I was always hearing about New York: it was in either my future or my past.

CP: Did you associate New York with show business?

DC: Especially when I got my first summer-stock job. Two guys who had been in the East opened a summer-stock theater in Lincoln. When they produced *The Winslow Boy* they called the principal of my junior high school in search of candidates for the title role. He suggested me, and I got the part: I looked right, and I could do a convincing English accent. I guess it was hanging around those New York actors in the company that seemed so glamorous, talking about "Remember that night we went down to the Village?" I realized that must be Greenwich Village, and I thought longingly, "I go back to school when fall starts here in Nebraska, and they go back to New York. Crap."

Somehow I got hold of *The Empire City*, a collection of stories about New York—everything from the famous E. B. White piece to stories by Fitzgerald and Ben Hecht. I read all these things and then thought, "If I could ever get there, what would it be like?" That was when I was about thirteen or four-teen. I had no idea how you went about it; not until the possi-bility of going to Yale came up did I begin to see the path dimly.

More than anything else, *television* to me was the glittering East; it was the biggest, most wonderful, most glamorous thing I could imagine. I used to evolve little fantasies when I'd watch Sid Caesar and Imogene Coca on *Your Show of Shows*. I knew it was live, and at the end, when the stars took their bows, I used to think, "Now, those people, where do they go? They leave that stage, and they go out of a theater of some sort, and people actually see them; people lay eyes on Sid Caesar and Imogene Coca, and they can see them get into a car or cab and go home." And I used to think how lucky those stagehands were—those people in the world of glamour. I didn't picture myself necessarily as one of the performers. I thought, "If there were only some way I could get there, I'd be willing to work backstage just to see it and be part of it."

I apparently was never above creating an aura of big-time glamour around myself to impress friends at an early age. I was talking to Mary Huston (now Schuyler) on the phone recently, and she said, "What was the name of your uncle who was in the movies?" It seems someone had come to visit my family from out of town when I was about seven, and I told Mary he was my uncle the movie star. She had believed it until now.

I'm sorry that has all evaporated, that dreamy love of the glamour of it all.

CP: What do you regret about your childhood?

DC: Aside from the fact that it's over, I regret not knowing my grandparents better. I knew all four of them and liked them well enough, but I couldn't imagine that they were of any interest beyond their ability to provide money, candy, or other immediate gratifications. I suppose it's a rare kid who appreciates not only his grandparents' roots in the past, but also the fact that their roots are his roots. And that when grandparents die a treasure of family reminiscences and historical recollections goes with them to the grave. I would settle for an hour now with any one of mine.

My grandfather Richards, for example, my mother's father. He and my grandmother stayed with us to help out when my mother was dying, and he seemed to me then merely a tiresome and foolish old man, who got in my way when I wanted to get up or down the stairs fast and whose manners were disgusting at dinner. When I think now that he came from Wales to Kansas and Nebraska and South Dakota before the Wounded Knee massacre, and that I never took advantage of the fund of early western history that he lived and saw, it just kills me. He was a heroic figure of a man, noble and rough in countenance, a fundamentalist Baptist preacher with an impressive list of conversions to his credit, and one or two minor miracles. He once prayed a boy virtually back to life who was given up for dead after falling from a hayloft and impaling himself in the groin on an upright stake. He was always ready to harness a team to a wagon and drive a hundred and twenty-five miles to preach a funeral or perform a baptism while standing waist-deep in a muddy river.

I can remember him in his eighties doing a full day's work in the broiling Nebraska sun. He had a passionate hatred of weeds, and when he had weeded his own acreage to his satisfaction he would weed the ditch for half a mile or so in either direction. He also weeded his neighbors' lawns and acreages when their appearance offended him. And he had an almost childlike capacity for amazement. In his last years my mother gave him a subscription to *Life* magazine. He thoroughly enjoyed it, but after a year he made my mother stop the subscription, because he couldn't understand how anything so impressive could be turned out every week and how we could afford to send it to him. I have a pair of Sioux moccasins that were given to him by an old Indian. They are burial or ceremonial moccasins, and they are unlike any that I've ever seen, because of an unusual amount of *black* beadwork. An Indian I showed them to said, "They must have belonged to a very great warrior." I often gaze at them and wonder if they belonged to Red Cloud or Spotted Tail—and if there is a reliable trance medium who could put me in touch with my grandfather, so I could hear him tell the story of the moccasins in that rich, melodious Welsh accent of his.

That voice haunts me still. He died in his late eighties, of complications after some little girls ran into him with a bicycle and broke his hip. I can hear him saying, with slightly trilled *r*'s,

"I really can't understand why the Lord has sent me this suffering." I also have a clear memory of sitting on a porch beside him looking up into a blue Nebraska summer sky and asking him how far away heaven was. "Far-r-rther than we can see, Dickie. Far-r-rther than we can see."

A few years before he died he sat down and typed up his life story, *In His Service (Being a Record of My Labors in God's Vineyard)*. It circulated for a few years among family and friends, along with some of his poetry. Then my uncle Lloyd Richards put it together as a book and mimeographed it, so my grandfather could circulate it even more. I've read it over and over, and parts of it always move me to tears. Here is an excerpt from the year 1892, when he had his first personal experience with the Holy Spirit.

*I was splitting up blocks of wood into stove wood south of the house that afternoon, and whilst I was working I was thinking in my heart all the time on the promise we had made to the Minister. [To pray that day at 4:00 p.m.] Then when four o'clock came I stuck my axe into the block of wood and walked down to the barn, and as I was walking along, suddenly a dark cloud seemed to come over me, and I was very much burdened in heart. After I got into the barn, I stopped and began to think why it was that I should feel this way.*

*Then I looked back over my life, and said, I have always tried to live a Christian life and take part in Christian work the best I knew how. And then I began to think of the life of Jesus, and the work He did, and the sacrifice He made to save the human race from sin and death and hell. Just then a voice seemed to say to me, "Your life can only be likened to filthy rags compared to the life of Jesus." I knew that was a scriptural reference: Isaiah 64:6 "But we are all as an unclean thing, and our righteousness is as filthy rags."*

*Then I said, "Lord, give me a righteousness that I will be acceptable with you." Then I went over to the southeast corner of the barn and fell upon my knees and said, "Lord, have mercy upon an unworthy creature like me." Just then it seemed that I could see Jesus hanging on the cross, His head hanging low in death.*

*I cried out, "Yes, Lord Jesus, and You died for me," and the love of God filled my soul and I said, "There, now I know from experience that my sins are all blotted out." And my soul was filled with the love of God and peace was upon me.*

*That day, that hour, four o'clock, I shall never forget, when in that humble barn I had the experience that I had been looking for even before leaving Wales to come to America. Yes, now I know what it means when Jesus said, "Verily, verily I say unto you, except a man be born again, he cannot see the kingdom of God." Now I see it and feel it and know it.*

Later that year, a minister told him that God had been "pressing upon [him] to urge Mr. Richards to become a minister." Disturbed by this, and by his lack of college training for the ministry, my grandfather waited for a sign. One day he decided to abandon his plans to husk corn and "consecrate this day to the Lord."

*I took the horses off the harness and turned them out to pasture. I went to the house and got my Bible. Then I went to the barn, got a horse blanket, and went out in the middle of the cornfield, where I would be alone and undisturbed. The first thing I did was to spread the blanket on the ground and lay my Bible on the blanket. Then I went down on my knees with my face in my hands and my hands resting on the Bible. I prayed to the Lord to give me the light and the true understanding of His Word: that if He had called me to preach his gospel, I might have the true light and wisdom to lead the lost into the fold of Jesus.*

*Whilst praying after this manner for some time, strange to say, I went into a trance. I do not know how long I was in this condition but whilst under the spell, I felt a hand taking hold of my side and shaking me and saying in plain words, "I want you to preach the gospel." Then I rose to my feet, and the glory of God was so bright I could not see anything else, and I was saying, "This is heaven; this is heaven!" Then the glory and brightness began to vanish and finally disappeared. I said, "There, I am in the world again." It made me think of Jacob when he saw the ladder that reached to heaven and said, "The Lord is in this place, and I knew*

*it not." That heavenly voice and that heavenly vision will never
be lost to my memory.*

In order to increase attendance at his regular church meetings, he would hold impromptu services in any public place
that would have him. He seemed to find low-down pool halls
a favorite challenge. Once, in Wagner, South Dakota, he sang
a solo to get the assembled ruffians' attention, and then brought
them the Lord's Word.

*I had very good attention. They seemed to be very much in-
terested, so much so that they asked me to come again. Some of
the men in this hall challenged me to go to the other hall, which
was run by a Bohemian. Quite a few Indians patronized that place.
I went there, and as I did in all places, I first went to the proprietor
and introduced myself, explaining my custom of holding meetings
in such places where I might have permission. This is what he said:
"If you can hold a service in a place like this, you are welcome to it."*

*Most of the patrons were Bohemians or Indians. I walked up to
them and said, "If you people will listen, I will sing you a solo and
give you a little talk." At all but one table the men threw their
cues down on the table and came up to the front. I went up to
those who were still playing and said, "If you will stop playing for
a few minutes, I will sing you a solo."*

*An Indian said, "Just a minute." When he got his ball into the
pocket he sat down on the side of the table. I sang them a solo
and gave them a talk, then sang another solo, and they seemed delighted. The Indian who had continued playing stepped up to me
and handed me a quarter. I said, "No thank you, I don't want your
money. I came for your good."*

*He said, "You are welcome."*

*I said, "I believe that!" Then I invited them to our meeting at
the Baptist Church. As I left they shouted, "Come again!"*

CP: Have you sorted out what it is that stirs you so about
this remarkable man?

DC: He had no doubt about how he would spend his life,
and he had the satisfaction of seeing people change and lead

happier lives as a result of his efforts. I envy him that. Also his capacity for backbreaking work to clear any obstacles that stood in his way. That I did not inherit.

CP: You don't seem to have inherited his piety either.

DC: Reading his account of his life always makes me wonder why I'm not more religious, if in fact I'm religious at all. It seems strange to say, but I can see myself having his experience in the cornfield. Unfortunately, I'm skeptical enough to know that even if I did have that experience I would suspect that it was self-engendered in some way and that it was not necessarily a proof of God's existence. Is this the price of too much education, perhaps? I know my grandfather expected to meet his Maker in the most literal sense when he died, and if he didn't, and there is no such Being, it is a cruel joke on him. But his life still would not have been misspent, because of all the misery he transformed into joy. Perhaps, if there is a God, He appears to and intervenes in the lives of a few extraordinary individuals like my grandfather and is bored stiff with the rest of us.

This is my religious problem: it would be wonderful to believe in the most fundamental way. It would make life easier, it would explain everything, it would give meaning where none is apparent, it would make tragedies bearable. If I went to a revival meeting, I have no doubt I could be one of the first to go down on his knees. It seems as if the only religion worth having is the simplest possible religion. But something about the fact that all it takes to make it so is deciding it *is* so puts me off. Knowing it could instantly make me much happier makes it somehow unworthy of having.

In Italy once I had a close shave. I had wandered into an empty little church in some town on the Amalfi coast. Near the altar there was a statue of Christ. As I was idly looking up into the face of it, the eyes moved. That's all there is to the story. It rooted me to the spot for a moment, and I tried to make it happen again but couldn't. There now.

CP: Did you go to Sunday school as a kid?

DC: Yes, and later to church, and they both bored my ass off. At Sunday school nice old ladies told me I was one of God's lambs or whatever, but even then I wondered if any of it was true, rather than just "good for me." I used to wonder why, if it "wouldn't hurt" to go to church, it *would* hurt *not* to, and the answers were never satisfying. I think my ultimate thoughts on the subject are that I am sorry I am not religious, that I know I could be in the next instant if I chose to be, and there's the rub—and that I hope there is a God for Grandpa Richards's sake, but don't much care if there is one for mine.

CP: You mentioned what would happen if you went to a revival meeting. But in a sense a revival meeting has come to you, in the person of Billy Graham.

DC: I like Billy Graham as a man; I always enjoy talking to him. He sent me a modern Bible once, which I am grateful for, and which is an abomination. It sent me smartly back to the King James Version, which in turn sent me to the King James Version in French, which is so sublimely beautiful it could make Jim Aubrey weep. I think Billy Graham truly believes in the God of the Bible. And, unfortunately, in one or two others.

CP: Your wife describes you as a closet Indian.

DC: Squaw speak with forked tongue.

CP: Having seen your closet, I know what she means. It's full of buckskins, beaded knife sheaths, feathers, hair-pipe necklaces, and what not. So is the rest of your apartment. You've also gone fairly intensively into Indian lore, done some traveling in Indian country, publicized Indian plights and culture on your show (especially through the appearances of the late Dr. John Neihardt), and the last time we went for a walk in the woods I noticed that you were able to move silently without snapping any twigs underfoot. To what do you attribute all this?

DC: I've had a reawakening of passionate interest in the West. I don't know why it happened, but I do know what the instruments of the reawakening were: having Dr. Neihardt on my show and reading Dee Brown's *Bury My Heart at Wounded Knee*, and through reading it getting Dee on the show and becoming acquainted with him. I'm delighted that I've been able to boost the sales of both men's books, and in Neihardt's case to do a little reawakening of my own. His *Black Elk Speaks* had been gathering dust in university bookstores for years, but the entire edition of fifteen thousand copies sold out in the week after he and I discussed it on my show, and a new edition was rushed through the presses.

As a kid I used to hang around the old Historical Society in the basement of the state Capitol and gaze for hours at the Plains Indian artifacts. The only way I can put it is to say they spoke to me. I could never understand how other people could walk past them and not get what I was getting, but I knew they weren't. It must be the way an art lover can tell when other people know nothing about great painting and feel nothing when they look at a canvas. Without getting too wispy about it, those artifacts involved my emotions and tear ducts in a way that went far beyond finding them interesting or attractive. I used to play around with the idea that I was at Little Big Horn in a former life.

CP: On which side?

DC: Hmmmm. Good question.

My parents used to take me each summer to Greeley, Colorado, where they were working on their master's degrees at what was then Colorado State Teachers College. In July a couple of Greyhound buses full of Indians would come and dance on the campus, plugging Cheyenne Frontier Days. I was only a preschooler then, but I can still vividly remember some of their faces, the details of the way they painted themselves, and the melodies of the songs. I was sent into a state of near hyperkineticism by their visits. I realize now that, since that was in the early 1940s, some of the oldest men who came to dance could have been in the Custer battle. As late as the thirties, you know, some of the older Cheyenne and Sioux who were in on the Custer kill would not go to a Custer anniversary observance, for fear that the sight of them might anger the bluecoats all over again and they would be shot.

I loved those trips to Colorado. We would always set out in the morning before the sun came up, to avoid the heat—this was years before air conditioning—and the thrill of dressing and having breakfast in the dark, then piling into our 1938 De Soto and turning the headlights west—it was all I could do to get my breath. When you get to the foothills of the Rockies and then abruptly enter Big Thompson Canyon, it's awesome even for an adult. For me, the first time, as a kid of four, it was terrifying. I became hysterical, because I thought the sheer cliffs on both sides were going to fall down on us. I don't know whether my parents wrapped me in a wet sheet or what, but when they finally calmed me down I wanted to get back on the plains immediately.

Once I got over the initial shock, I came to love the mountains, although they could, and still can, scare me some. Once we were visiting in the cabin of an old character who had been in the Buffalo Bill show, and I suddenly noticed that all the adults were acting strange and had gone quite pale. Someone said, "Cover up the bacon on the stove," and Elmer, the character, loaded a rifle. A grizzly had roared outside, and there were stories that a few days earlier a hungry bear had torn open a cabin, and one of its occupants, in the next canyon. It's shocking for a kid to see the adults frightened. In this case, however, the grizzly went away. Somewhere there's a snapshot of all of us, out in front of the cabin, labeled "After the Grizzly." When it was over, I felt I had endured a real western adventure, and used to embellish the story with sounds of clawing on the shutters and still other details to make me wondrous in the eyes of my audience.

For me, the mountains always had a mystery about them.

One summer, in Colorado, a friend of a distant relative and his wife were out for a Sunday drive near Estes Park. She got out to pick some wildflowers, and he walked down the road in the opposite direction to look at something. When he came back she was gone. They never found hide nor hair of her. This had a terrific effect on me, and whenever I was out alone I would try to imagine what horrible thing came at her and hauled her away, and what I would do if I saw one coming. I always carried a rock.

I have a tremendous yearning to see all the things I saw as a kid again—the West, Colorado, the mountains—a kind of nostalgia for it all that I haven't come to terms with. Even the weather. I hate the effete eastern establishment winters. Give me a good old-fashioned plains winter, where locomotives are buried in snow. Weather in the West is truly ferocious. People who haven't lived there can have no idea of it. I miss the violent electrical storms, where the lightning jars the earth. A cavalry unit once got caught on the open plains in a Nebraska rainstorm and nearly drowned on horseback. They were in what's called a downspout, the horses couldn't move, and the mounted riders had to form roofs over their noses with their hands in order to breathe, because there was no space between the raindrops.

There was so much about Nebraska, so much beauty and history, that I didn't fully appreciate when I was there. It was that stupid notion that if anything good had ever happened it couldn't have been in my own boring home state. I didn't realize till I left that Crazy Horse had been killed in Nebraska, that the major trails to the West—the Oregon Trail, the Mormon Trail—went through the state, that Lewis and Clark passed through, that Buffalo Bill's ranch was there, that the Red Cloud Agency had been there, that the Cheyenne came through the sand hills on their tragic attempt to regain their homeland, and that the first reports of Wounded Knee were telegraphed from Rushville. I even learned a few years ago, in reading Oscar Wilde's letters, that he was not only in Nebraska but in my home town of Lincoln, where—ironically, when you think of what was going to happen to him—he spoke of the forlorn looks of the prisoners in the penitentiary. If they taught us any of this in school, I was asleep. All I knew was that someone named William Jennings Bryan, who lived in Lincoln, had once run for president, and I assumed that that was all there was worth knowing.

CP: It's ironic, now that you're where you dreamed of being, and now that you've become who you dreamed of becoming, that your mind keeps turning back to the place where you did all the dreaming.

DC: And if I were a kid in Nebraska today, Dick Cavett would be one of the people I'd be dreaming about becoming. Sickening, isn't it?

CP: Are we on the verge of some fundamental truth here?

DC: I'm afraid so. Quick, put on an old Spike Jones record.

CP: Now that we've discussed Nebraska, what topic would you like to go on to?

DC: Iowa?

# PART TWO
# FITZGERALDIAN FANTASIES

What can you say about a college that has a song entitled "For God, for Country and for Yale" and is unhappy about the order of the billing?

—DICK CAVETT, in his night-club act

We were sitting in the first balcony of the Shubert that night, instead of the second. It was a slight extravagance we allowed ourselves for productions that promised to be more than routine. In this case I suppose the attraction was the subject matter. The play was *Tea and Sympathy*, Robert Anderson's rather dewy portrait of a prep school student wrongfully suspected of being homosexual. The final scene was sure-fire for a New Haven audience, with the housemaster's wife preparing to go to bed with the boy in order to reassure him of his masculinity, slowly unbuttoning her blouse and saying, "When you talk about this later—and you will—please be kind. . . ."

"Come on," Dick said as the curtain came down. "Let's go back and meet her."

Ron Wille and I followed Dick as he wove expertly through the crowd, down to the lobby, along the side of the orchestra seats, behind a side box, and through a door leading backstage. This was standard procedure with Dick after a show at the Shubert, trooping back to the dressing rooms to talk to the stars. Our quarry this time was Maria Riva, who played the housemaster's wife and who at the time—the mid-fifties—was a prominent TV actress. She also happened to be Marlene Dietrich's daughter.

We knocked on her dressing-room door, were admitted, and went through the usual compliments and pleasantries. Then Dick lapsed into only slightly broken German, and he and the actress began chatting and laughing away between themselves. Ron and I exchanged glances. Yes, we should have expected this.

At length, after the conversation switched back to English, Dick said, "Miss Riva, we were wondering if you'd like to see the Yale campus tomorrow. You could visit a typical college room and sort of check the authenticity of the *Tea and Sympathy* set."

Ron and I looked at each other again. We had been wondering no such thing. Where did he get these ideas? We could hardly believe it when we heard Maria Riva say, "That sounds like such fun. I'd love to. Why don't you pick me up in the lobby of the Taft at two tomorrow afternoon?"

We still didn't believe it when we arrived at the Taft the next day. But there she was, striding out of the elevator with an opulent fur slung casually over her shoulder. "Will I need this?" she asked. "No? Too warm?" Without looking, she flung the coat into the air behind her, where it sailed into the waiting arms of a bellhop.

"But this won't fit my wife," the bellhop said.

"Keep it anyway." Maria laughed. It was just the sort of glamorous gesture we expected of Dietrich's daughter. Leaving the lobby, we did our best to *saunter* and not to break into a skip or to hop up and down with glee. We didn't want to look like college sophomores, but like suave, mysterious young men who could fill bellhops and passers-by with wonder and envy at our easy intimacy with a gorgeous actress.

It was a Saturday in November, and because of a big football game at Princeton the campus was half-deserted. As we headed past Nathan Hale's statue and across the freshman quadrangle Dick kept looking from side to side, glancing up at dormitory windows, checking over his shoulder. He was hoping to be spotted, wishing there were more students around to see us.

No doubt Maria was fully aware of being on display. She probably enjoyed playing up to the giddy expectations she must have known we had. She, no less than we, was taking what today would be called an ego trip. In the library, when some figures carved in the stone near the entrance to the rare-book room suggested sexual positions to her, she said mischievously, "I often marvel that men are so concerned to have the dominant position in sex. The woman is always dominant, you know, no matter what the position, because she *encloses* the man." This was heady stuff, especially for the rare-book room.

Back in Dick's room, she looked around appraisingly. "On the basis of this, I'd say our set was quite authentic, except that it may need a little more dirt. I must speak to the designer about that."

For the next two hours, as we sat and talked, Maria took pains to show us she was no broad. She had a Ph.D. in philosophy from a European university, she told us, and had lectured at Fordham. She discoursed, and quite well too, on literature, psychology, drama, music, and even something to do with electronics.

Our heads swam with the famous names she dropped, and with the faintly indiscreet inside dope she revealed. "A child trapped in a woman's body" was her description of one movie star. Of a leading lady of the New York stage, she said, "She can accept being an actress, but she can't accept being a woman." Maria gave the impression that her theatrical friends came to her as their unofficial analyst, a role that was becoming a bore to her on the *Tea and Sympathy* tour (her production was the road show, not the Broadway version). "After all," she said, "I can't unbutton my blouse for everybody in the cast."

She told us of a test that her mother had for people. If, without finding them ridiculous, you could imagine them in their underwear or seated on the toilet, they were okay. "I have the funniest mother in the world," she said.

She described parties at her Manhattan apartment where household names took off their jackets and shoes and sat on cushions spread around the floor, where Hemingway traded gibes with her mother, where Judy Garland sang while Benny Goodman and Harold Arlen accompanied her. "And you all must come," she said. "Next time you're in New York, call me up. Promise me you will."

Dick, our ringleader, inevitably took the initiative on our side of the conversation, flattering Maria with his memory of her TV roles and dispensing show-biz tidbits of his own. When she mentioned a movie performance that might get an Academy Award that year, Dick said, "But what is an Academy Award performance? If John Gielgud doesn't deserve an Oscar for *Julius Caesar*, then who does?"

"You must distinguish between an Academy Award performance and an Academy Award *role*, which is far more important in winning an Oscar," she said. She gave an amusing account of the uncanny effect that roles involving cripples, mutes, alcoholic frenzies, deathbed scenes, and courtroom recantations seemed to have on Academy members. Then she and Dick were off, comparing notes and trying to top each other with appropriate examples, from *Johnny Belinda* back through *The Lost Weekend* to *The Song of Bernadette*.

On the way back to the Taft, Maria put her arm around Dick's shoulder and confided, "Next time I come up here, I'd just love to bring Mummy. She'd strut around and enjoy every bit of the commotion she'd stir up." Next time? Mummy? If

Dick had been connected to an electrocardiograph machine at that moment I think he would have broken it.

In the lobby, after we arranged to buy Maria a ham sandwich and a malt around the corner and have them sent up to her room, so she could eat while she rested, she shook hands with each of us. "You know, I'm going to give a bad performance tonight because of you. I should have rested instead of doing all that talking. But it's all right. It was worth it. And don't worry. I have several levels of badness I descend through before I'm awful."

We returned to the campus in a hallucinatory state, walking the sidewalks at the same time that we had a sense of floating over the elms and Gothic spires like the ecstatics in a Marc Chagall painting. On the way, we made two vows: to follow through on Maria's invitation to one of her fabulous parties, and to make a regular practice, for the rest of our college careers, of entertaining stars from the Shubert. We never did either, of course.

My mind goes back to this episode whenever I think of Dick at Yale. It wasn't a significant episode in the sense that it changed anything or led anywhere. But it was thoroughly typical. Its motifs were the motifs of Dick's college life. The relative indifference to conventional campus events, for example, as shown in the fact that he hadn't bothered to go to Princeton for the football game. The immersion, already, in show business. The backstage savvy, the knack for wangling meetings with performers. The bedazzlement with big names. The surprisingly intellectual tenor of our afternoon's conversation. And, finally, the yearning for that wider and richer world that was New York, a world where Judy Garland might lean on the baby grand in one's apartment and Hemingway might sprawl on a cushion on the floor.

People who know Dick as a TV star usually assume that he must have had a glittering career at Yale. Not so. Yale isn't really the kind of place where a single undergraduate can dominate. "Big man on campus" was not only a phrase we never used, but also a concept that had no meaning for us. There may have been a few students who loomed large by filling several key functions at once—editor on the Yale *Daily News,* member of Skull and Bones and of some classy fraternity like Fence Club, crack debater, charity organizer, that sort of thing. Yet, prior to Dick's and my time, probably the last person to have stirred the whole university with the force of his personality and ideas was Bill Buckley, who graduated in 1950. Even when we arrived four years later professors were still shaking their heads over Buckley and saying that if only he possessed the common touch he'd be a truly dangerous man.

Normally, if you stood out at Yale, you stood out in some particular area, maybe two. The campus was a huge arena in which all four thousand contenders were broken down into small clusters milling and jostling under imaginary placards that read "Politicians" or "Swimmers" or "Scholars" or even "Noncontenders." If I can say this without sounding derogatory, it was like a dog show at which there were only best-of-breed competitions, not best-of-show. This diversity, this localization, was to Dick and me positively liberating; it was one of the glories of the place.

Dick competed, then, in the short-haired-actor category. He played in and directed radio dramas on WYBC, the campus station. He took part in the comparatively informal entertainments got up by the Saybrook Players, a troupe in the residential college where he and I lived as upperclassmen. He appeared in six or eight major productions of the campus-wide theater, the Yale Dramat. All of this made him well known only in Yale theater circles. Otherwise, he went to his classes, indulged his modest recreations, made side trips to New York—in other words, made no big splash.

When I mentally chart our time at Yale I picture Dick slightly off to the side—not out of things, but apart from the mainstream, and very self-sufficiently so. How else can I describe somebody who, unable to concentrate amid the deafening silence of the designated study halls and reading rooms, used to go off and study by himself on a park bench on the New Haven Green or on a couch in the lobby of the Taft? Dick always had an air of knowing his own business and blithely going about it. And that business rarely had anything to do with the Old Yale Fence or the tables down at Mory's or any of the other sacred relics of campus life. Dink Stover he was not.

He showed no interest in "heeling" the fashionable undergraduate institutions, like the Yale *Daily*. Like me and a good many other public school graduates, he had been enervated by good citizenship in high school. Dance committees, publications, language clubs, student councils—all good for the record, our high school counselors told us, all counting for something on our college applications. Well, now that we were in college we swore off them. Our time was going to be our own, and if that meant staying in our rooms for three straight days, except at mealtimes, in order to plow through a two-volume history of the movies or listen to the complete jazz recordings of Charlie Parker, then, dammit, so be it.

In sophomore year, pledge time for fraternities, Dick waived them too. Yale fraternities were nonresident anyway, and thus even more purely social than fraternities at, say, a state university. "What do we need with fraternities?" Dick asked me. "We can get nude, drink beer, and throw up on each other right here in our rooms."

In our upperclass years, when the names of our classmates began turning up on the election lists of honor societies, institutions like the Pundits, and, above all, the Secret Societies, Dick looked up with no more than mild surprise. "It mystifies me what apparatus is conducting these people into these things," he said, "what streams these people are swimming in that I'm not only not in, but not interested in, and not even aware of." These people and these things were, of course, the core of Yale by some standards, the very essence of Old Blueism. Dick's attitude toward them was the attitude of an anthropologist toward the tribal rites of a people he lives among—bemused, clinical, friendly, separate.

And sometimes less than friendly. He and I both were repelled by Old Blueism when it swirled up into a vortex of raucous beer blasts, social snobbery, and boola-boola spirit. Worst of all were the days, especially during football season, when alumni swarmed over the campus. Who were these flushed, slightly crocked minor John O'Hara characters who gabbled beneath their blue-and-white-striped tents at the Bowl, caroused in Fraternity Row, and invaded the college dining halls trying to assume a proprietary mien that didn't fit (pathos there) and making insensitive remarks to professors like "Well, still teaching English 15 after all these years, eh?" We swore we'd never be like them. Which is one reason why neither of us has ever gone back to a reunion, or gotten roped into more than one or two alumni functions over the years.

Was Dick happy at Yale? Fifteen per cent of the time, no. And the other eighty-five per cent of the time? Joy, contentment, and delight are among the words that come to mind.

Dick has often said that his years there were the happiest of his life—while he was experiencing them. I'm not sure whether I understand what he means by that qualification, or whether *he* does; but I do know what kinds of experiences prompted the feeling. Sitting on the roof of Saybrook College on a golden, spacious afternoon, jazz from somebody's phonograph floating on the air, a good book in hand. Coming out of a literature seminar in which Richard Young had induced the illusion not so much that the Karamazovs were like us, but that we were somehow Karamazovian. Relishing a guest lecture in which Mary McCarthy managed to seem entirely charming while wickedly making fools of the academics who questioned her from the floor. Returning to our rooms after a new Bergman film, building a fire in the fireplace, and talking until we, the fire, and a deli bag full of knishes and pickles were exhausted, convincing ourselves that we had raised the bull session to new heights (but of what?). Being in on the

first performance at the Shubert of a play that was destined
to be a hit on Broadway and far more than a hit, like O'Neill's
*Long Day's Journey into Night.*

"You know," Dick would say at times like these, "it's sometimes incredible to me that I'm here at Yale. Me. At Yale. All
the way from Lincoln, Nebraska. And I have the feeling I'm
going to look back on these times and see them as a perfect
bliss that I'll wish I could recover, but never will be able to."

My God, the leisure. Does anybody ever fully appreciate
how much of it he has at college and how little he's going to
have later? I don't mean only leisure to do nothing, but leisure
to do *something*—read, play a fugue, go to the movies, write a
short story, learn glass blowing, shoot baskets. Dick and I
luxuriated in it as much as anybody we knew, yet I think even
we underestimated it. One reason was that we spent so much
of it fretting about whether we ought to have it or what we
ought to do with it. We might have been better off drifting
through it thoughtlessly.

Instead we picked away at clichés about college being a
"preparation for life" or about graduation marking the moment
when we would "go out into life." Wrong, all wrong, we said.
This isn't preparation; this is *it*. We're already out into life.
We kept trying to rally each other to an ordering of priorities,
to decisive choices and purposeful motion. What are we doing
sitting around talking about Edmund Wilson or Groucho Marx
or Porfirio Rubirosa? we asked. We ought to be making up
our minds to *become* them and buckling down to the appropriate studying or writing or practicing. Time is passing. We
adopted as an inspirational text Rilke's *The Notebooks of Malte
Laurids Brigge,* in which a character becomes so obsessed with
the passage of time that he imagines he can feel it on his face
like a draft; he becomes dizzy because he senses the whirling
of the earth under his feet, and finally he retires permanently
to bed.

These sessions ended the way most such sessions end—
with us suffering a mild form of the Rilke character's fate. We

were so overwhelmed with all there was to do that we couldn't decide where to start. We made most of our resolutions and exhortations without stirring off our duffs.

"I for one am going to seize the bull by the horns and take a nap."

"Yeah. You go ahead. I'll come up with a plan right after this next beer."

The theme has remained constant with Dick right up to the present. In his early years in New York, with a comedy-writing deadline looming up, he would wander into the Metropolitan Museum, find a back stairway where he could read *Death in Venice*, then tread homeward chanting, in rhythm with his steps, "Get to work, get to work," and finally veer off into a movie. Nowadays he worries that he ought to be making better use of the money and influence that TV stardom has brought him, ought to be more disciplined and enterprising. "My life," he groans, "is in danger of becoming one long Sunday afternoon."

There is your characteristic Cavett attitude—mocking, playful, and serious all at once. Dick is genuinely concerned about the Sunday-afternoon tendencies of his life. At the same time he deeply enjoys them. And in the end, realizing that it is all a bit of a joke on himself, he is happy to leave the conflict unresolved.

I was kind of a curiosity at Yale. The other fellows weren't accustomed to mingling with poor people, and periodically one of them would ask to have his picture taken with me.

Then my Nebraska clothes set me apart. I remember I actually wore brown-and-white shoes. They were impractical, though. The white one kept getting dirty.

In my freshman year I guess I was a sucker for anything. I needed a tux for the freshman prom, and I went bargain-hunting at a store with a GOING OUT OF BUSINESS sign over the door. They had been going out of business for some time. The words "going out of business" were chiseled in stone—and the u's were v's.

They certainly saw me coming. The store's sharpest salesman sold me a khaki tuxedo.

We were both midwesterners in the East, nonaffluent public high school graduates at a university that still took its tone from prep schools like Andover and Groton, raw green recruits in the sanctum of Old Blues. As freshmen, our manners were too open, our vowels too flat, our suits too loud. We felt like strangers in a closed society where everybody but us knew the rules. How could we decide what kind of an account to open at the Yale Co-op or where to find cheap furniture for our rooms? How were we supposed to know that only idiots and exchange students from Latvia signed up for contracts with the student laundry and dry-cleaning service, which turned out to have perfected a fearsome process for converting wool to the texture of linoleum?

There was not only Yale to cope with, but also New Haven. Far from being the snug New England port its name suggested from a distance, it was a rugged industrial city of 75,000. The university lay quite close to the center of town, not out on the rolling, grassy fringes we might have imagined. The campus was sliced up by busy streets and blanketed by fumes and grime and the roar of trucks. Beneath our neo-Gothic leaded windows pranced girls from nearby Hillhouse High School chanting, "If you can't get a date, get a Yalie." One of our classmates, Dave Breasted, was robbed and stabbed one night on Chapel Street, not far from Dick's freshman quarters in Vanderbilt Hall. We were learning the meaning of strained town-gown relations.

The prep school graduates around us seemed forewarned and forearmed against such things. Presumably they had prior access to the folk wisdom of the campus. They seemed to arrive fully equipped with self-assurance, a circle of fifty friends, and a detailed knowledge of local geography and the university bureaucracy. It was as if they had been readying themselves all their lives for this moment, which some of them had.

Our being there was more nearly accidental. Dick's was due to Frank Rice, a teacher in an Omaha high school who was a friend and former college classmate of his parents. Rice had earlier spent a year doing graduate work at Yale as a John Hay Fellow. It was only at his enthusiastic urging that Dick decided to take College Board exams and apply for admission to Yale instead of coasting along to the University of Nebraska. As a result, Dick won the Louis H. Burlingham Memorial Scholarship, and is convinced to this day that everything that has happened to him since has happened only because of Rice, a burden of responsibility that I hope Rice is up to.

Despite the fact that we were admitted, that Dick had a scholarship, that we were physically *there*, we were afraid to put our trust in these superficial appearances. We secretly suspected that we had been enrolled only as a result of a clerical blunder in the admissions office and that, with our paltry provincial educations, we would never be able to keep up with the academic pace. Surely the day would come when the error would be discovered and we would be expelled. We studied frantically to avoid being found out.

The prevailing mystique of that era at Yale was summed up in the slang term "shoe." To be shoe you had to be cool, correct, and casually knowing. You had to wear, unostentatiously, the right clothes—khakis, charcoal grays, Harris tweeds, button-down collars, narrow rep ties—but, beyond that, you had to have, without straining for them, the right friends, the right memberships, the right *tone*. Was it Dick who dubbed the excesses of this already excessive attitude "overshoe"? In any case, as a fellow outsider I was attracted by the way he parried it, with an irony so light that his targets may not have felt a thing.

"Where did you prep?" the shoe types would ask him.

"I didn't," he would say. "I highed."

It was distinctly unshoe, Dick found, to be a scholarship boy—particularly the kind of scholarship boy he turned out to be in freshman year. In return for his money, he was required to put in fifteen hours of work per week for the university. He had asked to be assigned to the scholarly editing project that members of the English department were carrying out on Yale's collection of Boswell papers. Instead he was given a more usual freshman scholarship job, as a bus boy in the Trumbull College dining hall. It galled him to have been rejected for the Boswell papers, and it galled him even more to have to wear a little white jacket, slop dishes, and be called "boy" at Trumbull. Worried by the inroads that the fifteen hours per week were making on his studying, condescended to by the Trumbull upperclassmen, badgered by the vinegary New Haven women who made up the kitchen and waitress staff, Dick several times stopped just short of spitting in the soup cauldron out of sheer spite. At least he claims that he stopped short.

At one point during freshman year that very shoe institution the Yale *Daily* ran what Dick considered a needlessly supercilious piece about Barbara Bel Geddes, who was then appearing at the Shubert in Graham Greene's *The Living Room*. Dick protested in a letter to the editor. "Many of my friends are in the entertainment business, some stars, some not, and I know firsthand that this type of interview article is not appreciated," he wrote. He went on to say that "the lay public snaps hungrily at anything having overtones of 'inside dope' and exposing a celebrity as a louse. For the sake of better theater-Yale relationships, please put a stop to this sort of banality in the future."

In an editor's note following Dick's letter, the author replied that his piece had been not an attack but a "friendly pat on the back" for Miss Bel Geddes. Then, trying to clinch the point by knowledgeably citing an old French motto, he made a gaffe by quoting *"Honi soit qui mal y pense"* as *"On y soit qui mal y pense."* So it seemed Dick had the last laugh. But he didn't. An upperclassman named David Lloyd did.

Lloyd, impersonating an editor of the *News*, telephoned Dick and pretended to take a great interest in his friendship with the stars; he implied that the *News* might want to run a feature on Dick. Guilelessly, Dick unfolded half of his life story and bared at least one-fourth of his soul. After which Lloyd skewered him, just before slamming down the phone, by saying, "Well, Mr. Cavett, let me tell you, you're full of shit!" As the connection was cut Dick heard what sounded like a roomful of laughter at Lloyd's end. At his own end, Dick's roommates were sitting in the room listening, and although he tried to fake an amicable close to the conversation, when he put the phone down he was hot with humiliation.

Of such odd things are friendships made, for Dick eventually became fairly close to Lloyd. Ebullient, and wittier than his phone call to Dick might indicate, Lloyd was a fellow theater buff and a prolific writer of comic songs and patter. He once wrote an original musical for the Saybrook Players, in which Dick played a somewhat raunchy leprechaun. Lloyd was a fixture in the Saybrook common room, seated at the piano amid a circle of friends, joking and singing his own songs. It was in the effervescence of one of these moments that Dick told him, "You could be the Noël Coward of our generation."

Years later, they worked together as comedy writers on the *Tonight Show*. And to show how bygone bygones can be, after Dick got his own show he hired Lloyd as chief writer. Or could that have been a subtle form of revenge?

Thanks to Yale's mania for cross sections, both Dick and I were paired with at least one freshman-year roommate who was an eastern prep school product. Dick roomed with Jim Carney of New York City, who seemed to run true to type when he instructed Dick that the best thing about going to Yale was that it enabled you to say for the rest of your life that you had gone there. This proved to be an ironic pronouncement for Carney, who within a year dropped out under mysterious circumstances, as indeed did my roommate. (Failing grades? Fathers ruined on the market? We never found out.)

Before Carney departed, he led some expeditions to New York that, for the kid from Nebraska, were realizations of marvelous Fitzgeraldian dreams. One weekend he got Dick a date with a girl who lived on Park Avenue and whose father was Errol Flynn's lawyer. For overnight accommodations, he put Dick up at the Manhattan town house of a friend, François Landon, whose father was an art dealer who shuttled, domestically and professionally, between Paris and New York. Right inside the door of the town house was a famous Van Gogh. In the living room there were sparkling conversations, servants gliding in and out, and a brief appearance by François's father, in a dressing gown, accompanied by a woman who was later identified to Dick as his mistress. François was younger than Jim and Dick, a senior at Jim's old prep school, yet he struck Dick as being surpassingly mature, suave, sexually experienced, and in every way like Louis Jourdan. The party they were all going to was black-tie, and when François slid back his closet door Dick noted not one but *several* tuxedos. The only thing François seemed to lack was a place in the following year's class at Yale, which he was afraid he wouldn't get because of his grades. "Well," Dick thought, "that's at least one thing I've got on him."

For months afterward Dick relived this weekend in his fantasies, sifting and savoring its glamorous moments, projecting himself into a similar setting in future years—seeing himself, garbed in a dressing gown, welcoming some old Nebraska friend like Tom Keene to his New York apartment while Tom looked around in awe and murmured, "All this . . . yours?"

Meanwhile Dick was unaccountably pierced with homesickness. Lying awake at night, he longed to be back in his own bed in Lincoln. When his parents sent cookies he nibbled them a crumb at a time so they would last for weeks. The crisis came late in the fall at Freshman Commons, the class dining hall: somebody took the storm coat that Dick's father had given him. For two days Dick stood outside the Commons at every mealtime watching nearly a thousand freshmen come and go, hoping to pick out the culprit. He made a poignant figure, coatless, dwarfed by the building's massive colonnade, yet determined, implacable.

At last the student who had the coat got in touch, having

found Dick's name tag in the collar. But getting the coat back was more disheartening than losing it. It seemed the guy had been smashed the night it happened. His friends had lugged him out of the Commons hollering and puking; one of them had mistakenly grabbed Dick's coat and thrown it on their fallen comrade just as he catapulted his macaroons. Next day he had the coat washed; the lining shrank, and the entire front of the coat drew up in a sort of pucker. When Dick saw it and thought of his father giving it to him, he just wanted to wrap it around himself and start hitchhiking toward Nebraska.

The pangs passed. By Christmas vacation Dick was back in his *chez*-François guise rather than his puckered-storm-coat guise.

There is no more compleat Yale man than the freshman home at Christmas, and no more intolerable one. Every morning Dick donned his full uniform—Yale blazer, narrow rep tie, gold collar pin, and all—and strutted around Lincoln like a peacock. "Don't you want to relax a little?" his parents asked, in what Dick then thought was a naïve question, but was more likely satirical. He dropped show-biz names like hailstones and played his new LP of Yale songs loudly enough to be heard in the next county. When he was with high school friends he managed, whenever he pulled out his wallet, to oh so accidentally spill out of his pocket a book of Stork Club matches or to expose the package of rubbers without which no freshman wallet was complete. (The rubbers were a New York memento too; he had bought them at Gray's drugstore on Broadway, believing, perhaps correctly, that Catholic interests had gotten them banned in New Haven.)

Much of this I learned only later, after we became friends. We had met, at the beginning of freshman year, in the usual way: through his voice. Dick sat next to me in an 8:00 A.M. course on Major English Poets from Chaucer to Eliot, and at that hour I felt rather than heard him, like one of those bottom organ tones that give off only vibrations. When the teacher, Cecil Lang, assigned everyone in the class to memorize and recite the first fourteen lines of Chaucer's prologue to *The Canterbury Tales* ("Whan that Aprille with his shoures soote . . ."), he too was bowled over by Dick's voice, as well as by his delivery and authentic accent.

"Tell me, old man," said Lang, "what do you plan to do after college?"

"Oh, I don't know," Dick said. "Show business, I guess."

Lang seemed somehow disappointed. "I see. Well, I hear you can make pots and pots of money at that."

Dick and I were also in a freshman geology course taught by Richard Flint (inevitably nicknamed Rocky)—part of the smattering of science that Yale considered essential to the well-rounded gentleman. We were among the handful of students who were able to fill in the names of all the states on the blank outline map of the United States that Flint passed out on the first day. Score one for the public schools.

Gradually we cemented our bonds of common midwesternism, of shared anxieties. Dick admitted what an adventure it all seemed to him and told me that when he sallied forth from the Vanderbilt Arch into a typically gray, drizzly New Haven day for his opening lecture, a mental sign lit up in capital letters: MY FIRST DAY OF CLASSES AT YALE.

Two simple souls, we confessed that we felt a tingle of naughtiness when our teachers swore and talked dirty in the classroom. When Cecil Lang, let alone Chaucer, spoke of screwing and farting and of a woman's "queynte," it was a long way from Dick's matronly English teacher at Lincoln High skipping over a passage with the prissy explanation "Shakespeare saw fit to get a little smutty here." We liked the frankness--there was an implication that this was the way men of the world talked among themselves and that we were therefore MOTW—but we never got completely used to it. Even as late as senior year, in Joel Dorius's Shakespeare seminar, we felt a little jolt when Dorius said of Antony and Cleopatra's gamboling, "What are they doing here? They're fucking in public, aren't they?"

We were equally titillated and flattered by Yale's liquor

policy, which allowed liquor, but not bars, in all undergraduate rooms. When Dick asked a campus cop what the definition of a bar was, the cop said, "I suppose it's when you have blinking lights and girls serving the stuff."

At official functions the university acknowledged our sophistication to the extent of serving sherry, as we learned when the Yale president, Whitney Griswold, held a reception for freshmen at his home. At the age of eighteen, in a state where the legal drinking age was twenty-one, and in a life where the only booze you'd previously consumed in a private home was the dregs of your parents' crême de menthe on cracked ice, it was hard to take even a glass of sherry off a silver tray without feeling a little daring or furtive. Dick had both feelings, he later reported, but after he drank the sherry they went away, along with all other sensation. The next thing he knew—also according to his later report—he was in the reception line. He heard a voice saying, "Mr. Cavett, President Griswold."

He blurted out, "Nice to meet you. I voted for you."

Throughout the next four years—in fact, the next twenty years—Dick remained one of the worst drinkers I have ever known. A thimbleful of beer and his eyes rolled like the cherries in a slot machine; he began talking to lamp shades. He was not above turning this incapacity into a point of principle. After all, drinkers did terrible things, like throwing up on other people's storm coats. He was genuinely awed, and a little revolted, the first time he saw one of our classmates creep down to the dining hall at noon with a colossal hang-over. The poor fellow was pale, his hands trembled as he tried to down some tea and toast, and he admitted to Dick that when he had awakened in that condition he had felt it necessary to read the Bible.

I too followed the classic collegiate approach to the new-found freedom to drink, an approach that I rationalized with one of Blake's Proverbs of Hell: "You never know what is enough unless you know what is more than enough." Once, at a party in some fraternity house where I had emphatically discovered what was more than enough, I saw Dick at the other end of the room. He was standing on a small platform, and he looked so clean and bright and sober amid all the smoke and din that I wondered for a moment if he was about to deliver a temperance speech. Lurching toward him, I somehow ended up literally at his feet. He glared down from a physical and moral height, his Baptist grandfather's blood rising in him, and sneered, "God, you're disgusting!"

Whenever I tell this story, Dick denies ever having said such a thing. He invariably turns to whomever we're with and says, "I leave it up to you who is the more reliable witness, a sober person or a drunk."

But our different drinking habits were a passing issue. It was only later, after we began rooming together, that we settled down to the serious business of becoming irritated by each other's quirks. I found that he made up for his abstemiousness with gluttony. He was ready to eat a full meal at any hour of the day or night, even if he had just finished one. While busing dishes at Trumbull College he would become so ravenous at the sight of all those other people eating that he would palm some bread or a chop off a tray, duck down to the basement to devour it, and return before anybody had missed him. Yet he never gained any weight. I decided that inside that wiry, hundred-and-thirty-five-pound frame there was a very fat man screaming to be let out.

Dick had the sleeping habits of somebody who had recently been bitten by a tsetse fly. He rarely took less than nine hours at night, and often supplemented them with one and two-hour naps in the daytime. Ron Wille, the third man on our date with Maria Riva, did the same thing, but with Ron it was a stylishly Oblomovian gesture. With Dick it was a biological necessity. He couldn't conceive of people staying up all night to study for an exam, couldn't believe it was physically possible. When he occasionally awoke in the morning to find me hunched bleary-eyed over my books, he always suspected that I had merely gotten up early in order to make him think I had endured the night.

One night about ten, as I was reading at my desk in the narrow little bedroom we shared, Dick reached across in front of me and snapped my lamp off.

"Dickie's going to bed," he announced, and vaulted into his upper bunk.

We exchanged a few words over whether Dickie's absurdly early bedtime should dictate the schedules of his roommates. Then I took some reading into the living room and put a record on the phonograph—softly, as background. Immediately Dick stuck his head through the door and complained about the music.

"I never heard of anybody who couldn't sleep with music playing in an adjoining room," I said.

"Congratulations. You have now."

That was about as violent as our quarrels ever got. Many of Dick's flashes of temper were like heat lightning, passing quickly without bringing on a storm. Yet it was a real temper, and it flared especially when he felt he was being passed over or taken advantage of. This I attributed to his shortness. He had some of the feistiness of the bantam. It made him a good man to have along when dealing with waiters, salesclerks, or bureaucrats of any stripe.

During freshman year Dick had a run-in with the freshman dean, Harold Whiteman, who once was described by an undergraduate columnist as "Yale's postnatal drip." Dick wanted to be transferred out of an astronomy class, where he wasn't equipped to do the necessary mathematics and his grades were plummeting. His argument was that Yale had known his math background when he arrived and that putting him in astronomy was like putting him in an advanced course of a language he didn't know.

Whiteman didn't seem to see his point. "Do you really think math is difficult, Mr. Cavett?" he asked.

"It is for me, especially since I haven't had very much of it."

Whiteman picked up his pen. "Well, just give me a problem and I'll show you how it can be done."

Here Dick became angry, in the way that he does, his whole body stiffening, his face drawing tight until it looked like parchment stretched over a frame, his language becoming exaggeratedly prim and precise.

"I'm not interested in a display of your math prowess, Dean Whiteman, but in my lack of it."

The meeting ended badly. Dick stayed in astronomy, scraping through with blind guesses on the math problems.

Trim and self-possessed as he appeared in public, Dick turned out in private to be about as organized as the Italian high command. He could focus one faculty only by letting all others lapse into vagueness. While he concentrated on something he was saying to his roommates he unconsciously unbuttoned and removed his shirt. (I have waited in vain for years to see him do this in an important meeting or on television.) The logistics of going to a movie could undo him. "Let's see, I have to go by the bursar's office first, so if you go to the theater and get the tickets . . . but then I might be late, and you'd have to go inside, and I might not be able to find you . . . maybe you should come with me to the bursar's office—no, then we both might be late . . . oh, I can't cope. . . ."

Though I was hardly fastidious, I was appalled by the deterioration of our tiny bedroom (and periodically Yale's room inspectors shared my view). Dustballs rolled across the floor like sagebrush. The top of Dick's desk was a Sargasso Sea in which papers, whole books, could be lost for weeks. All the drawers in his dresser were pulled out, and from them a motley stream of socks, shirts, and underwear cascaded to the floor. As a roommate, he left only one thing to be desired: a maid.

There were a lot of unbelievably smart guys at Yale. I mean guys who could walk down the street humming a crossword puzzle. For guys like me, who were worried about academic failure, Yale had what were called "gut" courses, courses that almost anybody could pass. I took one in the Old Testament. If you had a rough idea of the plot you could get through.

In that course I was reassured to meet at least one student who was dumber than I, a fellow named Clarence. Clarence had only gotten into Yale through influence. He came from a very old family. In fact, they could trace their family tree back to the original lungfish that crawled out on land.

But Clarence was hopeless. The final exam in the Old Testament course was a multiple-choice quiz on which the toughest question was: "Lot's wife was turned into a pillar of: (a) salt; (b) pepper; (c) margarine." Clarence missed that. He answered it "no."

Is Dick Cavett an intellectual? If I had one point of IQ for every time I've been asked that question within a six-month period, I'd be a genius. He certainly passes for one by the standards of commercial television. But then, as Judith Martin once observed in the Washington *Post*, being an intellectual on a talk show may consist simply of egging on Gore Vidal, rather than Zsa Zsa Gabor, to say something silly.

But you roomed with him in college, people persist; you should know. Well, the word "intellectual" is a loaded pistol. I wouldn't point it at a friend. I'd prefer to say that Dick has a good intellect. And a mild streak of Puritan conscience. And a schoolteacher for a father. Put them all together and you have a Yale student who works hard and gets good grades, often good enough to qualify for the dean's list. The imposture that we worried about in freshman year was never unmasked.

Yet there was something almost incidental about Dick's academic achievements. He wasn't grimly piling up credits. He hadn't the slightest interest in progressing to an advanced degree. ("It isn't the bright students who go on to graduate school," one of my teachers once told me, shortly before I went on to graduate school. "It's the persistent ones.") Nor was he a burrower, exploring the deepest labyrinths of a subject. Quick and curious, his mind moved, as in the Yeats line, "like a long-legged fly upon the stream." He had little in common with either the grinds or the brilliant weirdos.

The latter type, of which neither he nor I had had any experience in high school, was exemplified for us by Dick Higgins, a tall, pale spirit who always dressed very formally in dark clothes and had a wild corona of curly hair. Higgins affected to be far beyond the rudimentary challenges posed by course work and into avant-garde experiments of his own. He would flash the first page of his latest short story in front of you and then snatch it away before you could read any more than the opening sentence, which was usually enough. I remember one that began: "The rain came down like snot." Or he would announce to anyone who would listen that he had started a string quartet that abolished the concept of pitch, since each note was a glissando.

One morning in the Saybrook dining hall Higgins sat down next to Dick with a weary sigh and said, "I spent the whole night drinking Pernod and reading John Donne's sermons, arguing furiously with Donne in the margins."

"Gee," said Dick, somewhat at a loss. "I'll have to try that."

Dick was as interested in the extra as the curricular, and he worried because there was never enough time for all the plays, lectures, paperbacks, and the like that beckoned. One of our doleful exercises was to try to top each other's list of great unread books; it sometimes seemed that Yale assumed we had read them all, whereas they were what we went to Yale *for*. Dick managed to get through *War and Peace* before graduating only because of a salutary case of measles, which enabled him to spend two days in the Yale infirmary reading solidly from waking to sleeping.

The literary, the dramatic, the philosophical and psychological—these pretty well defined Dick's academic orbit. But his greatest facility was in languages. When it came to conversational French or German, he had the knack of a Caesar—Sid, that is, not Julius. Except that he wasn't faking. This gift was to earn him his first network television appearance, on the *Jack Paar Show* in 1961. One of Paar's guests was the then Miss Universe, a German girl who spoke no English, and Paar brought Dick on, as "one of our young staff members," to translate. Something must have been gained in translation, for Dick's English version of the girl's remarks got several big laughs.

Dick has always had a prodigious gift for wordplay—anagrams, spoonerisms, puns, palindromes, anything that requires quick feats of recognition and rearrangement. He could glance at a book by Oscar Wilde and say, "Do you realize that an anagram for 'Oscar Wilde,' which could also be the first line of a suppressed poem by him, is 'O lad I screw'?" Or he could take the name of a contemporary writer and spoonerize it into a description of somebody who crucifies members of the Church of Jesus Christ of Latter-day Saints, that is, Mormon Nailer. If the conversation turned to one of Sol Hurok's coups in bringing Soviet artists to the United States, Dick would remark, "You know, if you met Sol Hurok at a cocktail party the best way to open the conversation would be to ask, 'Have you booked any good Reds lately?'"

This sort of thing became part of the aural background of my life at Yale, like traffic noise. There were the Harkness bells, the rattle of beer cans on stairways, and Dick's voice relentlessly breaking up and re-forming familiar names and expressions. We both met a fellow named La Fontaine, who had in him a little of the pixie as well as the braggart. It wasn't long before Dick was referring to "the fey bull of La Fontaine." When we marveled at a promiscuous girl of our acquaintance who, because she was Catholic, never practiced birth control yet never became pregnant, he hit upon the simple explanation: immaculate contraception.

His invention was tireless, and therefore also tiresome at times. You might have had a serious point to make about Salvador Dali, or you might have wanted to mention Dali only incidentally on the way to some other point, but it was no use. The mention of the name set Dick off: "Did you know that 'Salvador Dali' is an anagram for 'Slav laid Roda'?"

"Hmmm," you could say, as noncommittally as possible.

"Or 'Roda laid Vals'?"

"Yeah. Well—"

"Wait. Better yet: 'Dial Roda's lav.'"

"Stop, stop!"

Actually, Dick was as much at the mercy of the anagrams that came to him as we were. They weren't calculated; he never paused to figure them out. They were formed instantly in his mind by a sort of synaptic seizure. He had only to glance at a marquee with Alec Guinness's name on it to know somehow that "Alec Guinness" was an anagram for "genuine class." And once he had one anagram, variations on it might follow in waves —"mister" became "merits" . . . "mitres" . . . "remits" . . . "timers" . . .

This ability was a reliable icebreaker; failing anything else to say to somebody he'd just been introduced to, Dick could always do an anagram on the person's name. In recent years he has done this occasionally with guests on his TV show, although his audience probably doesn't realize how spontaneous it is. When greeting Theobald the Futurist, for example, Dick informed him that "Theobald" was an anagram for "bad hotel" and "hot blade." The mental patterns involved in these tricks may in fact be a part of what has always made Dick a good conversationalist—his deftness at making unlikely connections, at reshuffling familiar elements.

Yet even at Yale he realized that his most brilliant anagrams were feats for which the world had little use. He used to say, "I'm highly qualified to win a lot of money on a game show that will never be invented." Much as he enjoyed his penchant for wordplay, he sometimes regarded it as a curse. He professed to be a little worried when he read in a psychology textbook that compulsive punning was a symptom of the prelude to schizophrenia. But soon he appropriated even this diagnosis into his comic lexicon; just say the phrase "prelude to schizophrenia" to him today and you'll get a laugh, if not a net thrown over your head.

For myself, I have never regarded his wordplay as anything more ominous than the sound of some very good mental machinery idling or, when the jokes are really good, playfully revving. Most of his friends at Yale, I think, would gladly have exchanged it for their own particular neuroses, especially when he was using it to humiliate us at competitive word games.

We spent many hours at such games that might otherwise have been devoted to more respectable pursuits, like harassing the campus cops or mortgaging our futures at the five-cents-a-point bridge table that was maintained in Pierson College. We used to improvise limericks in rotation, one line per player, to see who could come up with the best rhymes. Dick became bored with this, for in the time it took some clodpate to think of a single line he could sometimes complete one or two complete limericks. He also had an inexhaustible capacity to improvise rhymed couplets in iambic pentameter—awful stuff, usually, but perfectly parsed; and very useful if he should ever forget his lines while acting in an eighteenth-century play.

Another game that he and I invented had no name, but was a sort of verbal dominoes, reminiscent of a game played on the old *It Pays to Be Ignorant* radio show. The first player would mention a well-known person, and the next player would have to think of a well-known person whose first name was the same as the last name of the previous one, and so on. The hitch was that, after the first name, no names could be said aloud; each had to be evoked through a brief description. Thus:

"Thomas Mann."

"No, you're thinking of a surrealist painter and photographer" (Man Ray).

"No, you're thinking of a drummer with Glenn Miller" (Ray McKinley).

"No, you're thinking of the author of *Andersonville*" (Mac-Kinlay Kantor).

For this, my parents were paying two thousand dollars a year.

In the classroom, Dick was drawn to teachers who were personalities, who had a histrionic flair. He went around collecting them—following up on campus legends or rumors about this lecturer or that seminar leader, sitting in on friends' or roommates' classes, sometimes signing up formally to audit extra courses. He fastened eagerly on a teacher's catch phrases or facial tics or rhetorical gimmicks. Once he had made the man come alive in his imagination as an almost Dickensian character, he could make the subject come alive through the man. It was not a bad way of learning. He can still "do" several professors today; their language and mannerisms are part of his and my vast repertoire of private jokes.

One of his favorites was Paul Weiss. If Socrates had been reincarnated in New York's garment district, he would have turned out to be Weiss. A bald, gnomish little man, whose manner was by turns comical, belligerent, and judicious, Weiss was an unabashedly old-fashioned metaphysician who taught that there were more things in philosophy than were dreamt of in our heaven and earth. He was also intrigued by the theater and theater people; he was the only professor we knew of whose cocktail parties were frequented by a Broadway actress (Janice Rule). It was inevitable that Weiss would take Dick up. In the years since then, Dick has returned the compliment by repeatedly having Weiss philosophize on his show—surely a first of some kind.

Maynard Mack was another favorite. Mack was a Pope scholar as well as one of the campus's foremost lecturers on Shakespeare. He spoke in a nasal twang and perversely anglicized the names of all the characters (Gloucester was "Glauchester," Bolingbroke was "Bowling-broke"), yet he had the features of a gray eagle, and when he narrowed his eyes to slits and gazed over our heads as if glimpsing some far horizon, he could be a spellbinder. At least he spellbound Dick, who used to go out of his lectures in a state of high exhilaration.

Then there was Bernard Knox, a bluff Britisher with a bull-dog jaw, who made Greek tragedy seem really Greek and really tragic. Dick came up with a story from somewhere that Knox had been a commando during World War II, specializing in demolition. This invested Knox with a combined aura of don-nishness and derring-do, like Jack Hawkins in *The Bridge on the River Kwai*. Knox too followed the theater, even though he considered that it had all been downhill after Euripides. I re-member him visiting Dick backstage at the Dramat after a performance of an undergraduate musical based on *Cyrano de Bergerac*. He had compliments for the performance, but he typically dismissed the original Rostand play as "a load of Hottentot rhetoric."

Nothing about these men impressed Dick more than their farewell messages to their classes at the end of term. The drama of the occasions appealed to him as much as the import. Mack put the bleak wisdom of Shakespearean tragedies into this-worldly terms. He cited Phlebas the Phoenician in *The Waste Land*, who after drowning

*Forgot the cry of gulls, and the deep sea swell*
*And the profit and loss.*

*.    .    .    .    .*

*He passed the stages of his age and youth*
*Entering the whirlpool.*
                    *Gentile or Jew*
*O you who turn the wheel and look to windward,*
*Consider Phlebas, who was once handsome and tall as you.*

"Years from now," Mack said in his dry, almost rasping voice, "when you're standing at the Astor Bar, and you're on your second martini and third wife, consider Phlebas, gentle-men, who was once handsome and tall as you." Well, the Astor Bar is no more, and Dick is still on his first wife and probably has never had a second martini; yet he can recite Mack's peroration today with an intensity that shows how deeply it still stirs him.

Weiss evoked the death of Socrates for his class. After inculcating philosophic speculation in us all year, he warned nevertheless that "the contemplative life is haunted by the specter of hemlock."

Weiss also delivered an unusually somber speech at our senior banquet, a few weeks before we graduated. Not only did he tell us that his generation was leaving us "a miserable heritage . . . a world torn, tensed, broken in every way." Also, he went on, "I cannot say that I really believe—because I do not think that you're any different from what we were in 1913 or 1927—that you will make any or much of a difference to the world we pass on to you." The best he could offer was the *hope* that we would make it "a little less miserable."

There were members of our class who resented this speech and felt that it cast a pall on the banquet; they wanted more of the traditional flowery uplift. Not Dick and me. We applauded the absence of bullshit, the willingness to treat us as mature realists. In this I think we were being true to the impulses of our generation, the so-called silent generation. We didn't want to have any illusions. Tell us the worst, was our attitude; strip us, flay us. We were more than ready to believe that our heritage was miserable—a few fragments, as *The Waste Land* put it, to shore against our ruins.

Of course the label "silent" was misapplied. It didn't describe our generation so much as our period. I think Dick and I and our contemporaries eventually came to realize that the quest for no illusions was itself an illusion; that the belief that the worst news was necessarily the truest was itself false; that what had seemed definitive traits of our generation mostly defined the mood of the time.

For all this took place, you must remember, during the Great Doldrum. The reverberations of the Korean War had died away. The campuses of Eisenhower's America had not yet been jarred and swamped by the now familiar list: racial tensions; the drug culture; protest; violence; Mick Jagger; Consciousness Three, or at least Two and a Half. In the gap, we were caught with our aspirations down. We had lost the old faith that any-thing could be achieved within the social and political system except the most immediate and selfish goals—job, salary, con-tentment within our individual caves. We had not yet caught the new faith of the angries and the mystics, the sitters-in and the droppers-out who were to follow us—the faith that some-thing transcendent could be achieved outside the system or in-side one's head.

So it was a time for shoring up. Camus and David Riesman were our prophets. Security was our byword; that didn't always mean a job with IBM, but we knew there would come a time, as Lenny Bruce told us, when we would have to "grow up and sell out." Our fable was *Lord of the Flies;* Tolkien had barely been noticed by then, and Hesse was still considered old, not new.

We had what we melodramatically called riots—mob scenes at intersections, with streamers of toilet paper flying overhead —but no issues were involved. College was a place where we had come not to confront the great issues of the day, but to evade them temporarily. It was an enclave where relevance was blessedly irrelevant. Dick and I could get worked up about the Hungarian uprising or Adlai Stevenson's rude reception at Yale during the 1956 presidential campaign; yet when the fore-runners of student activism appeared, under acronymic banners like SANE and CORE, when the first demonstrators took off for Birmingham or organized a picket line in front of a Wool-worth's in New Haven, we remained sympathetic but aloof.

One day at the end of 1957 a Japanese professor who was a Fellow of Saybrook College sat down with us in the dining hall and asked how sputnik had changed our lives. Dick looked at me; I looked at him. We both saw in each other's eyes a reflec-tion of what we felt: perfect blankness. Sputnik was a headline item, of course, a conversation piece. But changed our lives? Ask us in ten years—and meanwhile pass the salt, please. Gen-erally, we left current events to the drones in the Political Union. Dick freely admitted that he went for months, maybe years, without reading anything in the newspaper except the theater pages.

I wanted to invite a girl to the campus for a big football weekend, so my roommate fixed me up with a blind date. You know the old vaudeville gag "She was so ugly that her face would stop a clock"? My date had stopped sundials. It was easy to recognize her when I went to meet her at the railroad station. She was standing amidst a group of people who had turned to stone.

It turned out she was attending Bennington on the Gertrude Stein wrestling scholarship. Her major was guerrilla warfare. She spent a lot of the weekend telling me about a term paper she had written for a religion course trying to prove that there *was* room at the inn—but it was restricted.

By Sunday I really didn't know what to do with her. I asked her if she'd like to go to a movie, and she said yes. So I gave her the money.

Nowadays, as Dick's and my contemporary Holden Caulfield would say, they've got goddam *women* at Yale, for Chrissake. When we were undergraduates, a casual remark by the director of admissions that Yale might benefit from going coed prompted every headline writer in the nation to express facetious alarm. A "Keep Yale Male" movement was organized by students and alumni, and campus theater troupes whipped up dozens of feminist and antifeminist satires. President Griswold felt constrained to reassure an anxious world that "we are nowhere near deciding the question."

At that time girls were allowed in the rooms only between noon and 7:00 P.M. (11:00 P.M. on Saturdays). Now everything, including bathrooms, is coed, and cohabitation is an unofficial fact of campus life. When Dick revisits Yale today, he finds not only that his old freshman quarters in Vanderbilt Hall are occupied by girls, but also that above the door in his old bedroom a brass plaque announces: DICK CAVETT SLEPT HERE.

"What's more," says Dick, "I didn't put it there."

In our own benighted, precoed days, social life followed a simple pattern: long periods of monkish deprivation interrupted by occasional intervals of what were designed to be bacchanalian revels, but often turned out to be convulsions of forced hilarity and forced virginity, or slow-motion sequences of Antonionilike boredom. Study dates, coffee dates, any kind of relaxed everyday date—we scarcely knew what they were, lacking girls on campus as we did. Instead we had the institution of the Big Weekend. As a way of spending some time with a girl, it had all the spontaneity and simplicity of a De Mille spectacular, and a budget to match.

Weeks in advance, you had to find a date, through whatever divining rod your ingenuity could devise. Next you got her a hotel room in New Haven at special weekend rates (that is, double the weekday rates). Then you crammed the weekend calendar with a schedule of restaurant meals, sporting events, dances, milk-punch brunches, and jazz concerts that would have exhausted Scott Fitzgerald. Finally, the two of you tried to find some way of slogging through the whole affair without becoming heartily sick of each other. Age may not have withered nor custom staled Cleopatra's infinite variety, but a Yale weekend could have worn it pretty thin. (The entire procedure was reversed, with similar results, when the weekend was at the girl's school and you were the imported date.)

My own solution to the problem arose from the dance and jazz bands I formed to play at these occasions, which afforded me a beachhead from which to make side forays. Dick's solution was to by-pass the problem entirely. In four years at Yale he never once went on a date to a girls' school, and he only rarely broke down and invited a girl to New Haven. Hats off, gentlemen. Nor did he resort to such local alternatives as the Nursing School, Albertus Magnus College, or Hillhouse High School, all of which, rightly or wrongly, were viewed as the frontiers of desperation.

What was left? Deferring the matter of girls until after graduation, like the draft? Allowing himself to be kept by an older woman on the faculty? No, Dick's expedient was the Yale stage, the logical gathering place, come to think of it, of the liveliest and best-looking girls in town.

I saw little in Dick of the dry-throated, moist-palmed suitor he claimed to have been in high school. I do recall that at the freshman prom, his first and last prom at Yale, he expressed a fervent wish that "the dancing would be over." But as he got to know girls in Dramat productions—Drama School students, mostly—and as he began pairing off with them in rehearsal breaks and cast parties, he at least conveyed the impression of a certain charm and ease.

At one Drama School Christmas party I inadvertently knocked over a partition screen and to the assembled revelers revealed Dick locked in an embrace with a New Haven girl and would-be actress named Beverly Davis. This charming tableau won a hearty round of applause. Dick naturally accused me of deliberately embarrassing him, but I blamed the Drama School's vodka punch. And, in my defense, I must add that I was hardly the only one to be clobbered by that punch. A little later in the evening an actor named Paul Asselin attacked the Christmas tree in the corner of the room, wrestled it to the floor, and managed, just barely, to subdue it without electrocuting himself on the lights.

Sometimes Dick would bring a girl up to our room and, when the moment came when she seemed disposed to give him a back rub, would make frantic silent signals to any of us who had not already cleared the premises. Not that he was—at that point—a full-fledged swordsman, wit, and breaker of hearts. He was not capable, for example, of being blasé about the frequent visits that Jane Fonda, then a Vassar student, made to one of the guys who lived upstairs from us; he listened as breathlessly as the rest of us for the click-click of her high heels on the tile corridor outside the guy's room—*after hours!* Yet in his own way he was doing better than we were.

Or than I was, anyway. When I tried to share in Dick's success I usually ended up making him share in my lack of it. One night, when he and I were walking along a street near the campus, two girls pulled up in a car and asked directions for a New Haven address we'd never heard of. After a couple of minutes of joshing, we suggested, rogues that we were, that we could better help them by getting in the car and pointing out the way. They agreed, and we hopped in—but both in the back seat, a bad start.

We drove around aimlessly for a while, Dick and I making pointed allusions to West Rock, a traditional parking spot, the girls seeming evasive and finally a little bored. Suddenly the girl who was driving pulled over to the curb and said she wanted to check the engine, which was "acting up." Then, improbability piling on improbability, Dick announced that he had to relieve himself and faded into the shadows.

The driver and I began peering under the hood. This was the time to make a move, right? Wrong. All I got for it was a near miss on my fingers as she slammed down the hood and on my toes as she jumped back in the car and roared away into the night.

Enter Dick, out of the darkness, to find me standing alone in the middle of the street in a strange neighborhood, all explanations seeming somehow superfluous. As we made our way back to the campus we consoled ourselves that with a little added business it would have made a good Laurel and Hardy episode.

From a roommate's vantage point, all of Dick's conquests took place offstage. The evidence for them was convincing but circumstantial. Occasionally I would awaken in the morning and notice that the upper bunk in the double-decker bed we shared was not sagging. No Cavett. Aha! Around noon he would amble in, his collar open, his manner radiating well-being. By suppertime he would allow himself to be coaxed into telling me and the others about it. Then, withholding only a few of the most explicit details, he would spin out a narrative that, while appealing primarily to prurient interests, certainly struck us as being full of redeeming social value.

It was typical of Dick that he made the most of these anecdotes. He was a great magnifier. Everything seemed more vivid and intense when he described it. Friends of his you

hadn't met sounded so witty and audacious, experiences of his
you hadn't had sounded so fascinating—often it was only when
you caught up with these people and things yourself that you
realized they took on some of their life through Dick's appreciation.

Nowhere was this better demonstrated than in Dick's account, at the beginning of our sophomore year, of his sexual
initiation the previous summer. Reduced to its essentials, the
episode consisted of familiar and mundane ingredients—an
amiable slattern, a bunch of callow boys, a shadowy rendezvous.
Yet by the time Dick got through with it, it sounded like
*Tristan und Isolde*. I don't mean he falsified things, or even
merely overstated them. I really believe that his ego, vitality,
and verbal powers conspired, and still conspire, to heighten his
sense of life. It is part of what makes him such good company.
And if you are a friend of his, it is pleasant to imagine how he
must make you sound to others.

One of the girls whom Dick met at the Drama School was
his wife-to-be, Carrie Nye McGeoy. Carrie Nye—she used both
names, in the southern manner, as in Mary Beth or Janet Lee; a
little confusing after she also shortened her stage name to just
Carrie Nye—was a banker's daughter from the delta town of
Greenwood, Mississippi. She came to Yale from Stephens College, in Missouri, and over a period of three years played dozens
of roles that established her as perhaps the Drama School's
most gifted and stylish actress. She was in everything—original
one-acters by Yale playwriting students, major Drama School
productions, plays ranging from *Marco Millions* to *The Way of
the World* and from Garcia Lorca's *The House of Bernarda
Alba* to Tennessee Williams's *This Property Is Condemned*.

She also appeared in several of the Dramat productions
that Dick was in—among them *The Crucible* and *La Ronde*.
Often her parts in these productions were bigger than his, a
pattern of apparent overshadowing that was to prevail for
several more years.

In the years since her marriage to Dick, Carrie Nye has

delighted in telling interviewers that her and Dick's meeting at Yale was loathing at first sight. "He thought I was Zelda Fitzgerald and I thought he was Frank Merriwell. We were both sadly mistaken," she will say. "He was an extremely serious-minded young man. His idea of a good time was to go drink sherry in his room and read Dr. Johnson's dictionary."

When Dick was interviewed by *Playboy* magazine in 1971, he claimed that he and Carrie Nye had not met at Yale at all, but in a brothel in Paris. "I asked her to leave her tawdry profession and marry me, as I was planning a career combining the best aspects of podiatry and fortunetelling. She said that hers seemed a more honest trade, but she told me to keep in touch. A year later, she appeared in New York, married to a UN delegate, and we had a brief liaison in chambers I kept for that purpose at the Hotel Alamac. Her husband was recalled to Paris by a combination of international tensions and chronic gastroenteritis and eventually forgot her, so I married her."

After all that, the truth is bound to be disappointing, and it is. For the first couple of years after they met, they paid scarcely any attention to each other, much less did any loathing or wooing away from tawdriness. The closest they came to socializing with each other was at a Beaux-Arts ball at the Art School. Carrie Nye was there with a group of friends, all acting very cool and sophisticated, while Dick and a classmate named Dave Adnopoz were distinguishing themselves by setting off firecrackers in various corners of the room. For some reason, Dick kept asking Carrie Nye to dance the tango with him. Carrie Nye persistently declined, though whether because of the firecrackers or some prior knowledge of Dick's dancing, she will not say.

Dick at least acted with her in plays; he occasionally saw her serious and hard-working side. Most of the rest of us saw only her Zuleika Dobson side. To us she was, in local terms, a star, and we saw her through the haze of glamour that stardom generates. A Mississippi blonde, mercurial, a trifle flamboyant, she was a vivid presence on our gray campus, especially compared with Smith girls in their sensible sweaters and loafers. She must have gone to every prom that was held while she was at Yale. She turned out at garden parties. She gave poetry readings. She was much fussed over, spoiled, and petted.

What even her numerous beaux (her word) probably missed was the extent to which she played up to all this with a deliberate frivolity that at times approached a put-on. Maybe we all missed it, which would mean that she really had put us on. All I know is that after one of Dick's and my roommates met her at a party he announced that behind her façade she "wasn't all she was cracked up to be," and the rest of us, including Dick, were content to let that verdict stand.

It wasn't until after Dick graduated, and both he and Carrie Nye were acting at the Williamstown, Massachusetts, summer theater, that Dick realized she had been granted a truly unfair allotment of brains along with her beauty, and some serious interest developed. And it wasn't until their second Williamstown season that Dick worked for two weeks in a local lumberyard to earn the money for an engagement ring. Over the next four years their love was a many-splintered thing, but they were finally married in New York late one afternoon in a quick, private ceremony squeezed between performances of *The Trojan Women,* an off-Broadway production in which Carrie Nye was playing a leading role. It was June 4, 1964, and if you can remember that date you're doing more than either of them has ever been able to do.

The Yale library, besides being a gloomy Gothic pile, always loomed in my mind as an ominous and threatening institution. I returned from Christmas vacation one year to find a stern letter from the library saying that some missing books had been found in my room. I was summoned to the librarian's office to answer charges that I had stolen them. I immediately sensed that he meant business when I reached over to shake hands and he pulled out one of my fingernails.

"What makes you so sure those books are mine?" I asked him.

"We have our methods. You're an English major, and the books are novels and poems." I gave a mocking, bitter laugh. "Everybody knows that English majors don't read novels and poems; they read criticism." Then I went too far. I told him I resented his "Gestapo tactics."

"You shouldn't have said that," he said. "You'll be sorry you did."

Two weeks later my aunt disappeared in Germany.

The library story is an exaggeration, of course. Dick's aunt didn't disappear; she was merely held for ransom. But any implication that he was virtually mesmerized by the shadowy alcoves of the Sterling Memorial Library is correct. Two of his favorite private studying preserves were there—one on a roof top outside a window in the stacks, the other in a lounge for female employees that was unused after 5:00 P.M. After his freshman year of being a bus boy, his scholarship job was there too. He drew the assignment of assisting the curator of the Yale Musical Theatre collection, Robert Barlow, whose trove was housed in the library basement. Down there, Dick rummaged through old scores and programs while listening to Barlow's eccentric, biting commentary on shows past and present, and for Dick this was not work at all.

Through his acting Dick got to know another librarian, Herman ("Fritz") Liebert, who was a patron of the Dramat. Liebert, I suspect, was the source of the insider's knowledge that Dick dropped offhandedly about realms of the library beyond the ken of most undergraduates—the rare-book room, the little scholarly mill where the Walpole letters were being stitched together, and that most fabled bit of arcana, the Zeta collection of pornography (which was said to be even better than the Vatican's).

But even this relative intimacy was not enough for Dick. He seemed to want to come to terms with the library physically, as if its stony vaults and passageways might have a message or say "boum" to him, like Forster's Marabar Caves.

One midnight he persuaded me to linger with him in some hiding place inside the building while it was darkened and locked for the night. Then we crept about for a few minutes, stumbling and whispering in the blackness. I don't think we were seeking anything in particular, unless it was a simple Tom Sawyerish thrill—but we did find that. All those spiky chandeliers and empty chairs and tables, felt more than seen, had an eerie expectancy about them. And our nerves were kept jumping by an occasional startlingly loud click or creak (but no "boum").

We realized as we started to leave that we had neglected to plan how to get out. After some anxious moments, during which we speculated about whether mice would bother us if we spent the night on the leather couches in the Linonia and Brothers Reading Room, we finally wriggled out through a narrow leaded window beside the huge wooden main doors—fortunately undetected by watchmen or campus cops. Our relatives in Germany were safe.

Our library prowl was the capstone of a minicareer of sneaking into university buildings at night. Lecture halls, architecture drafting rooms, laboratories—Dick led the way into them all (not by breaking, just entering), and I and whoever else we had recruited would follow, grope around, disturb nothing, depart, and consider the time well spent.

Dick was also a great roof man. If there was a way to be found to clamber out onto the top of a building via window, trap door, or fire escape, Dick would find it. He spent more time on roofs than a cat burglar. (Good God! Do you suppose . . . ) Where he preferred having a few accomplices when he poked around in buildings, he enjoyed being alone when he went up among the crenellated battlements of Saybrook College or the Payne Whitney Gym. On fair days, he always said he wanted to get a little sun while studying. But on inclement days or at night—well, I leave that to the Freudians.

I realize these outings barely deserve the name of escapades. Next to the drunken students who cleaned their fifth-floor room one night by throwing all the furniture out the window; next to the Yalie who successfully ran for a campus office at Harvard under an assumed name; next to the freshman who made the bells atop Battell Chapel ring at odd hours by shooting at them from his window with a twenty-two rifle; next to the class ahead of ours that introduced a horse onto the dance floor at their junior prom; next to all these, our own pranks were feeble gestures—poor things, but our own.

At the time they struck me as very midwestern, extensions of boyhoods spent climbing bluffs and exploring haunted houses. Even now Dick is fascinated by derelict resorts, abandoned warehouses, deserted buildings of any kind. But why should the Midwest have a corner on boyishness? The fact is, these pranks were also just plain silly. And silliness was always a major theme in our friendship. We seem to have agreed tacitly that there was ample seriousness around us already and that we need not add to it unduly, at least not when we were relaxing together.

This remains true today. Part of what Dick and I offer each other is an escape into inconsequentiality, no small thing. Our wives and our colleagues don't understand it, so it must be worth while. We can interrupt something important, something serious, and talk to each other on the phone for thirty or forty minutes without once touching on a subject of substance or conveying a speck of information. Our conversation is often a skein of private jokes, persiflage, and jabberwocky. Dick may need this even more than I do, now that he is caught up in the all-too-consequential pressures of TV stardom and I have slipped into the Eddie Albert role in his life—the faithful holdover who knew him when. But at Yale it was the other way around.

Then I was more often the one who needed decompressing and deflating. I would hold forth about a writer until my pomposity became a little too much for Dick to resist, as it did one evening in the Saybrook dining hall when I subjected a table of friends to a slightly moist appreciation of Dylan Thomas. Just as I got to the part about Thomas always being able to keep the child alive in himself, Dick interjected, "But where did it get him?"

"I know," I said. "He died at thirty-nine."

"Yes . . . strangled on a Yo-Yo."

When a perception of the ridiculousness of things overwhelmed both of us at the same time, our behavior could be beneath the consideration of any sane or sober person. Throughout the latter half of our senior year I treated Dick to some unflattering mimicry of the voice and platform mannerisms of Alexander Witherspoon, whose lecture course on seventeenth-century English literature I was laboring through. At year's end, when I was getting ready to go to Witherspoon's rooms in Berkeley College for my final grade, Dick asked to go along, so he could meet the source of all my comic turns.

"No," I said. "You'll laugh."

Dick bristled. "I'm a trained actor, and an actor never breaks up."

I relented. But no sooner had Witherspoon let us in and begun discussing my final exam than I heard, from Dick's direction, a loud snorting sound followed by an unmistakable wheeze of laughter. I glanced over and saw him giving a very bad imitation of a man coughing into a handkerchief. So much for an actor's training. Somehow there didn't seem to be anything else for me to do but to begin laughing too. As Witherspoon stared at us uncomprehendingly, I thought, "My God, here we are about to graduate, and we can't control ourselves any better than this."

In truth, not even our graduation was spared. During the solemn baccalaureate ceremony in Woolsey Hall, Yale's retiring chaplain, the Reverend Sidney Lovett, known to generations of students as Uncle Sid, stood at the lectern to read a Bible passage. As he turned one of the pages the paper's edge scraped across the microphone, producing a roar from the loud-speakers that shook the hall. Neither Dick nor I had to say anything or even exchange a glance to know what the other was thinking. Jehovah's thunder, casually invoked by Uncle Sid, like some fumbling wizard who sets off fireballs and earthquakes without meaning to. Once again an actor's training was of no avail. We passed on from Mother Yale giggling like a couple of choirboys.

One thing we all had to do when we arrived at Yale was to have posture pictures taken, for some unspecified reasons—sadism, blackmail, I don't know. Everybody in the freshman class had to go into a room in the gym while stark-naked and have his picture taken from various angles. You got three provocative poses. The reactions were interesting. One guy fainted in line . . . another tried to go through twice . . . one guy tried to get his photo retouched. . . .

Vassar also had posture pictures, and in 1956 they were stolen. Years later they turned up on the black market in Paris. And they didn't sell.

Occasionally there were thefts from the Yale files too. We were never sure where the pictures were ending up, but one time my fat roommate, Chris, got a call from Mr. Male Magazine offering him a chance to be their comedy fold-out of the month.

The posture pictures were part of a battery of physical tests that required each freshman to jump eighteen inches off the floor; do eight pull-ups, twenty-five push-ups, and fifty sit-ups; broad-jump eighty-six inches from a standing position; vault over a five-foot bar while touching it only with his hands; and swim one hundred yards. In the course of this ordeal I lost my balance, my dignity, and finally my breakfast. Dick, the boy gymnast, breezed through, and looked especially flashy on the vault over the five-foot bar, which, as he approached it, appeared to be as high as he was. Even his posture picture was approved, though I believe he stopped short of passing out autographed glossies.

So, while the likes of me were still putting in three remedial sessions a week at the gym, Dick was free to go out for a sport or take up whatever outside activity he wished. Naturally he decided to join the gymnastic team.

Alas, there was no gymnastic team. Yale, which offered more-or-less organized competition in every sport from polo to fencing, had no gymnastics. There was only a gymnastic club, which tried to set up informal meets with other clubs. But what was that to a former Nebraska state champion? The afternoon when Dick learned all this was virtually the beginning and end of his nonacademic career at Yale. Deprived of the opportunity to flaunt his triple-rear dismount, he had no interest in any other activity.

Except the theater. But the theater was no mere activity for Dick. It was a low-grade obsession. What excited him about coming to Yale in the first place, as he admitted, was "getting to the East, next to show business, going to New Haven, the town where the Broadway shows try out." And he got next to show business in every way he could—at the Shubert and in New York, in his conversation and extracurricular reading, and even in his academic work; senior year he changed his major from English to drama in order to take a few more courses in it.

There were times when I believed he saw everything through a proscenium arch. He came backstage once after a campus jazz concert in which my band had played. I expected him to say something about the music. What he said was, "You really had them with you." After a moment I realized he didn't mean the musicians in my group, but the audience. Even a jazz concert was another form of theater.

Dick's acting career on campus was successful, but not spectacular. With his mismatched physique and voice (looking like a juvenile, sounding like a tragedian), he always had trouble finding suitable roles. His performances in dramatic parts were solid and craftsmanlike—I remember particularly the moral fervor of his Reverend Hale in the Dramat's production of *The Crucible*—but sometimes they tended a little toward stiffness. He was more comfortable in character and comedy parts, especially old men. These brought out his better side as a performer, and they brought out his skills with that old childhood hobby, theatrical make-up.

In the Dramat's musical version of *The Great Gatsby* he played a brash young society photographer in the first act, a pathetic old man from Minnesota—Gatsby's father—in the second. Two effective vignettes, and each so different from the other in make-up, gesture, and emotional tone that they might well have been played by separate actors. In *The Lady's Not for Burning* his doddering chaplain was a hilarious study in agitated senility. In the musical *Cyrano* he not only managed to make himself up to be plausibly paunchy as the pastry chef, Ragueneau, but he actually sang a few songs as well—a feat that I, from my position in the orchestra pit, applauded nightly as a triumph over a splayed sense of rhythm and an ear that, if not tin, was at least alloy.

One of his most interesting performances, in *La Ronde*, was not even in the script. During the scene changes between the play's amorous episodes, he came out in black tie and mustache as a sort of pantomime emcee. His appearances consisted of semi-improvised magic tricks and slapstick; in one he even got away with walking into a wall. Some of these bits were skillful enough to be cited later by the notoriously rigorous Constance Welch, who told her acting class at the Drama School that they displayed "flawless timing." (Timing, yes; but I still say his musical rhythm is the metrical equivalent of cubism.)

Dick as comedian and character actor emerged further in his summer session at Williamstown. While Carrie Nye was doing Blanche DuBois in *A Streetcar Named Desire*—the best Blanche, bar none, that I have ever seen on the stage—Dick was enjoying his greatest success in what might be called the title role of *Charley's Aunt*. He was also getting an inordinate amount of satisfaction out of a secondary role, the Japanese butler in *Auntie Mame*, for which he experimented at the make-up table with a construction of nose putty and nylon that gave him authentic Oriental eyelids.

Above all, comedy was the thing. No textbook of Dick's was more carefully pored over than Steve Allen's study of a dozen classic comedians, *The Funny Men*. Studying was never too important to be interrupted by the opening monologue on a Bob Hope show, for which Dick would set aside whatever he was doing and bolt downstairs to the Saybrook buttery, which doubled as our TV lounge, or, if necessary, halfway across the campus. He plotted and intrigued like a Borgia in order to get access to TV lounges where no raucous majority of sports fans or *Dragnet* addicts could prevent him from catching an appearance by Groucho Marx or Jack Benny or an old movie of W. C. Fields'.

He was forever being one or another of these people. Instead of wasting energy simply pacing around our living room, he would practice the distinctive saunter with which Hope made an entrance. Calling to one of us from an adjoining room, he would use the inflections of Benny: "Rochester . . . oh, Rochester . . ." If one of us made some such innocuous remark as "I feel like a sandwich," up would go the imaginary eyebrows, down would go the imaginary cigar, and we would be Grouchoed: "Funny, you don't *look* like a sandwich."

I recall that when Ed Wynn scored a success, at about that time, doing a dramatic cameo in a movie called *The Great Man,* Dick felt that all the to-do over a comedian proving capable of a "straight" role was patronizing. Any really good comedian could do that, he argued; if you have the kind of consummate theatrical skill it takes to make people laugh, then you certainly ought to be able to use that skill to obtain the somewhat cheaper effect of making them cry. He quoted Shaw, who once saw an eminent tragedian do one of his plays in a careless, slipshod fashion, as if slumming. "What you're doing on the stage is all very well for tragedy," Shaw told the actor, "but comedy is serious business."

If we roommates could never laugh enough at Dick's witticisms to make him completely happy, we could never take them seriously enough to suit him either. As a result, we were subjected to mock indignation (sometimes not so mock) in a variety of veins. There was the stunned disbelief at the abyss of ignorance yawning before him: "I just can't conceive of somebody who doesn't know who George Abbott is." Or the sad shrug at the hopelessness of stunted souls: "Well, all I can say is, I don't see how you can count yourself an educated, aware, adult human being unless you've seen at least one Marx Brothers picture." Or the aggressive prosecuting attorney: "Do you mean to sit there and tell me you don't recognize the name Percy Helton? I submit to you that you've probably seen him a hundred times without knowing it."

The visual-trivia game of spotting character actors like Percy Helton was a specialty of Dick's. It was a common experience to be walking down a street with him and have him suddenly nudge you and indicate a blue overcoat that was disappearing around a corner. "Don't tell me you didn't recognize Henry Daniell!" (Years after we graduated, when Dick made his first trip to Hollywood, he was to end a letter to me with this P.S.: "So far I've recognized Eduardo Cianelli, Percy Kilbride [twice], and George Tobias. Wow!")

The symptoms were clear. Acute professional mentality, with complications. Like the more blood-sworn novitiates in the Drama School, he began to think of himself as being "in the business." He began to invite New York agents up to see him in Dramat productions, to invoke the talismanic names of the big producers, and to use that most plaintively yearning word in the actor's vocabulary, "interested." ("There's a guy at MCA who's very interested in me." "I hear Cheryl Crawford is interested in taking the show to New York.")

He devoted his final two college summers to apprentice work in the Oregon and the Stratford, Connecticut, Shakespeare festivals respectively. Prior to our senior year, I cut short my summer at home in Minneapolis to see him deliver his one line in the Stratford production of *The Merchant of Venice*—"Gentlemen, my master Antonio is at his house and desires to speak with you both"—a sacrifice, as I pointed out to him, of nearly one day of vacation per word. He felt it ought to be worth every day to me, since I also got a chance to see Katharine Hepburn in the role of Portia. Professionally speaking, he had now "worked with Hepburn," and that gave him a big boost psychologically, if in no other way. On his mantelpiece at Yale he casually propped up a picture of the two of them smiling and chatting together at a rehearsal, as if he had absent-mindedly set it there on the way to putting it somewhere else—but it stayed there all year.

To Dick, Yale's most storied football exploit was nothing compared with the glory of a Yale actor winning a New York role. Bradford Dillman, then a recent graduate, got a minor hero's reception when he came through New Haven in *Long Day's Journey*. If it was an exact contemporary who got a break, the pangs of envy, vicarious excitement, hatred, and a dozen other conflicting emotions were all the sharper. For example, when Bill Hinnant took a year's leave of absence from the university to do *No Time for Sergeants* on Broadway. Or when James Franciscus (known as "Goey," a nickname I assume he has since dropped, for obvious reasons) was cast in a play on the old *Studio One* TV series. I remember that on the morning after the *Studio One* broadcast Dick wondered why the whole campus wasn't talking about such an earth-shaking event, instead of only a sprinkling of faithfuls in the Dramat green room—or, as Dick saw them, unfaithfuls.

Hinnant and Franciscus also were cast in a movie while they were still undergraduates. It was called *Four Men with a Gun*, and Dick went to see it when it played, briefly, at a New Haven theater. It was trash, but I know the important thing for Dick was that they were up there, Billy and Goey, *in the movies*.

For all his professional outlook, Dick never completely fell in with that fierce, desiccating actor's penchant for finding a backstage motive for everything (venal, sexual, or both) and for explaining away other actors' performances ("Oh, Gielgud was all right, I suppose, if you like that sort of thing; it was just the same old Gielgud devices"). He could relish gossip and analyze acting technique without shrugging off the mysterious reality of talent and unique stage moments. If a performance moved him, he was not ashamed to say so. Which is another way of saying that he remained, in the best sense, a fan.

Nor, for all his cultivation of contacts, did he ever seem embroiled in the calculated, close-quarter maneuvering of the casting office. He merely used to say, "I guess after graduation I'll go down to New York and just see what happens." That was his general strategy; the specific tactics were all improvised.

But what improvisation! One of the truest comments I ever heard Dick make about himself was, "I have a talent for taking advantage of situations." Broadly and deeply defined, it may well be his greatest talent.

What were the situations? Receptions at the Drama School for guest speakers like Sir Tyrone Guthrie, Moss Hart, or Jason Robards, Jr. After-theater dinners at Kaysey's, where performers like Maurice Evans and Geraldine Fitzgerald would turn out to be at a nearby table. Sometimes they were self-created situations: rehearsals at the Shubert that he had snuck into to watch Alfred Lunt work, or Shelley Winters, or Dennis Price. Vigils outside the Shubert, where he might spot Basil Rathbone coming out the stage door after a performance or Grace Kelly going in the front door to see the play.

Always, always, in these situations, Dick had the brass to go up to these eminences and the wit to have something to say when he got there. If he ever felt his nerve slackening he exhorted himself, "Do it, do it! This is one of those moments."

He led many sorties backstage at the Shubert like the one to meet Maria Riva. One of the best was after the opening performance in the tryout of *My Fair Lady*. Unlike many of the shows that go on to do well in New York, this one was instantly recognizable as a superior piece of work and a sure-fire smash. Backstage was a bedlam of well-wishers and popping flash bulbs. Dick and I and two other guys with us couldn't even get into Julie Andrews's dressing room because it was so full of people. Dick stood outside the door and gazed in at her as she laughed amid that noisy throng, and his face reflected the mixture of admiration, exasperation, and jealousy I knew he was feeling.

"Do you realize," he said to us, "that she is just *our
age* . . . and now she's a *star!*"

Rex Harrison was even more besieged in his dressing room,
so we looked in on Stanley Holloway, who played Liza Doo-
little's father. After the initial greetings, while the rest of us
stood transfixed by the spreading conversational vacuum, Dick
recalled that Holloway had played the gravedigger in Olivier's
film of *Hamlet* and threw out the cue for the scene with Hamlet
in the graveyard: "How long hast thou been a gravemaker?"

Holloway looked blank for a second, then drew back his
head and roared. All went well after that, at least for Dick; the
rest of us remained about as scintillating as costume manikins.

It wasn't until after a later performance, one of several
that Dick went to during *My Fair Lady*'s run at the Shubert,
that he met Harrison. As he slipped through the door leading
backstage he came upon Harrison lounging against a wall and
sipping a Scotch, and they fell quite easily into a relaxed shop-
talk.

The peak of Dick's *My Fair Lady*-watching, however, was
a little masquerade he pulled off in order to see a performance
from backstage. Wearing a topcoat over his shoulders, theatrical
style, and carrying a copy of *Variety*, he strolled brazenly
through the stage door one night and took up a position in the
wings, trying with all his might to look as if he belonged there.
Considering how young and collegiate he was at the time, he
must have given a remarkable performance, for he was undetected by the surly stagehands who had thrown him out so
many times in the past.

He had hoped only to see the opening number, but to his
delight the entire first act went by, and then most of the second
act. Technicians worked unconcernedly around him. Actors and
actresses brushed past him as they made their entrances and
exits ("Little slow that time . . . do you suppose it's our accents that are bothering them?"). He was there while it was
all happening; he was seeing how it all worked.

Finally, shortly before the final curtain, the rough hand that he had been expecting all evening came down upon his shoulder. The chief stagehand recognized him and, to the accompaniment of a shower of obscenities, flung him into the alley outside. But before slamming the stage door the stagehand gave Dick the satisfaction of knowing that his disguise had worked. "I saw ya carryin' a copy of *Variety*," he said, "an' I thought you was connected with the show."

More and more, in our junior and senior years, Dick went down to New York in search of bigger and better situations to take advantage of. He announced himself at agencies, saw shows and rehearsals, and sometimes tested the wiles he had learned backstage at the Shubert (they were enough to get him into Judy Garland's dressing room at the Palace). He hovered at stage doors, reconnoitered actors' watering places, from Sardi's and Downey's to the Stage Delicatessen, even staked out the homes of stars whose addresses he had ferreted out (including Maria Riva's). You can bet *he* never let the likes of a Henry Daniell pass unrecognized on the street.

New York offered more of everything, including rebuffs. Yale had been applying an RCA grant to cover part of Dick's scholarship. Since RCA owned NBC, naturally NBC would want to encourage a student whom it was, in effect, underwriting. Q.E.D. But when Dick dropped by NBC one day to give the network an early look at its protégé, he was met by a politely bored public relations man, who sent him away with a pat on the shoulder ("At least it wasn't on the fanny") and two tickets to the *Mister Peepers* show.

Dick took every advantage of his connection with Yale. The name alone was leverage. In a world that fed on fame, a famous university carried some weight. When accosting a star Dick would say, "You know, you have a lot of fans at Yale."

Usually the star's indifference would immediately change to an intrigued "Oh, really?"

The university administration would have been appalled to know how many offers and invitations Dick made in its name.

Dick Cavett with his parents,
Grand Island, Nebraska, 1937

With his friend
Mary Huston,
Grand Island, 1940

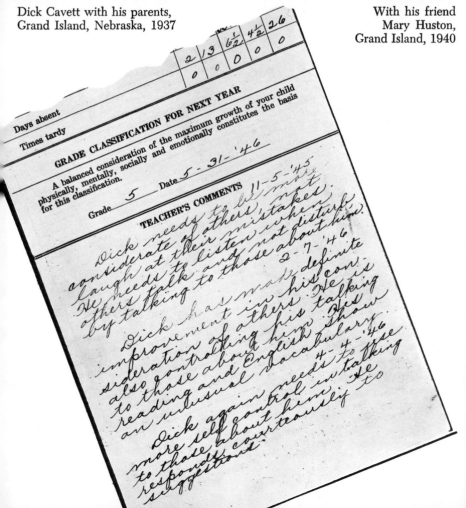

| | | $6\frac{1}{2}$ | $4\frac{1}{2}$ | 26 |
| 2 | 3 | 0 | 0 | 0 |
| 0 | 0 | 0 | | |

Days absent

Times tardy

GRADE CLASSIFICATION FOR NEXT YEAR

A balanced consideration of the maximum growth of your child physically, mentally, socially and emotionally constitutes the basis for this classification.

Grade 5 Date 5 - 31 - '46

TEACHER'S COMMENTS

Dick needs to be more 11-5-'45
considerate of others, not
laugh at their mistakes.
He needs to listen when
others talk and not disturb
by talking to those about him.

Dick has made definite 2-7-'46
improvement in his con-
sideration of others. He is
also controlling his talking
to those about him. His
reading and English show
an unusual vocabulary.

Dick again needs 4-4-'46
more self control in talking
to those about him. He
responds courteously to
suggestions.

(Opposite page) Winning the International Brotherhood of Magicians award, St. Louis, 1952; in *The Winslow Boy* in summer stock, Lincoln, Nebraska, 1953; Lincoln High School graduation portrait, 1954

(This page, from top) With Sandy Dennis, at far right, in high school play; as the Stage Manager in high school production of *Our Town;* escorting Lincoln High School homecoming attendant

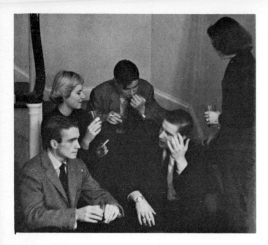

The Yale years, 1954–1958: *(clockwise, from above)* At an undergraduate party; playing murderer (the man on the right) in Oregon Shakespearean Festival; with guest lecturer Peter Ustinov; rehearsing with Katharine Hepburn at Stratford, Connecticut, Shakespeare Festival; chatting with Moss Hart at Dramat reception

With Carrie Nye in *Cyrano* at Williamstown, Massachusetts, 1958; as the Japanese houseboy in *Auntie Mame*, Williamstown, 1958; playing a wounded German soldier in an army training film, 1959

*Williamstown Theatre Foundation, Inc., Williamstown, Mass.*

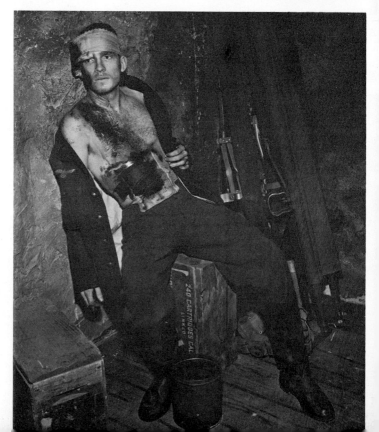

As Charley's Aunt at Williamstown (peeking through the curtain: Carrie Nye)

A guest appearance on the *Alias Smith and Jones* TV series, 1972

The comedy act: At Mister Kelly's, Chicago *(above)*,
and as Johnny Carson's guest on the *Tonight Show,* both 1965

Once, after reading an article about Jackie Gleason's interest in ESP and spiritualism, Dick wrote to Gleason offering him the facilities of the Yale library for research in those fields. Gleason didn't respond, which was probably Dick's good fortune.

Dick dangled the bait of a Yale appearance before several performers, but probably his biggest catch was Peter Ustinov. One evening at the end of senior year Dick and a friend named Bart Giamatti were waiting in the Saybrook dinner line, talking about Ustinov's scheduled reading that night at the YMHA Poetry Center in Manhattan. On an impulse, Dick and Bart dashed away from the dining hall and took a train to New York to attend the reading.

Afterward they met Ustinov, and Dick invited him to come and talk to the Drama School. Ustinov accepted. A date was set, which happened to be the day before Dick's comprehensive final exams. Next day Dick presented the plan as a *fait accompli* to the dean of the Drama School, Curtis Canfield.

When the day came, an assemblage of students and faculty waited outside the Yale Theater to watch Ustinov's arrival. The appointed hour passed; Ustinov was five minutes late, ten minutes, twenty minutes . . . a half hour. The greeters were getting restive; Dick was awash with flop sweat. Suddenly Dean Canfield broke away from the crowd and stalked off, raising his fist in the air and shouting, "Fiasco, Cavett!"

Dick reeled with panic. He thought, "Have I neglected my comprehensives only for this?"

But ten minutes later Ustinov tooled up the theater driveway in his Alfa Romeo, to raucous cheers from the front steps, none more heartfelt than Dick's. And for the next twenty-four hours Ustinov was delightfully "on" every minute, doing, as Dick put it, the equivalent of fourteen *Tonight Show* appearances as he passed from lecture hall to library to cocktail party to faculty lounge. Moreover, Dick did pretty well on his comprehensives.

It was no accident that Dick gauged Ustinov's brilliance in terms of *Tonight Show* appearances. Just as television epitomized the glittering East to Dick when he was a boy in Nebraska, it shimmered as the most potent and glamorous medium of show business for him when he was at college. Many of the shows he scrambled to see were TV shows; the stage doors he haunted, TV-studio stage doors; the stars he sought out, TV stars.

He saved some of his most audacious infiltration techniques for TV sound stages. Applying the lesson of his backstage caper at *My Fair Lady*, he found that if he carried an envelope bearing the appropriate network logotype and strode around purposefully enough, people would assume he was on official business. He could move among the cameras at rehearsals, stepping over cables, hobnobbing with writers and producers; maybe a Gleason or a Berle would sweep by ("Hi, how's it going?"). In the corridors that fanned out behind the studios he could pass unchallenged, pushing open door after door; maybe a Caesar or a Benny would be behind one of them.

"What do you want to get out of meeting those people?" I asked him. "What is it you're after?"

"I can't say exactly. I just know I want to get close to it all, get close to those people. Sometimes I have a sort of premonition that I'm going to meet one of them and that I'm going to be able to make him be interested in me. It's a sort of tingling sense that *something is going to happen.*"

To me, that was Dick's real graduation from Yale, his real commencement. Not promenading down an avenue of elms holding a diploma, but, rather, pushing open a door in a TV studio, clutching his camouflage envelope, eager, tense, ready—for what?

"When I open those doors there could be an executive meeting, a rehearsal, a tryst—anything," he used to say. "I just keep pushing them open because I have to find out."

# PART THREE
# LOOKING UP

CP: I was in the army, in 1960, the first time I saw that three-room rummage sale that passed for your Manhattan apartment. I came up on a weekend pass from Fort Meade, in Maryland, and I remember that the taxi driver hesitated to take me to your address on West Eighty-ninth Street until I assured him that I knew somebody there. He indicated that it was a neighborhood in which booze, women, and human life were all cheap. Then, when we got there, he wouldn't pull away until I was safely inside your building—unheard of in a New York cabbie. It was so incongruous to have crawled under live machine-gun fire and tossed grenades around and been gassed in basic training, and then to find real fear in the middle of New York City.

DC: As I recall, you made it to my charming fifth-floor walk-up—or run-up—relatively unscathed.

CP: Propositioned on the second floor and chased by muggers on the third, but I guess it could have been worse.

DC: I always wondered why I had so few visitors.

CP: What are your memories of living there?

DC: Poor and varied. My parents took me back there once, after seeing me in Williamstown, Massachusetts, in summer stock, and had nightmares for weeks when they saw where I lived. I had very little trouble, although a guy next to me dropped to the sidewalk once from a zip-gun shot, and one day, as I was reading the *Times* in my tiny living room, a crowbar tip came through my front door. I decided that the illegal police bar would hold awhile, and I peeked through the viewer and saw two guys with slim mustaches working on my door. "Hmmm," I thought, and eased the phone off the hook and dialed the police. I whispered to the cop on the phone what was happening, and he kept yelling, "Can ya gimme that address again?" I whispered, "Oh, fuck it!," hung up, and pounded on the inside of the door. The guys went tearing down the stairs, and the police did arrive ten minutes later. When I got out on the street there was a cop standing in front of the building who had been there the entire time, supervising a polling place across the street.

CP: Who was being elected?

DC: I hope it was a new police commissioner.

CP: Was it always as harrowing as that?

DC: Not quite. At night I watched TV, read, went to the New Yorker movie theater, or watched my Puerto Rican neighbors make love in the apartment directly across the air shaft. The nights were hot, the windows were open, and by getting on the roof I could simultaneously arouse, educate, and frustrate myself by taking in the erotic circus that took place almost nightly on the queen-size bed just below. When either they or I tired, I would sit by the chimney and, like Gatsby looking at the light on Daisy's dock, gaze at the East Side skyline, resolving that someday I would live over there, by hook or some other means.

When my hyperactive neighbors moved out they were

replaced by another bunch, who gave parties instead of making love, and the din was murderous. I got their number by looking through their window at their phone with binoculars, and I called and complained about the noise one night. They yelled something into the phone from which I thought I caught the word "gringo" and the Spanish word for goat. I missed the verb. The din continued until two o'clock, when my patience snapped and I decided to smash their window. I reasoned that if I climbed up on the roof they would not know it was their immediate neighbor who had done it. I took a full bottle of Seven-Up and, allowing for the angle, heaved it straight through the glass portion of their dining-room window, which was right across from one of my windows. Instantly an empty beer can, propelled with terrific force, smashed through my own window. I had somehow thought it would be clear to them that the bottle came from above, and that that plus the fact that my apartment was dark would protect me and my premises. Wondering where I had miscalculated, I went to bed miffed, marveling at the combination of sex and violence that the apartment across the way now symbolized.

A month or so later I got into a similar battle with the newest tenants of *Casa Grande*. A loud party again, only this time I was smart. I went *into* their building, out on the roof, tied a full bottle of Seven-Up to a cord, and swung it out and in again so it smashed through the *back* window of their apartment, which didn't face mine at all. When I got back to my own apartment, exultant at my ingenuity, my same window was smashed anew, and a beer can lay in the middle of the floor. I did an Oliver Hardy take to an unseen camera and went to bed.

CP: In your night-club routine you used to tell a joke about your nasty New York landlady. You said she was so mean to some newly immigrated Puerto Rican tenants that she sold them their mail. Was the landlady real, and what were some of her other exploits?

DC: No, she didn't exist, and, like theologians with an unjust God, I had to invent her.

CP: Perhaps we should mention the reason you were living on West Eighty-ninth Street in the first place.

DC: You mean the fifty-one-dollars-a-month rent?

CP: No—your quest for a glamorous career in show business.

DC: Oh, that. Yes, like a million people before and after, I came to New York to break into the theater. And it did seem glamorous. Of course, getting the first job I ever auditioned for in New York gave me a slightly false impression of how things were going to go. It was a movie made by the Signal Corps in the old Paramount studios on Long Island, where the Marx Brothers made *Cocoanuts*. I read for the part—a foppish West Point student in the time of Sylvanus Thayer—came back to town, and sat by the phone until the agent called and said I was hired. I thought, "This is a snap. One reading and I'm in a movie. What a good way to make a living."

It felt like the movies. I got up at six, took the subway to Long Island, got made up, costumed, and filmed. I came home from my one and only day of shooting, lay soaking in the tub, and thought, "I've made it." I was "in films." I gave myself a week off, knowing that it's important to keep the momentum of a career going but not wanting to overtax myself, and thinking, "If I want to work again, I will." There I was in New York, with unlimited time and nobody to tell me how to spend it. It was like a paid vacation.

CP: Soon it was more like an enforced one, wasn't it?

DC: Yes. When I began making rounds I discovered they weren't looking for any more foppish West Point nineteenth-century types, and they especially weren't looking for people who had played eighty-year-old chaplains in college productions of *The Lady's Not for Burning* with half a pint of hair whitener on their heads. They were looking for people like our fellow Yalie James Franciscus. Remember him at Yale in the title role of the musical *The Great Gatsby?* He was signed for a movie before he even graduated. Somehow the talent scout overlooked my three separate character-role turns in the same production, despite my changing my hair color twice each night and executing two masterful character make-ups. And to think I helped Franciscus with his spelling.

CP: You mean his writing?

DC: I mean his *spelling.* Remember the *Mr. Novak* series, where Franciscus played television's first English-teacher hero? Seething with jealousy, I would sit home nursing the secret that I had saved Mr. Novak's ass in Mr. Kernan's seminar at Yale by correcting his atrocious spelling on weekly papers, so he wouldn't flunk out. "Is this the sort of man we want playing an English teacher?" I would mutter, while penning anonymous hate mail to the studios about him. I alone knew that whenever Mr. Novak wrote on the blackboard they had to use a stunt man.

CP: You used the phrase "making rounds." Do you want to describe what that entailed?

DC: I used to trudge around town to various agents' offices, going through the foolish motions of leaving off a photograph and a résumé, the latter a work of semifiction, in which you put everything you'd ever played in high school or church basements under the heading of summer stock and tried to make it all look as impressive as possible. When you listed the television shows you'd done, you omitted the fact that you were an extra. One of the paradoxes that trapped the fledgling actor was that if you had a short résumé you looked inexperienced, and if it was long it raised the question "Why haven't I heard of you?" And one of the most discouraging things was that you'd see people you considered established actors making the rounds too, just as mournfully. I used to see Dane Clark, every single day I made rounds, walking up and down Fifty-seventh Street. I'd wonder what the hell *I* was supposed to get if *he* couldn't get a job.

CP: Was that more discouraging than running into established actors who *were* working?

DC: It's hard to say. Occasionally I'd see one of the giants on Fifth Avenue, and it was exciting, and then depressing, because they seemed as far removed from one's world as the literal stars in the heavens. Once, waiting for a traffic light, I noticed I was standing next to Paul Douglas. I had just seen him in a movie, and I mentioned the fact and said, "Where would *you* go today, if you were an actor looking for a job?" He looked at me as from a great distance, sucked his teeth audibly, and said, "I couldn't ansuh ya." The tooth sucking, the New York accent, the indifference, all seemed glamorous. I decided I had accomplished enough for that day, talking with Paul Douglas, and went home to my electric skillet. And the roaches.

CP: Your roommates, as it were.

DC: Yes. I had gotten to know a couple of the larger specimens, and they provided a modicum of company.

CP: No other roommates from time to time?

DC: Mine was not a spectacularly romantic bachelorhood, if I catch your drift. For the better part of it I was committed off and on to my future wife, to whom I was intermittently true in my fashion, and somehow unemployment, substandard living, and an uncertain future are not the best psychological base from which to wage romance. Besides, my roommates, the roaches, were great antidotes to amorous projects. I doubt if there is anyone who has lived in modest circumstances in Manhattan who hasn't had a seduction or two spoiled by a roach stomping across the anatomy of one or more of the parties involved at the worst moment. These insect walk-ons could, so to speak, unmake a scene.

CP: If you don't have an illustrative example for that generalization, you'd better make one up.

DC: How did you guess? Once I got invited by one of my few Yale friends to a party on the East Side. One of those crowded, pre-freak-era parties where much booze is loaded away and people break off in groups to go to the Village for aimless wandering in search of kicks. I decided the hostess was fair game and stayed on after everyone else had left. Just ahead of the moment when gallantry required an offer of help to clean up the apartment, I left, suggesting that after a morning's sleep we meet in Central Park and discuss how I was to get my new bookcase lacquered.

It was one of those Sundays when the vernal sunshine, the buds, the birds, the nascent leaves, and the whole equinoctial bit contribute to a sense of the sap rising in the trees and in the loins. The whole world seems a scented boudoir. We did get my bookcase lacquered, a job that was sufficiently protracted by intermittent sallies forth for wine, until it was mutually agreed upon that it was too late for returning to the East Side. Discreet fade to black. The following morning, brunch included a Sara Lee chocolate cake, which my co-lacquerer had purchased and was in the act of opening and cutting when some crumbs fell to the floor. She bent over to pick up what she took to be the largest one, and it ran under the refrigerator. Thanks to thick walls, no one responded to the scream, but what had promised to be a healthy, extended, and much-needed April fling never got back on the track. She remembered a previous engagement, or possibly marriage, and departed. *La cucaracha* strikes again.

CP: That's the saddest thing I ever heard in my life. Did you make the East Side party scene often?

DC: I did find myself mysteriously invited once or twice to

a posh bash by some Westchesterishly nasal undergraduate who had met me at a Dramat party and who had his parents' Park Avenue pad for a month or so while they cavorted in Europe. I would go along out of curiosity as to just how such people lived, and in hopes of meeting someone rich and strange who would take me away on a yacht or something.

CP: How were the girls at those parties?

DC: They were either ugly and rich or beautiful and rich. The latter always seemed to have that mysterious blond streak in their light brown hair, stood with a martini glass to one side and one toe pointing in the air, were slightly taller than I was, or seemed to be, and gave the impression that if I touched them they would call a cop. They gave off a vague air of ambitions foreign to me (I always sensed they had tagged me instantly as "not Social Register") and an infuriating way of making me desire them.

CP: Did you ever act on your desire?

DC: Yes, to little avail. Once or twice, apparently by appearing to promise a novel experience of a slumming nature, I would lure one of these well-coifed society chicks away from the Tiepolo we had been chatting in front of, down the elevator, over to the West Side (where she had been before only on the way to Europe), and into my Dickensian digs. She usually referred to my dwelling place as "quaint" or "disarming," whereas "dirty" and "depressing" would have hit the nail more squarely. After she had consumed a pint or so of the vodka I could ill afford, and to the strains of my transistor radio, I would succeed in getting part, most, or, in one case, all of her smart toggery off when something Woody Allenesque would happen. The heat would go off (or on, in summer), the landlady would have to get in to get at Mr. Lottman's fuse (why Mr. Lottman didn't have his own fuse I never learned), or there would be a visitation of roaches in the bed, which cooled everything.

Barring these mishaps, she would decide this was just too

sordid a setting and would say, "This is silly. You'd better take me home." Knowing, as every young man does, that this line is merely a tactic, a temporary dodge, a face-saving protest merely for the record, and the cue to get rough and insistent, which is What Every Woman Wants, I would hear myself say an abject yes. She would say, "Don't bother seeing me home. Just put me in a taxi." And I would say, "Don't be silly," when what I meant was, "*Do* be silly and haul-ass home on foot in the goddam blizzard for all I care." We would suit up and climb into a cab, which I could afford less than the vodka, knowing that I would spend the half hour after delivering her to Sutton Place freezing on a subway platform with a migraine of the gonads.

CP: Do you suppose the prevalence of roaches in your apartment had anything to do with your general housekeeping habits?

DC: Well, as you should know, I am not naturally neat. Over the years, my apartments have had to be gutted whenever I moved out. Once I *had* to clean one in order to sublet it, and it hadn't been touched in two years. An old Yale actress friend, Brita Brown, came over, in answer to my plea, to help clean it and could scarcely conceal her horror. She has spoken to me only once since.

Still, I feel the roaches were just part of the scene, not my special burden. My memories of all those early years in New York are mainly of roaches and agents. Neither of which a young actor can, apparently, live without. The difference is that you have all you want of the former and it is hard to get the latter—although the city is crawling with both.

CP: In laying siege to the agents, didn't you have any help from veterans of the process? Any help or advice from older actors, for example?

DC: The advice I remember most vividly came from the actor John Newland. He was the first celebrity I recognized on the streets of New York in 1954, when I hit town on my way to Yale. Newland had been host, director, and sometimes star of Robert Montgomery's TV dramatic show that summer. He always reminded me of our family friend Frank Rice, who was the reason I went to Yale, and somehow it seemed appropriate that I should see him on my first day in New York. I was coming up the Rockefeller Center promenade around dusk, and, like a zoom shot in a movie, I spotted Newland across the street, strolling alone up Fifth Avenue. I instantly approached him, and he looked somewhat irritated. Displaying my gift for the offbeat, I opened with, "Are you John Newland?" He replied, "I am that man," a locution I found a touch lofty, but not enough to dampen my excitement. Undaunted, I said, and you can bet that every syllable of this is accurate, "I think you're a wonderful actor, Mr. Newland. I'm going to Yale in a few days, and when I get out I hope to be an actor someday like yourself." He must have thought a bad script had come to life. I'll never forget the next two lines of dialogue.

ME (*eagerly*): Do you recommend acting as a profession?

NEWLAND: No. It's a rotten damn game.

I don't remember clearly what happened next. I seem to see myself rooted to the sidewalk by that and Newland continuing into the dusk along the sunset-lit avenue. I seem to remember, although the scene should end here, that he waved without looking back and said, "Good luck," and later I tried to remember that he had said to keep in touch or look him up when I came back to New York, but I knew that he hadn't. I think I went instantly back to the Roosevelt and up to my student-rate room (is it possible it was three dollars a night?), and wrote a letter home about meeting John Newland. For years, whenever my intentions to act or go into show business were mentioned my father would quote Newland on what kind of game it was.

CP: What about your Yale connection? Since you didn't drop out, like your freshman-year roommate Jim Carney, you retained that lifelong opportunity that he used to speak of, to be able to say, "I went to Yale." Did that turn out to be worth a hill of beans to you, or even a handful?

DC: When Carney said that to me, I revealed one of my layers of naïveté by asking him when such a matter would come up. He said, "Are you kidding? There isn't a law firm or business in New York where you won't get past all the people sitting in the waiting room just by saying, 'I went to Yale.' It's an open Sesame." Of course that revealed one of his layers of naïveté too. But at the time I only remember wondering why he didn't realize that I didn't want to get into, let alone through, the waiting room of any law firm in New York.

The next time some guy told me there wasn't a firm on Wall Street or Madison Avenue that wouldn't give me preferential treatment because of my Yale sheepskin, I said, "But I don't *want* to get into any of those places." He blinked incredulously and said, "Then I don't know what good it would do *you*."

CP: But there were waiting rooms you did want to get through—booking agencies and the like. Did saying you went to Yale have any effect there?

DC: It had an effect, but not the right one. It would cause eyebrows to be raised, pencils to be laid down, and the situation to seem to be put into a whole new light. Sometimes the person involved would suddenly become conscious of his grammar. But the question it would stimulate was inevitably, "Then why are you fooling (or fucking) around with show business?" (I was fooling.) This would be followed by dire prognostications of no success, recitations of statistics on how few people make it, and their asking me if I could introduce them to James Franciscus.

You've got to remember what kind of place these agencies were. If Sir John Gielgud called one of them the secretary would say, in a nasal accent, "Whom shall I say is cwalling?"

The voice would say, "Gielgud." Then the secretary would say into the intercom, "Gil Good is cwalling."

Then, as you and I have discussed, there was no graceful way to say you went to Yale, no neutral way to read the line. It always got a reaction: "*Wow!*" or "*Well!*" or "I *see.*" Or else it got such a transparent attempt *not* to be impressed that *that* was embarrassing. And there was always the problem (there still is) of whether to say "when I was in college" or "when I was at Yale." If you say the former they ask where, and it looks like you were saving it for impact. If the latter you run the risk of "La de da" or "Am I supposed to be impressed?"

I recall Jonathan Winters saying to me once, after revealing that his father had gone to Yale, "I love these guys who say, with upper-nasal resonance, 'When I was at school in New Haven.' I always want to say to them, 'Was that New Haven Polytechnic?' "

The whole problem would remind me that there were guys to whom getting into Yale, or into the other two, was in a true sense everything in life. It meant the rest of life took care of itself. Some of their parents had had the good taste to dress them in miniature Yale sweaters when they were kids.

CP: I assume one of the reasons you were fooling around in show business was that you were repelled by the thought of fooling around in anything else. I remember your saying that you couldn't conceive of going into some of the jobs and professions that our classmates were going into. Why? Was it the apparent boredom of these other jobs? Their highly structured daily routine? The fact that you had to wear a tie while doing them?

DC: And shoes in many of them. I think it was simply lack of attraction. I could not conceive of where the satisfaction lay in any of the so-called professions. Obviously jobs that, as they say, help people, like medicine or psychiatry, have an intrinsic satisfaction, but a little voice told me they were not for me. I can imagine that there is a satisfaction of a kind in setting up a business and making it succeed that I can almost understand, like putting a toy car together and seeing it go, but I just knew in my bones I did not want any of the imbecile jobs my fellow Yalies would sacrifice the left side of their souls for. They had all the appeal for me of Devil's Island. I would think, "It's just lucky that show business is there, that someone invented it, because if it weren't, where would the thousands of people go who wouldn't fit in anywhere else?"

CP: I always thought those people went into teaching or journalism.

DC: Let's leave journalism aside, since one of us was allegedly involved in it. I can imagine the pleasures of teaching, but I also know it is full of drawbacks. And from what you've told me of graduate school, I wouldn't last a month. I would be one of those ninnies who thought it would be an extension of undergraduate life, and when the shock of that disillusionment wore off I would be left having to pretend I was seriously interested in slaving to push back the wall of knowledge in some obscure area, when, as far as I was concerned, that wall was fine where it was. I never could get over the fact that one of my friends from Nebraska, Marvin Breslow, wrote a dissertation at Harvard on a period in history that took less time to occur than it took Marv to write about it.

CP: Remember Woody Allen's telling you that he never in his life had to earn a living? He meant, I guess, that he had never had to do the same task over and over again for a daily wage. Wasn't that always one of the appeals of show business to you too—that even if things were going badly you were relatively unshackled? That you could be a sort of worker bee, free to fly off on your own and do your dance, and never have to be a drone stuck in the hive?

DC: Say, when you're through with that metaphor can I have what's left of it?

CP: Take it all. Please. But why are you evading the question?

DC: For all the usual reasons. I guess the gypsy nature of the business is part of its appeal for me. Making a lot of money suddenly, then none, then a little, never knowing precisely where the fates will whisk you next. I like that.

CP: Let's see what we have so far. You were trying to get into a rotten damn game where you had received little or no encouragement, where your Yale education was of no use to you, and where you had no particular friends or contacts to help you out.

DC: Wait a minute. I never said I didn't *pretend* to have big-name contacts. One of my early attempts to use my wide circle of famous momentary acquaintances to propel myself forward involved going into David Susskind's offices, a place where I had gotten an "extra" job or two, and deciding to accost the first person who came out. An efficient-looking lady appeared, and I told her I could get Jack Benny to appear on Susskind's *Open End* show, if anyone there was interested. Who the hell I thought I was going to say I was, or how I would then get Jack Benny, I had only the dimmest notion, but I used to do things like that. Perhaps sensing I was a fraud, she said something vague, but also indicated she was connected with *Open End*. "Are you the secretary?" I asked. "No, I'm the producer." I blushed, mumbled that I would keep in touch, and walked out *under* the closed door. The elevator was unduly long in arriving, and before it did she came out and also waited for it. Sweat began to pile up above my collar, and by the time we reached the ground floor several people's lives had flashed before my eyes. To this day I get a hot flash when the name Jean Kennedy comes on the screen at the end of Susskind's show. The phrase "male chauvinism" had not yet been invented, though it should have been that day.

CP: And your peculiar radar did keep leading you into encounters with big names on the streets of New York. You really did have a wide circle of momentary acquaintances with the famous.

DC: Yes, in a manner of speaking. One day, for example, I was plodding around Manhattan making the rounds of the casting offices in the Broadway area, and suddenly I realized the man I had fallen in step behind was Anthony Quinn. He looked terrific—open shirt, dark tan, and big aviator-style sunglasses. Like a lost tourist, he was carrying a note and looking confusedly at street numbers. I took a deep breath and asked if I could help, and he said he was looking for a costume company with a name like Karinsky's. I said I thought it was in the fifties, having no idea what I was talking about. I suggested checking the phone book in the booth on the corner. While looking up the number, with Quinn standing outside the booth, I could feel my pulse beating in my ears, and I wondered, "Is this my big moment? Should I ask him to get me into the movies? Invite him to Yale? (Although I was no longer there, I figured if he accepted I could arrange something.) Ask if he wants to go fishing? (I didn't fish either, but I figured I could find somebody who did.) Shoot a little pool? (Where?) Take a swim? (Ditto.)"

What I actually did was tell him the address. He thanked me and ambled on, out of my life (until years later on my show, of course). I stood there thinking, "Shit. There's Anthony Quinn going to get a costume for his seventy-sixth movie, and I ain't done nothin', and the sands in the hourglass are running apace." I decided to chuck the rounds for the day and walk home through Central Park. I thought how undemocratic it was that if Anthony Quinn walked into a casting office they would leap to their feet, tug at their forelocks, and drop everything to get him a coffee and Danish, whereas if I walked in they would think, if they bothered to look up at all, "Here comes another one."

I decided it was only Quinn's height and physique and talent that made him a big star anyway. Except for those minor assets, we weren't so different. I began to hate him. If he were here now, I decided, I'd give him a push off the sidewalk. Who wanted all his problems anyway? I wasn't sure what they were, but I hoped they were enormous. He probably wished *he* had a little apartment on West Eighty-ninth Street and nothing to worry about except whether to make rounds or not. I looked around for a movie to go to—any movie, as long as it didn't have Anthony Quinn in it.

CP: It sounds as if your rounds consisted mainly of heading back to your apartment.

DC: Sometimes whole weeks would go by and I wouldn't even *leave* the apartment. I developed a curious neurosis that took the form of a psychotic need for sleep—if it's possible to have a psychosis stacked on a neurosis. I decided I was in need of fourteen, sixteen hours of sleep a day to ward off mysterious diseases. And when I did get up I couldn't always bring myself to leave the apartment unless I was out of food. If I had one thing to do, like take out my laundry, it became a day's work, and I felt I couldn't be expected to do anything else that day. Also, it was then that I went on a binge of reading Henry James, which I decided it would be bad luck to break off. I convinced myself that I couldn't step outside my door until I had read all of Henry James.

CP: That's odd. When I was in graduate school I convinced myself that I couldn't read another word of Henry James until I had stepped outside of academe.

DC: Poor Henry. Did he deserve either of us as posterity? Sometimes I actually did make rounds, and usually I got a tiny job just as things looked blackest. Whatever was governing me then was a curious combination of neurotic incapacity and laziness, but also a weird sense that I would make it anyway, even if I didn't abide by the rules. Somehow, I felt, they will come and get me and make me famous, whether I work at it or not.

CP: You were that convinced that you were going to be famous?

DC: Yes. And on the other hand, no. I did have this sense

of inevitability, that somehow, somewhere in the future people would be taking my picture, recognizing me, asking for my autograph, and writing me fan mail. It was weird, because the rest of the picture was blank. I had no idea what I would be well known for, just that I would. At odd times, friends or acquaintances would suddenly predict this. Mary Jean Parsons, a friend from the Yale days, was sitting with me once during a rehearsal of a play we were in at Yale, and she gave me a long look and said, "You know, don't you, that people are going to *pay* to see *you* someday?" I allowed as how I didn't know this.

Even before college, back in Lincoln, I was talking one day with Bob Johnson, a local radio announcer, and suddenly, changing the subject completely, he said, "I just got a sudden feeling you're going to get out of this town and go places the way Johnny Carson did. I can feel it." At that point I had never given it a thought. Another time, at the end of my season at the Hayloft Summer Theater, I told one of the actors how much I envied him going back to New York while I had to stay in Lincoln and go back to high school. He said, "Dick, I have a feeling you're going to go further in this business than I ever will, and I can tell you right now I hate your guts for it." I said to him jokingly, "Well, if I do I'll always give you a job." And he said, "Isn't that charmingly condescending."

CP: If that actor came to you today would you give him a job?

DC: If his nails were clean.

CP: At least you didn't say, "Let him eat cake."

DC: That too.

CP: Seriously, would you give him a job?

DC: Yes—mine.

CP: Okay, what about the times when you *didn't* feel you would make it?

DC: They were at least as frequent as the others. I felt that I was one of those people who were always just a little bit off-center in terms of what was wanted, that I fit no known category. That I would unjustly go unrecognized while mediocrities made it all around me. The fact is, mediocrities and worse make it all the time, so the phrase "make it" has no value. People who don't make it feel their lives would be rosy if they did, and those who do are startled to find they still have all their old problems, plus a few new ones, and begin to wonder if they'd be happier if they hadn't made it. My, my, Dickie, how profound. Why don't you sit on a tack?

CP: That's supposed to be my line. Before leaving this one, did you set standards below which you would not descend, even if it meant not making it?

DC: It's easy to say now that I wouldn't take a job on *Let's Make a Deal* playing host to the people who dress up as hamburgers and radishes, but I would have once, and probably would have been happy to sign a ten-year contract. I hope to God someone would have chopped my hand off before I did so, because after a month or so I would have been puking all the way to the bank. But the point is, my commitment was merely to get into the business, not anything so hifalutin as to have an Emmy-winning talk show. And if I had become the host of *Let's Make a Deal* I would have felt I had succeeded at something infinitely more interesting than the jobs some of the frat-house assholes we knew at Yale scrambled to get into.

CP: Meanwhile you had to settle for being the face next to the famous face, in crowd scenes, walk-ons, and so on. I remember you called me long-distance to tell me to watch for you as an extra on the *Sergeant Bilko* TV show.

DC: And the call cost more than I made. That was one of my first jobs. I got it because I had impressed the casting director somehow. When I went in, he said there was nothing, and we somehow got to talking about the meaning of Tennessee

Williams plays, and he said, at the end of a half hour or so, that I ought to be doing something other than making rounds and that he was going to get me a job for the following day. He made a call, told me where to be, and I left with the illusory feeling that I could talk my way into work whenever I wanted. I reported to the Bilko studio the next morning and found I was one of a dozen extras in a college-classroom scene. At one point I sidled up to Phil Silvers and reminded him that years before, when he played Omaha in *Top Banana*, I had come back to his dressing room and gotten his autograph on a picture. "And here I am on your show," I concluded, a little too brightly. "What for?" he said, a little edgily. "To give back the picture?" I looked around at the dinginess of the studio, noticed that, although Silvers was a big star on a big series who had everything I wanted, he didn't seem ecstatically happy, nor did his footsteps leave a glowing print on the floor as he passed. It was hard to relate all this to the thrill of having been in his dressing room at the Orpheum in Omaha. He was on a chaise in a dressing gown then, and the fact that a phone call came in from Ed Sullivan while I was there sent shock waves right through me.

CP: Memories of Omaha weren't enough to get Silvers to put you in a close-up?

DC: No, but I can give a small example of how I sometimes had an instinct that gave me a slight edge over the competition. I got a call one morning to report immediately to a studio across town as an extra on a Susskind revival of *Body and Soul.* I asked what I was, and they said a fight fan. I dressed quickly, gulped some breakfast, and was out the door when something told me to go back and get a tie. (I'd been told to wear either a sweater or a jacket.) When I got there they were arranging a shot near ringside, where the first few rows would show, and suddenly David (Mr. Susskind then) waded in among the extras and said, "Who the hell dressed these people? These are hundred-dollar seats, and I only see two people with neckties!" I quickly pulled my tie from my pocket and waved it in his face, and he lifted a tieless extra from beside Franchot Tone and put me there instead. As a result, I was in a two-shot with Tone, and all my friends saw me. It's not much of a story, but that small voice that said "Take a tie" as I left my pad was often there to give me a slight edge.

A slightly different example had to do with exploiting something as a conversation starter with someone I wanted to meet. I was on my way to a rehearsal of the last live *Playhouse 90* production in the history of the world, Robert Shaw's *The Hiding Place*. The stars were Trevor Howard, James Mason, and Richard Basehart, and I had wangled a job as an extra—a young Nazi at a Bund meeting. As I got off the subway train I saw, horrified, that a man had somehow fallen or jumped so that he was wedged between the train and the platform. I ran for a cop, who summoned medical help and a priest, and after forcing myself to take a good look at the man—a thing I do at times like this to try to overcome a squeamishness I am somehow ashamed of—I went to rehearsal. I'd always been crazy about Trevor Howard, but had never met him. I found him in his dressing room and said, "I just had a terrible experience . . ." and told him the story. Later I did the same thing with Basehart and Mason.

This led to my joining Howard and Basehart for lunch in a nearby restaurant. The play had about twelve sets that stretched over an acre or so of studio, so each man apparently assumed that I must be a featured actor in some scene he was not in. Otherwise why was I eating with him and not from a trough with the extras over in the corner? I remember the spiteful, envious glares coming from that corner as the two stars and I joked and chatted like old friends. It's a wonder the extras didn't wait for me in the alley.

I suppose you could say I was using another man's grave misfortune to advance myself, although you would be stretching a point. By the way, where did the silly idea come from that you must not speak disrespectfully of the dead? This is a hate-mail staple. The notion that, by dying, people instantly attain respectability, though they may have had none when alive, strikes me as silly. There is a widespread primitive notion that it's bad luck to speak of the departed in any tone; but the idea that it's poor sportsmanship to speak slightingly of someone who has added moribundity to his slight list of credits puzzles me. But let it pass—as the departed has.

CP: I recall that one of the things you tried in those days was to revive your magic act, even if not quite by popular demand. In fact, didn't I drive you in my battered Chevy to one of your bookings while on my way to some pressing business out of town? The place was a dingy building huddled among warehouses on the West Side water front. I felt sure that the next time I heard from you you would've awakened to find yourself working as a wiper in the engine room of a freighter bound for Bremerhaven.

DC: Correct on all counts except the freighter. It was actually bound for Rangoon. And instead of a wiper, I found myself, through some bizarre misunderstanding, signed on as the ship's surgeon. Fortunately there was another passenger on board, a lovely and mysterious mulatto woman, who—but seriously, to return to landlocked reality: it did strike me one day, like the light-bulb moment in a comic strip, that my magic act was the route to the top. It would show off the thing I could do that actors couldn't—stand "in one," downstage in front of the curtain, and be funny—and it paid well. It was the variety agents I should be seeing.

I got a list of them, and made a schedule and map for myself so that I could hit all their offices in a well-organized two days. Those two days are a vaguely blurred montage of cage elevators, yellowed autographed glossies on dirty walls, raspy voices, chomped cigars, and hair pieces that looked like a wedge of door mat perched on the head. I left off all my remaining eight-by-tens and actually got a job my second day. That was the one you dropped me off for. It was a place called the Seaman's Club, and it was a freebie, but an agent was going to drag his shiny serge ass, wig, and cigar over to see me.

On the bill with me were a ventriloquist whose lips moved more than the dummy's and a fattish lady of middle years who sang coquettish ditties and would occasionally lift her skirts to reveal legs that looked like bleached hams and chirp (with pathetic seriousness), "Not bad, huh?" I had not looked out front, and discovered when I got out there that it was not just that the acts ahead of me weren't so hot—there was scarcely any audience, and what there was was ninety per cent French sailors who understood no English. At first panicking, then realizing that at least here was a chance to impress my agent in an unexpected way, I did my act bilingually, to the delight of the sailors. Finishing, I packed and waited for the appearance of the man who was to offer me a string of club dates through the following January. He came back, and the fact that he had on his overcoat and hat boded ill.

I asked him how he had liked my act. "Lousy." I was stunned. "What was lousy about it?" I asked. "I thought I did pretty well under the circumstances." I remember fixing my gaze on what looked like Le Page's glue that secured his rug around the temples. You will have to take my word for what he said: "Your pace was lousy, and half the time I couldn't even understand what you were sayin'." We parted company, and I hauled my pathetic suitcase of magical delights aboard the subway and decided wherever you had gone (the army? newspaper job?) was a paradise compared with my pointless life.

CP: I think I had gone back to graduate school to read Henry James.

DC: Make that "demiparadise," then. I had one other club date before deciding that conjuring was not the best route to the summit. It was a synagogue on Long Island, and I arrived, as directed, at 7:00 P.M. The show, as usual, didn't start until two hours later. I followed two middle-aged ladies who did a puppet act that lasted for over an hour and a half, consisting of scenes from the Old Testament. When I finally got on, my opening line was, "For a minute there I thought we were going to get the New Testament too." It was greeted with silence and a perceptible wave of gloom. In the middle of my rope trick a rotten little girl in the front row threw a wadded-up napkin at me soaked in melted ice cream, which stuck, momentarily, to my suit. Her parents and everyone else looked on amused. I made light of it while suppressing a desire to drop-kick her into the cloakroom, drew abruptly to a close, collected my check, and headed for the cold and windy subway platform, having decided to drop my apparatus in the nearest manhole piece by piece. I forwent the dramatic gesture, but I did retire from magic that night.

CP: When Peter Shaffer's *Five-Finger Exercise* was on Broadway, you told me that you felt you could have played the part of the German boy who finds a home with a British family in that play. Were there other roles that you saw and felt you could've done as well as the actors in them, or would've liked to try?

DC: I think I could have done the German boy as well as the other actor *after* seeing him do it. I don't think I would have conceived the role as well, but I could have given a brilliant imitation of his conception of it.

I don't know exactly where I thought I was going in those days. I used to tell people that the life of a versatile character actor would be the most satisfying life I could imagine, and used to point to E. G. Marshall as my example. He worked constantly in all media, undoubtedly made a good living, didn't have the neurotic pressures of movie stardom, and was respected throughout the industry, as it's called.

In more of a comedy vein, I would really love to have been a second banana on a variety show, like Carl Reiner or Howie Morris with Sid Caesar, or Harvey Korman with Carol Burnett. Strange to say, as you may or may not agree from having seen my character-acting career, I am versatile enough for that. Constantly improvising and surprising myself and others in a variety of nationalities, ages, and characters would have been great fun. I think I am made for that kind of thing, or was. My wife will tell you that acting with me in a comedy was always trying for other actors. I could never seem to master my blocking, do the same thing twice, or even get all my lines right, up to opening night. Then, still quoting my wife, I would come together somehow in front of the audience, in ways that had not been glimpsed in rehearsal and that were as much a surprise to me as to everyone else onstage.

CP: While you were still standing at the back of the house watching actors in roles that you *might*'ve been able to play, your wife was actually onstage, in some cases on Broadway, and was having a pretty successful career. Was this a problem for you?

DC: Yes, there was a period when I was in danger of becoming Mr. Nye. I thought I could sense the disdain on the part of her Broadway friends that I was "no one," and began to get glimmerings of the chill existence of a man attached to a famous lady. Introductions would go, "This is Carrie Nye and, uh . . ." I would either supply my name or, in a more antic mood, say, "I hope you come up with it"—a move that generally failed to relieve the tension. I was later in a position to screw some of the people who had been more than condescending in those days, but didn't, when I realized I would get no satisfaction from it.

But I could clearly see her being swept along the Great White Way and up and out of my life, or else me swinging at photographers the way Elliott Gould did when he was married to Streisand. I remember getting a queasy feeling one day when she had to cancel lunch with me for one with her agent at the Plaza. With a couple of exceptions, she has never taken a job she didn't think was a good one, and she has no yearning for stardom. She is, in short, serious about acting.

CP: Today there are probably quite a few producers who

would be happy to cast you in a play or movie, giving you a chance to act with Carrie Nye if you wanted to. Can you see the two of you doing that? Being a sort of seventies version of Nick and Nora Charles, perhaps?

DC: I think it would be fun to act with her, but I somehow doubt that we will. We would probably collapse in a fit of giggling during the reading-of-the-will scene and be run out of town. That, and the fact that she could act me off the stage if she took a mind to, might inhibit me. Besides, she can be mean on the stage. Once, in a musical, she and I and the actor John Cunningham came to a dead stop. She looked accusingly at us until one of us came up with something, even though it was *her* line, which to this day she won't admit. But then, she will tell you *I* can be mean onstage too. Once, in a crowd-brawl-party scene we were in together, I was supposed to turn upstage, where she was standing with her back to me, and slap her on the behind. I apparently forgot the proper moment for this, or let it pass, and she decided it was not coming and turned face forward. Suddenly I remembered what I was supposed to do. I turned and slapped her on the front before realizing she was facing me. The audience gasped at this audacious bit of business. She claims it was intentional.

The other danger would be that she is so believable that I would do what I did once with Sandy Dennis and forget I was in a play. I would say, "Why are you yelling at me, Carrie Nye? I didn't do anything. Oh, shit—sorry, ladies and gentlemen," mutter "Fat-bloat, ahoy!" and walk into the wall in confusion.

CP: In any case, the little acting that you *were* doing was obviously not providing you with a living wage.

DC: Hardly even a dying wage.

CP: And I know you were not living off the immoral earnings of women. What *were* your techniques for survival?

DC: My lifesaver was having studied typing in high school.

It's nice to know even now that I can still make an honest wage at the keyboard if things go badly. I am an alumnus of Office Temporaries and spent many an arduous day pecking out labels and typing up sales records for a fat ten singles per diem. Only occasionally did my mind and fingers wander, causing contretemps that led me to fear I might have to turn in my ribbon. Once, it was discovered at the end of a day that I had typed scores of labels contrary to instructions, and my entire output had to go down the john. Next day my temporary employers requested someone else. But most of my assignments, as I said, were less drastically temporary than that.

Then for a time I worked as a spy. Not an actual CIA spook, but when I applied for it I reported to an office that had heavy iron caging on the door, and later I had to be finger-printed for the job. Behind the caged door sat a businesslike woman who had what I still thought of as the comic New York accent, from the telephone operators on the old Jack Benny radio show. She made sure the door was latched, checked behind the curtains, then instructed me in how to go into a major department store and pose as a customer, going through all the motions of almost buying something, then not buying it. After fifteen or twenty of these impostures, I was to skulk home and write up a report on each salesperson's attitude: did they make me uncomfortable, were they friendly, did they have nasty habits, did they suggest alternative purchases, did they seem convinced of the quality of the item, did they resent waiting on me, did they make me feel important, did they pinch my fanny?

There was one section of the form, after the "Check One" section, where you wrote a little paragraph describing your encounter with the salesperson. The boss woman, Miss Gallay, used to compliment me on the literary merits of my prose: "Scene: the vacuum-cleaner department of Macy's New York, five or six customers milling among vacuum cleaners, inspecting them, turning them over, fingering price tags. One sales-man, staring into the distance." "That's excellent, Mr. Cavett.

[She always inflected my name wrong and I would mutter *Cavett*, to no avail.] It puts me right there in the scene. I can see those customers, that salesman staring into space. If only all my people could write so clearly as yourself."

For this morally dubious but slightly creative activity I was given ten dollars a day. I figured it was good for me as an actor; I was getting on-the-job experience. I even considered putting it on my résumé: "Fifteen weeks in the role of customer at Macy's New York . . . good to excellent reviews." The real reward of the job, though, lay in those few times when I would get waited on by an absolute schmuck, or schmuckess, of the kind you get in real life. It was a pleasure to give them scathing reports. It was the kind of satisfaction I used to long for when I'd see some injustice being done and wish that, for that moment, I could be a cop.

CP: Was the scene always Macy's?

DC: Macy's New York was the plum. It usually went to the senior counterspies (sorry). For every Macy's assignment you drew a few Siberia gigs, which meant something like Abraham & Straus. That required a soul-killing subway ride to whatever benighted section of Brooklyn it's in; I have happily blanked it from memory. I remember something akin to panic when I would get there on the day of a sale and be assigned to the portion of the store where the sale was, presumably to test the salesperson under duress. The ladies, to employ a euphemism, would be held back by a chain and two or three strong men, and when the whistle blew they were released in a flying wedge to descend on the sale area. I would have to immerse myself in it all, and it was like being caught among cockatoos in a feeding frenzy. Some of the women kept their nails long and sharpened, and wore heavy, lethal-looking bracelets, the better to do damage to competing grasping fingers with. It was terrifying. Only those who have been through it can understand. I hope we have somehow made the world safe from sale days at Abraham & Straus, so that young men of future generations will never have to go through what some of us had to.

CP: It was experiences like that that persuaded you to come in from the cold?

DC: The job had palled in other ways too. I developed an aversion to the deception involved and began to sympathize with the probably overburdened and underpaid clerks, many of whom were probably out-of-work actors like myself. Eventually, when I had about forty dollars saved—forty dollars went farther in those days; about eight inches—I decided to give it up. When Miss Gallay called I answered in a Spanish accent and said that Mr. Cavett had moved to Akron.

CP: Having helped your father in Lincoln on one of his moonlighting jobs, collecting the proceeds from gum machines, you had the technical know-how to get those machines open, didn't you? I remember your telling me once that if all else failed in New York you could subsist by emptying pennies and nickels from gum machines on subway platforms. Perhaps you'd better not say whether or not it ever came to that. But wasn't it depressing even to have to joke about such a possibility? Didn't you ever suffer from a feeling of being down and out on the Upper West Side?

DC: Never completely out. Down and clinging a few times, maybe. Letters from my father at the time indicate a mild tolerance, but no great confidence in my ability to make it. I had periods of near depression, when I would quietly realize that he was probably right, but I wanted to hold out in New York for a few more years. I continued to harbor a vague hope that I would somehow land on at least one of my feet.

I'm not usually given to moods of deep depression. But I do remember once sitting on the edge of my bathtub on West Eighty-ninth Street, staring at the tiles, and thinking, "I'm not likely to get anywhere. I don't even feel like getting up and going to bed. I guess I'll just sit here until I rot." It was the closest thing to despair I can remember during that early period. I thought, "I've never understood how anyone could commit suicide, but if this feeling gets much deeper or won't go away, I can." I felt I would much prefer committing suicide at that moment to getting up and brushing my teeth and hauling my despondent frame into the bedroom.

CP: What pulled you off the bathtub?

DC: I got hungry. It's embarrassing—even in despondency I'm shallow.

But I must emphasize how atypical that low point was. I just don't have the temperament or metabolism for such moods. In some ways, most of that early time seems rather pleasant in my memory. I was in the city of my dreams, in the midst of the world I aspired to, and I felt snugly secure in my bachelor pad with my electric skillet, TV set, transistor radio, and stacks of dog-eared books. I knew that I could type my way out of total poverty whenever it struck, and occasionally fortune dealt me an ace.

Once, when I was down to my last subway token, I decided it was too nice a day to make rounds, that I deserved a day in the sun in Central Park. I went to a drugstore on Amsterdam Avenue near Seventy-sixth and bought some Sea & Ski for my near-albino epidermis with some change I found in my dirty laundry. The guy put it in a bag, and as I passed a litter basket I dropped the empty bag in and took two steps and realized something had caught my eye. I went back for the bag, uncrumpled it, and inside was a crisp new fifty-dollar bill. It was incredible. This meant two week's freedom. I started, out of conscience, to take it back, and then began to wonder how a fifty got there. All I could think of was that it was meant to be a pay-off, and the guy had gotten either the wrong person or the wrong bag. I decided it was the devil's money, and that to return it would be to contribute to a crime. To assuage my conscience, I decided I would go back in a few weeks and say a friend of mine had gotten a fifty there in a bag, and what was the story? If the guy wept and pleaded for its return I'd tell him I could get it back for him. I keep meaning to do this.

CP: I suppose it made up for a lot that New York was, as you say, the city of your dreams. No matter what happened, it was still the Big Apple.

DC: To say the least. It may be hard to imagine from some of the jokes I've done about it on TV, but when I first saw New York City, on my way to Yale, I flipped. I took the Pacemaker from Lincoln, changing trains at Chicago. I had about a half-hour layover and spent it strolling in the Loop. I loved Chicago; for me, up until then, *it* was Metropolis. Now I was going to the *real* Metropolis, and Chicago was merely a way station. The thought of New York made my scalp tingle. When I got there I walked through the tunnel at Grand Central with the words of the old radio show *Grand Central Station* running through my head, checked into the Roosevelt Hotel, which connects with Grand Central, and took my first steps onto the streets of Manhattan. I remember the overwhelming sense of it, and I have learned since that no other city in the world feels remotely like it. As I began to walk I was struck with some kind of half-assed destiny, a feeling that the city suited me, that I belonged there, and that the next few years were going to be thrilling. I took no more than ten steps and ran into a woman I knew from stock in Lincoln, a New York actress. A few months later she was murdered by the super in her building. Weird.

I was bone-tired, after two and a half days in a coach seat, but was so intoxicated by my first views of Fifth Avenue, Rockefeller Center, St. Patrick's, and Times Square that I could scarcely sleep that night. I kept going to the window and verifying that it was New York outside, and then lying in bed and watching the shadows on the ceiling and wondering if it was true that they stole your wallet out from under your pillow in New York, even in the best hotels. I put mine at the foot of the bed, under the covers, and dozed off.

When I awoke it was about 7:00 A.M. In a kind of trance, I realized where I was and remembered that if I were at home I would be watching the *Today Show* and that this was the very New York it came from. Then I remembered Dave Garroway, who was the show's host in those days, referring to "the people outside our Forty-ninth Street window," and how I used to wonder why those people waving to the camera were lucky enough to be where I wanted to be. I dressed, grabbed a doughnut, and looked for Forty-ninth Street. I found the NBC window, edged my way to the front, and, lo, a camera lens passed within a foot of my face. I thought, "I've made it! I'm on network TV! At this very moment I'm in New York and Lincoln." Various relatives saw me and wrote about it as if I had succeeded at something remarkable.

I went to several plays, and while I was watching them the thought would cross my mind, "Not only is this great, but when it's over I step outside and I'm in New York again." When I went to New York on weekends from Yale I would always catch the last train back to New Haven on my last night. On the way to the station I would stand at the shuttle subway entrance at Times Square and look at it and say goodbye to it. Nowadays I avoid Times Square like boils, but then it was Eden. I once bought a postcard of Times Square, at the late Hotel Astor, and stood on the island between Broadway and Seventh Avenue looking at the Pepsi sign on the postcard and then at the real Pepsi sign and trying to locate myself in the merging of the two realities. What has become of that foolish, foolish lad?

CP: The question is, what became of him then? Did he ever get into trouble in the wicked city?

DC: Aside from someone trying to sell me a marijuana cigar, almost never. I always acted as if I knew my way around.

Once Bob Leuze and I went down from Yale and saw a lousy singer in a club in the Village. When we asked how much a cocktail was they said a dollar and a half, so we ordered Cokes. When they charged us ninety-five cents apiece for the Cokes I was outraged. The manageress, a formidable dyke, came over and said, "What's wrong? Where are you gonna get entertainment like this for ninety-five cents?" I said, "The Nebraska State Fair!" slammed down a dollar-ninety, and stormed out with barely perceptible dignity. Thanks to the inflated Cokes, we had to walk all the way uptown to Grand Central in order to have enough money to get back to New Haven. I don't think I've enjoyed a Coke since. Or a dyke, for that matter.

CP: What did you do for entertainment, given the fact of your not having money, which is quite a fact, come to think about it—that's a question.

DC: I took walks in the park, after-dark strolls in neighborhoods I couldn't afford to live in, a small amount of prowling the water fronts—things like that.

I used to ride the Staten Island ferry from time to time, preferably with a young woman who had long golden hair suitable for blowing in the breeze on the windswept deck. Like Gerry Hempel—remember her? I used to call her when the urge struck and say, "Meet me at the Battery, and don't forget your hair."

Once I made the crossing with Maeve Maguire, the actress, and we decided to get drunk on martinis in a Staten Island bar. We must have succeeded, because I remember Maeve and me sitting on what seemed like church steps, laughing uproariously over God knows what, wondering if the steps were warm enough to sleep on if we missed the last ferry. I have no recollection of the return trip, but I assume she was lady enough to see that I got home safely.

The only other time I went to Staten Island proper, my wife and I decided to swim there. Our local delicatessen man recommended a beach he recalled from childhood, and after taking a cab, a subway, a ferry, a bus—a veritable *Boys' Book of Transportation*—we got there. It looked fine. We plunged in the water, and we had swum about eight strokes when we noted the remarkable fact that, of the three hundred or so people on the beach, we were the only ones swimming. Dismissing this as eastern effetism, we splashed merrily on until we both noticed what appeared to be swarms of bugs on our persons, but were in fact globules of oil. We decided we would swim through it, when I noticed Carrie Nye's hair changing color. In a sort of panic we headed for the beach. Our toes were gummed together into fins by the oil, and the soles of our feet had acquired a retread a half-inch thick that was like molten rubber. Apparently the entire population of the beach had watched in shocked silence as two figures actually ventured into the briny, or, I should say, the oleaginous. It took hours to get the stuff off, and for weeks I had a thin black sole of glop on my feet. As I was coming out of the water I said to one of the habitués, "Look at this. It's incredible." And he said, "Yup. Oil." That was the first conversation I ever had with a Staten Islander.

CP: You understood the folkways of the Manhattan Islanders better.

DC: I did, and I should have stuck to home. Sometimes I can entertain myself by reeling off in my mind a montage of the famous faces I glimpsed during early years in Manhattan, faces that have since passed from the scene. Thurber going into the Algonquin, T. S. Eliot getting into his overcoat in front of the Algonquin, Franklin Pangborn walking up Broadway one night right after I had seen him in *The Bank Dick*, Ward Bond crossing Forty-ninth Street, with a beer gut and cowboy boots and walking as if he had either a charley horse or hemorrhoids, Charles Laughton wearing an English cap and strolling through the theater district as people parted (groups, not individuals) in front of him and whispered, "There goes Charles Laughton," Ben Hecht hailing a cab, Basil Rathbone, looking

Holmeslike, with his dog in Central Park, Cedric Hardwicke entering the Royalton, Una O'Connor, whom I'd just seen in a Frankenstein film, Errol Flynn buying a paper, and the one who gives me anguishing regret, Fred Allen.

CP: Why anguish?

DC: I saw him coming out of the *What's My Line?* studio one rainy night, and I marveled that people were asking for the *other* panelists' autographs. I walked up under the marquee and told him I thought he was wonderful—you know, you can never think of anything else to say—and then he started walking alone toward Broadway in the downpour. I followed him, four steps behind. I didn't know he was aware I was there. When he got to the corner two bums came staggering out from a doorway, and one of them said, "You're the greatest, Fred." He turned and, in an aside to me, said, "Ah, my fan club is gathering." It was funny and bitter, and I remember thinking, "Fred Allen said something, and I'm the only one who heard it."

I wish to God I had followed him into the subway and struck up a conversation. When I think of all the third-rate celebrities I was forcing myself upon, why the hell I thought I had more urgent business elsewhere I don't know. I told myself, I suppose, that I was going to be in the East from then on and I could meet him some other time. He died a few weeks later.

CP: To add violence to death, what about the mangled man you started talking to Trevor Howard about? The actress who was murdered by the super in her building? That too is part of New York.

DC: Yes, and an excessive amount of it seems to have been thrown into my path. Going to and from work, moving about in New York, can be uncomfortably like crossing a battlefield. Once, coming home from my show, I heard shots and went around a corner just in time to see the police efficiently chalking onto the sidewalk the outline of a man they had just shot.

Another time, when I was a guest panelist on *To Tell the Truth* for a week, way back at the beginning of my television career, I walked past an old building on Fifty-third Street that was being dismantled. I remember the smell of wet earth and the sort of catacomblike chill you get when you pass one of these places, even on a hot day. The workmen were having their lunch, and I remember nodding to them as I walked past. I taped one of two shows, walked past them again, and went into the Stage Deli for lunch. When I went back, there was a mountain of rubble where the building had been and the dust was just settling. Seconds earlier the whole thing had collapsed on the workmen, and the ones it had missed were running around frantically pulling at timbers and chunks of wall. They roped off the area, and began digging and taking out corpses and injured. I retain a grisly image of a large flat section of wall being lifted away, revealing what looked like the bust of a man. It was a dead workman covered with plaster and buried to the waist. He was upright, and the plaster made him the color of a statue in a museum. I went through the usual gamut of intimations of mortality, musing that I had passed this man a couple of hours earlier and that when we nodded to each other neither of us expected to be dead in two hours.

At times like that, I always think of the Frost line from the poem about the boy who's killed in a buzz-saw accident—"And they, since they were not the one dead, turned to their affairs." What else could they—or I—do? And what was that Auden poem about Icarus that you quoted to me? You said you thought of it when you saw, from a bus, the doorman of a building lying in a pool of blood on the sidewalk, presumably knifed, while passers-by continued to chat and blow bubble gum and your bus routinely pulled away.

CP: It's *"Musée des Beaux Arts."* Auden describes Breughel's painting of Icarus, in which everything turns casually away from the disaster of Icarus's plunge out of the sky. He says suffering always takes place "while someone else is eating or opening a window or just walking dully along."

DC: That's it. And in New York, where violence is more dramatic and more ominous than that, it's still just part of the air of potentiality that the city has. Like that passage in Fitzgerald where he describes seeing Manhattan while crossing the Fifty-ninth Street bridge and feeling it a place where anything, *anything* could happen. I still have great affection for New York. It can thrill me still when I see it from the air on a clear night or come over one of the bridges and see that skyline—there is no other like it. I've gotten that kind of kick in London, Rome, Vienna, and other places I've been since, but never as strongly as when New York was rich and strange.

CP: When we talked about the part-time jobs with which you supported yourself while looking for work as an actor, we left out the most important one: your stint as a copyboy at *Time* magazine. I was not yet working at *Time* myself, of course, but I've since learned that your place in copyboy legend is secure, for having sent an empty beer can through the pneumatic tubes one night and for having spent most of your working hours in the library reading the files on the likes of Stan Laurel and Buster Keaton.

DC: I also have fond memories of making the airport trip to pick up or deliver photographs. It was always a great plum, not only because it got you out of the office for a long time, but also because you could take the subway and bus, spend only about a dollar, and then put in for seven dollars' worth of expenses when you got back.

The *Time* job gave me a modicum of definition, especially vis-à-vis Carrie Nye. Once I went to pick her up after a rehearsal of an ill-fated Broadway play called *Second String*— a title with ominous implications for me at that point. The stars of the play, besides Carrie Nye, were Shirley Booth, Jean-Pierre

Aumont, Nina Foch, and Cathleen Nesbitt. One of them introduced me to the others by saying, "This is Mr. Cavett. He works
for *Time*." It was better than merely saying, "He makes the
rounds and goes out with Carrie Nye."

CP: You assumed the *Time* label in a similar way when you
made your crucial contact with Jack Paar, didn't you?

DC: Ah, the fateful typewritten sheets of jokes in the *Time*
envelope.

CP: I realize you've told that story to interviewers to the
point of nausea and beyond. Do you want to give one final
rendition of it here and then never think about it again?

DC: No.

CP: I see. Well, good night, then.

DC: Why don't *you* tell it and give me a rest?

CP: All right. This was one day in 1960. Instead of going
about your duties as a copyboy, you were loitering in a corner
somewhere reading the newspaper. You came across an item
saying that Jack Paar worried constantly about his opening
monologue for the *Tonight Show* and was always searching for
more and better material for it. So, seeing your chance to become a real writer, like those slick pros who surrounded you
at *Time*—

DC: Excuse me. I had never for one second harbored a
desire to join the fraternity of ink-stained wretches, nor did I
see this as a chance to do so. I merely saw it as a chance to
bring about some kind of meeting with Paar.

CP: Yes. Seeing your chance to bring about a meeting with
Paar, you sat down at a typewriter in an empty writer's cubicle
in the Time and Life Building and—

DC: Actually I just cooked with the idea for a while, and
didn't sit down at the typewriter until I had gotten off work
and gone back to my apartment.

CP: Anyway, you wrote a few pages of what sounded to you like a Paar monologue. You stuck them in a plain envelope. Then, prompted by the little genie that always gave you an edge over the next guy, you took them out and stuck them in a *Time* envelope, grabbed a taxi—

DC: Subway.

CP: —for the RCA Building, and asked the receptionist where you could find Jack Paar.

DC: No, I knew perfectly well where to find him, since I'd nosed around the *Tonight Show* before. I took the back elevator to the sixth floor and explored the corridor where I knew Paar sometimes walked between his dressing room and the bathroom. Sure enough, he suddenly appeared around a corner. But you go ahead.

CP: I believe he took you for a *Time* reporter.

DC: His eye was caught by my *Time* envelope, and I assume he took me for a reporter, which I guess is what I intended. The impression wasn't hurt any by my saying, "*Time* is thinking of doing a story on you." I'd been watching the show and knew he had a cold, so I added, partly to demonstrate that I *had* been watching, "That's just what you need on top of your cold." He laughed.

I waved my envelope and said, "I wrote you some jokes you might be able to use." Looking only a little skeptical, he took the envelope and thanked me and went into his office-dressing room. Not knowing for sure what to do next, I decided to go sit in the studio audience and watch the show, or at least the monologue, to hear my jokes. You can imagine my surprise when Jack came out and took a folded piece of paper from his pocket. In an instant flashforward, I knew what was about to happen. He would say, "Everything I'm going to tell you now is true. A kid just came up to me out in the hall and handed me a monologue that's funnier than the stuff my own writers give me. If anyone saw which way the kid went, let me know.

Meanwhile, here are his jokes. . . ." But in fact what he had pulled from his pocket was a prepared bit that had nothing to do with me.

I began to get a queasy feeling and to eye the exit. Suddenly I heard one of my lines used as an ad lib. Then another one. Paar was working them deftly into the show. I began to emerge from my collar again and sit up. At the end of the show, I managed to get into the same elevator with him, and he spotted me and said, "Thanks, pal. You should do that again sometime." I graciously let a week pass, did, and the second time resulted in my getting a job. Which resulted in my being wherever I am now and not someplace else. That's the story.

CP: The definitive version?

DC: Yes. And you told it very well.

CP: When you took the job with Paar did you give up on becoming an actor? Or was it just the best prospect at the moment?

DC: I thought the Paar thing was right for me, somehow, and would open up vaguely defined doors to who knew what? It is remarkable that in all the time I worked on talk shows, and long after I began to appear on them, I never pictured myself hosting one. Talk shows were merely a means to something else. I remember once when I was writing for Carson I said to him, rather tactlessly, I now realize, "What do you go on to from this?" Meaning him. I realized I had embarrassed him with the question. I guess most people would settle for achieving the hosting of a network talk show, but for me it remained a steppingstone to some filmy beyond.

CP: With Paar, you started in the position of talent coordinator. You told me at the time that the job consisted of meeting and interviewing people who would grab your ass in one way or another to get on the show. With all due respect to your ass, could you elaborate a little?

DC: Sometimes it meant literally that. I remember one guy who was recommended by a frequent lady guest on the show. He was the lady's tax expert, in fact. I was assigned to meet him for lunch. By the end of the lunch, I guess he felt he hadn't sufficiently passed his audition with me. Suddenly, before my eyes, he suffered a diabolical personality change and began to offer enticements of the flesh and senses that would have made Fellini's cameraman blush. He had a young man with him, slightly deformed, who had a distressingly obedient air about him, and a skin tone that you see only on things that hurry for cover when you turn over a stone, and I fancied I could detect the marks of some sort of collar around his neck. The would-be guest went on to describe how adept his maid was at services beyond those generally required of a domestic, and he did it with a graphic skill that was beginning to unsettle my shrimp curry. I decided I was needed at the office and excused myself, marveling once again, as I walked back, at how much distance I had put between me and Sunday-school class in Grand Island.

CP: Beyond such enticements, if that's the word, what else did a talent co-ordinator's job consist of?

DC: Looking constantly for guests to suggest for the show, getting the okay to interview those people for a possible appearance on the show, and interviewing people who were already booked for the show in order to make notes for the host.

If the guest was a big star or a VIP of some other kind, the talent co-ordinator would go to him or her, usually at the guest's hotel room, and chat a bit about the appearance. A good talent co-ordinator does a certain amount of coaching, saying things like "Tell that story just the way you told it to me . . . and say the line 'And I can never face those people again!' just the way you said it." You had to assure the guest that his stories were not as boring as he thought (or claimed to think), and in some cases had to stay with him to see that he didn't get drunk before air time.

With Paar, you would then go to him and give him your

impression of the guest, or else the impression you thought it would be best to give him, knowing that there were problems he could easily handle on the air but that would scare him off a bit if you raised them ahead of time. Then you would meet the guest at the studio and hang around with him in the green room and dressing room, calming him whenever possible and sort of holding his hand until the dreadful moment when he stepped out between the curtain and the flat into the nation's bedrooms. Afterward the guest would come off and tell you that *you* made it all possible for him, and you would thank him and walk home thinking, "But *he* got to appear on television and I didn't."

CP: Enough of that thinking apparently leads one to write his own act and eventually become the person who walks out there, rather than the one who ministers to him in the wings.

DC: Apparently. I remember the day the irony hit me that for years I had wondered how I could get on the *Tonight Show* and suddenly, in becoming a talent co-ordinator, I had become one of the people I had always wanted to meet. I had the power to put anyone in the world on the show except myself. I had a sense of having jumped two squares when I should have jumped only one. It occurred to me a few times, when guests I was interviewing would say, "You ought to tell Paar to put you on the show," to do so, but I never had the nerve. Then the opportunity came up when I went on to translate for the German-speaking Miss Universe.

CP: Did it live up to your expectations?

DC: All I can say is that when I got out there I knew it was where I had always wanted to be. I had that old feeling; I knew how to get laughs, knew what to do with myself. I felt at home under the lights and in front of the camera. Would you like to hear a few bars of "Over the Rainbow"?

CP: Maybe a little later. Even though it buried you backstage, the job of talent co-ordinator gave you a splendid means of meeting luminaries of show business and the arts, which should've appealed to you.

DC: It did. I now had an excuse to do all the things I was attempting to do before—to visit Peter Ustinov at the St. Regis (to make a note or two about his upcoming appearance on the show), to have lunch with Kenneth Tynan (who wanted some firsthand impressions of Paar), and to be able to remind Noël Coward, when I ran into him somewhere, that I had met him before (backstage at the Paar show). My compulsions had been, you might say, legitimized.

CP: I suppose in some ways the most significant of all those meetings was the time the *Tonight Show* assigned you to look over a new young comedian at the Blue Angel.

DC: Always referred to reverently as the now-defunct Blue Angel, but in those days it was obviously still funct. Yes, there was this newcomer named Woody Allen playing there, and everything I had heard about him sounded good. I was dazzled by his credits, which included writing for Sid Caesar while still a teen-ager, and I had the feeling this was someone I would like to get to know, even though I had neither seen him nor met him. His sounded like one of the lives I would like to lead.

I got there just as the lights went down and he came on. His opening jokes were marvelous. They were not formula; they showed complex intelligence and genuine wit. It was marvelous just to see this high level sustained throughout his act, instead of the intermittent gems of good but lesser comics. Yet about a third of the way through the audience began to murmur and talk. Woody plowed on, his face largely concealed by the mike, and ended, more by excusing himself than finishing, and left the stage to polite applause. Somehow I felt there had been a kind of arc traveling from him, on the stage, to me, standing there in the back. I recognized immediately that there was no young comedian in the country who was in the same class with him for sheer brilliance of jokes, and I resented the fact that the audience was too dumb to realize what they were getting. They were mildly appreciative, but they would have preferred a folk singer, which they soon got. Woody had been casting pearls over the heads of swine.

CP: Even in the Blue Angel.

DC: I've never been able to discern any genuine taste on the part of the so-called better night-club audiences, like those in the Blue Angel or the hungry i. I've always felt that most of the stuff they swooned over and took to their bosoms was merely a higher brand of junk—acts that would throw in a reference to Proust or Kafka, thereby defining themselves as somehow rarefied. Lacking the gusto and true funniness of some of the so-called low comics, these acts and their audiences mutually flatter each other that they are somehow superior and protest too much that they would not want a big, crass, commercial acceptance, because it would involve lowering their standards and compromising themselves. I think we're discussing a phenomenon that has largely become passé, and less is the pity. But when I was coming up it was a trap and an irritation.

CP: Did you convey some of this to Woody that night?

DC: Yes. While the folk singer was on, I sought him out, and we sat down in the pink light of one of the lounge booths of the Angel, hit it off immediately, and talked until it was time for his late show, then went to his apartment and talked some more, and have been close friends ever since. A few days after he met me, incidentally, he got a divorce. None of the rumors, I might add, are true.

CP: You two would seem to be a rather unlikely combination.

DC: I guess we look different and have vastly contrasting social and ethnic backgrounds. But we have the same reactions to and estimates of a lot of things, which make us *simpatico* despite the miles between Brooklyn and Nebraska, geographically and otherwise. We both dug the Hope-Crosby road pictures as kids, appreciated comedy at an early age, had a serious side that made us seem a little odd to our friends in school, and tend to be amused by the same things now. Actually, Woody is much closer to being an intellectual than I am, and if he wanted to he could conduct a seminar on writing and comedy at any major university. He once threatened to publish a series of essays on comedy, and I hope he gets around to it. It's about the only form of writing he hasn't turned his hand to, except the novel. I wouldn't be surprised if he had two or three of them in a trunk somewhere—novels, I mean—and an epic poem or two that he isn't telling anyone about. I think too he would like to write and act in a serious film, but his comic image is so strong in people's minds that he has held off. I hope he does it anyway.

The only discomfort I felt in getting to know Woody was how ashamed of myself I would get when I saw how disciplined he was. He can go to the typewriter after breakfast and sit there until the sun sets and his head is pounding, interrupting work only for coffee or a brief walk, and then spend the whole evening working. I had the feeling that one day like that represented more work than I had done in my life. But even this discomfort proved to be a good thing, since exposure to Woody was what finally prodded me into getting an act together for myself.

CP: Meanwhile, back at the *Tonight Show*, you were soon helping Paar to get *his* act together, by writing comedy for him instead of being a talent co-ordinator. What was it like working closely with Paar?

DC: One, it wasn't all that closely, and, two, it was a little like living at home with an alcoholic parent. The family's (staff's) first question was always "How does he seem today?" I, for one, when I finally came to terms with it, found it enormously interesting and stimulating, and watching the other staff members gird for it was an amusement in itself. As you once pointed out, the relationship of a star and his staff is essentially that of a king and his courtiers. The politics and favor currying and jealousy and spitefulness of a talk-show staff would make the court of Versailles look sweet. If anyone on the Paar staff brought cookies to work and passed them around, no one else would bite into one without a food taster. Survival there, in some cases, depended not only on surviving yourself, but also on doing in everyone else.

A certain amount of this is endemic to television—the constant guessing and second-guessing in people who aren't sure of what their contributions and talents are, or why someone else isn't in their jobs, or how soon someone else will be. The medium is full of people who are desperate to retain positions that have certain trappings they enjoy: expense accounts, shoulder rubbing with the famous, prestige and glamour, higher salaries than they ever expected, and, from time to time, all the free booze and sex they can carry. But they aren't quite sure just how they got hold of the big cookie or when it is going to crumble suddenly. So already half their fun is spoiled because they lunch on Gelusil, although they can afford (or freeload) the Four Seasons. It's easier for the people who practice a specific craft, like make-up or joke writing, but if you're in one of the less precisely defined jobs, where your performance is not so easily assessed except that it either does or doesn't appeal to the star's mood, it's Ulcer City. Everything you wear, drive, live in, and are making payments on is made out of burstable-bubble material.

CP: But there was even more of this than normal with Paar?

DC: I'm afraid so. Once, when Jack was on my show for ninety minutes, I seemed to startle him by telling him publicly that he had made his staff nervous. "Panicked" would be a more accurate word. Not that he did it deliberately. It was just a natural consequence of his complex personality, which was hard to figure and hard to predict; it kept people off balance. I think his fascination with the big cats—I mean the jungle ones

—must have to do with an affinity with them in his own personality. He is instinctive, cagey, and suspicious, as well as appealing and attractive. He has joked about his alleged paranoia, and I think he does have a low-grade case of it that accounts for some of his more fascinating quirks.

For years people have remarked on Jack's tendency to overpraise guests as he introduces them, and haven't been able to understand why anyone in the business would keep doing it. The introductions are sometimes so ludicrous that he himself has to laugh, like the time he said about Florence Henderson that when she sings the nightingales hang their heads in shame. He realized, when he heard himself say it, that not only do they not, but also that he or whoever gave him that nauseating introduction *should.* Sometimes he gets going on an introduction and finds things to admire in the person that he didn't even know about when he started, until only Christ Himself could live up to it.

This has to do with a feeling I understood when I started doing this kind of show myself, that you want the audience to think you are bringing them the best of something, because if you are not it means either somebody else is or you are not capable of getting the best. It also shows that you recognize the best, even though you said someone else was the best (or, in moderate moods, "perhaps the best") last week.

CP: I'm not sure I see the connection with paranoia.

DC: Well, the people who like to psychoanalyze Jack would say that his intros are a form of neurotic hostility. He might say, in one of them, "Johnny Winters is pound for pound the funniest man on earth," and add that before the show Winters was making the stagehands laugh harder than anyone in history. The amateur Freudians would say that what Jack is doing here is saying, "This guy is capable of being great, he has been great all over the place in the past, and if he isn't tonight he must have something against *me,* because eyewitnesses can testify that he can be if he wants to be."

CP: Jinkies, I'm going to have to start listening more closely to introductions after this.

DC: Either that or don't listen at all.

CP: Didn't you ever lose your head, or your nerve, or your temper, or something, while coping with Paar's quirks?

DC: My temper, once. It was over two guests on the same show—one was someone I'd booked, and the other was Alexander King, whom Jack adored and I came to hate. King played on a couple of Jack's idiosyncracies, and went to him and poisoned his mind about my guest out of fear of competition. Although my guest's appearance went well, Jack, still under King's influence, called me into his office afterward and chewed me out. He was actually shouting at me. To my and everyone's surprise, I shouted back at him, made a caustic remark about his friend King, stomped out of the office, assumed I was finished there forever, and went to get my belongings. Paul Orr, the producer, assured me it would all blow over, and he was right. I honestly doubt if Jack remembers the incident or could tell you who the guest in question was. This quality of blanking out unpleasant things can be a blessing. If Jack has been accused of lying, I think it is because of this quality. He could probably pass a lie-detector test that he and I never had a harsh word when I worked for him, and if I played a tape of the incident for him he would be amazed.

He is a witty man, he has a quickly bored, fast-moving mind, and his lack of extensive formal education gives him a respect and sometimes excessive awe of the educated. I've seen him humble himself before certain people because of their book learning who were his inferiors brainwise. He is an omnivorous reader, and whenever he would see me with some learned periodical that, as an Ivy League grad, I still felt it a duty to drag myself through each month, he would note the name of it, get it, and read it more thoroughly than I had. I always liked that quality in him, though I'm afraid I put him through some pretty dreary issues of *Partisan Review*.

CP: Your stock with him must have soared after the Carrie Nye incident.

DC: I'm not sure it moved in either direction, but it was a funny incident. Before we were married, she came to a taping of the show because she wanted to see Noël Coward, who was a guest that night. Early in the show, Jack went out into the audience to play "Stump the Piano Player," a game where he would ask for a composer and a style and José Melis would invent something blending the two. Jack was naturally attracted to the glam-looking blonde on the aisle, although he had no idea who she was or that she and I were connected. He said, "Hello," and when she responded with the same word but in a voice deeper than his, the audience roared. Jack said, innocently, "Well, Tallulah!," a thing that sends her up the wall. He asked, with implied doubt in his voice, if she could name a composer. This question usually elicited names like Brahms, Beethoven, or sometimes Strauss. She leaned into the hand mike and intoned, "Glazunov." José collapsed on the keys, and Coward, watching on a monitor in the green room, spilled his tea breaking up with laughter. To this day she claims it was the only composer she could think of.

The next day I told Paar that she was my fiancée, and he said, "*Is* she?," in that way that only he can say it.

CP: After Paar's departure from the *Tonight Show*, you wrote for a series of interim *Tonight Show* hosts, and then started in with Johnny Carson when he took over the show. How did working with him compare with working with Paar?

DC: I could refer you to an article that appeared in one of the fan magazines under the title "Why I Never Liked Johnny Carson." In it you learn that Carson never spoke to me voluntarily, that after I'd worked for him for two years he still did not know my name, and that the photograph in the article of us smiling together at a Friars roast was an acting job on both our parts, because we could never abide each other's guts. The author of the article allows as how I may not remember having given him all this information, because he interviewed me at "a busy time of [my] life."

All of the above makes good copy, but I'm sorry to report that those articles are phony from beginning to end, and this one is no exception. It has a basis in truth: I did work for Carson. We didn't go fishing together on weekends, and I never slept over at his house, the two of us lying awake in our 'jammies eating the fudge we had made together, talking of our dreams and hopes and fears. But I found him to be cordial and businesslike, and to have himself well in hand as far as the show was concerned. And I would like to say publicly that just because everybody says he is a drug-addicted, sadistic Commie sex pervert, he never showed me that side of himself. I never knew or asked why those screams came from inside his locked office door, and I don't care to know.

CP: In other words, nobody's going to accuse *you* of bad-mouthing your old employer.

DC: Exactly. He did once call me, when I had handed in what he thought was a lousy monologue, and said, "I think you're capable of better work than this." I suddenly felt like a kid who has been rebuked by a favorite teacher. He was, need I add, right. I think it happened in a period when I was beginning to see daily joke writing for others as a dead end, a way of giving away something I ought to be saving for myself. I was beginning, about then, to cook on the idea of moonlighting on him and doing my own act. But I did try to improve my writing for him. I remember his doing smashingly with some of the stuff I wrote, and he would occasionally compliment me the next day on a specific line.

CP: One does hear reports that his staff isn't overly fond of him.

DC: I'm not sure that's a serious charge. He is not a man who seems to seek close buddies, and, if he were, the staff of his own television show would not be the ideal place to seek them.

CP: Are you saying that you agree with the frequent characterization of him as cold?

DC: A woman journalist, one of the most dislikable interviewers I've ever endured, once said to me, in an accusatory tone, "You worked for Carson. Why are you afraid to admit in print that he's cold?" I had had enough of her, and I said, "I'm not. He *is* cold. One day he was napping in the nude in his dressing room, and I shoved a thermometer up his ass and the mercury froze." Our interview ended a short time later. I don't think this got into print.

I knew very little about Johnny's personal relationships. I have heard that he has been manipulated and screwed more than once by trusted associates, to the point where he is defensively wary to what some find an excessive degree. I see this as a perfectly reasonable response. It is, I suppose, the sort of thing that happens to a person in show business that makes his former friends say, with heavy disapprobation, "Boy, has he changed."

While I'm at it, I'll do a short cadenza on the subject of changing. If you are going to survive in show business, the chances are you are going to change or be changed. Whatever your reasons for going into the business, it is safe to admit they form a mixture of talent, ambition, and neurosis. If you are going to succeed and remain successful, you are going to do it at the expense of a number of people who are clamoring to climb the same rope you are climbing. When you suddenly acquire money, hangers-on, well-wishers, and ill-wishers; when you need to make baffling decisions quickly, to do too much in too little time, to try to lead a personal and a professional life when you can't seem to find the time for either; when you have to kick some people's fannies and kiss others' in order to get to the point where you won't need to do either any more;

when you have to sort out conflicting advice, distinguish between the treacherous and the faithful or the competent and the merely aggressive, suffer fools when time is short and incompetents when you are in a pinch; and when you add to this the one thing you don't get in other professions—the need to be constantly fresh and presentable and at your best just at the times when you are bone-weary, snappish, and depressed; when all these things apply, it is possible that you are going to be altered, changed, and sometimes for the worse.

Unless you are one of these serene, saintly individuals about whom it can be truly said, "He or she hasn't changed one bit from the day I knew them in the old house on Elm Street." This is true mostly of those who have found others to do their dirty work for them. All I'm saying is that your demands and needs change, and if you don't change with them you don't survive. There are times when I've envied Carson's ability to say to someone, "This is a business. You're not pulling your weight. You're out." Faced with the same kind of decision, I usually wait a year or two, and nobody profits in the long run.

I went into Johnny's office on the day the news of Stan Laurel's death was announced. He was very fond of Laurel and had spoken to him a number of times by phone when Laurel was in the hospital. I went in to ask him if he wanted to say anything about Laurel on the show that night. He was sitting alone at his desk, and the second I entered he said, "You too?" I was not aware of looking particularly dejected, although I was (I also knew Laurel), but I could see that Johnny was clearly moved and had caught my mood instantly. We talked about Laurel for a while, and he asked me to put down some suggestions of things to say.

As I recall, a couple of them were pretty flowery. Johnny chose the briefest one and made it briefer. At the end of the show, he simply said, "A great comedian died today. His name was Stan Laurel and I'll miss him." I suppose some people regarded that as cold and brisk, but, as one who would rather be accused of coldness than of exploiting emotion myself, I understood.

CP: Even though you weren't consciously aspiring to host a talk show yourself, you must have used your vantage point in those years to analyze the performing styles of both Paar and Carson.

DC: I decided at the time that the thing that made Paar exciting on the air was the thing that, seen from another angle, made him exciting to work for. He worked with a kind of spontaneity that was startling for television, especially in those relatively early days, when everyone was slick, hair-sprayed, buttoned up, and observing the proprieties. Other people were natural, but he was unpredictable, which is quite different. Berle, Jerry Lester, and Jerry Lewis could be unpredictable as comics, but Jack in all his work let his own quirks, neuroses, suspicions, and dislikes play freely on the surface, along with his enthusiasms, instant reactions, and emotional knee jerks. Even for those who didn't like it, it was compelling, and you had to admit that it appealed, if only to a voyeur instinct. There was always the implied possibility in his manner that he would explode one day, and you might miss seeing a live nervous breakdown viewed from the comfort of your own bedroom. No matter who the guest was, in a two-shot your eyes were on Jack.

Another part of his appeal was that he instinctively asked and said things that you yourself, if you were not inhibited, would like to ask and say. Which is to say, here was someone who went through with things that many self-respecting people denounced as somehow "not done." Yet those same people watched him nightly and loved seeing him do those things. When attacked unjustifiably, and in some cases cruelly, by some cheap columnist, Jack would give as good as he got, with humor. The fact that he also did this when he was criticized reasonably just made him that much more fun to watch, at least for me. I still can't figure out why it just didn't seem the same when he came back for a year in 1973—whether it was Jack or the audience who had changed, or failed to change.

CP: And Carson?

DC: I'm sure that Johnny is as riddled with doubts about his identity as any of us who have gravitated toward comedy for a living, and I think it shows in his work. His style is an accretion of Bennyisms, Grouchoisms, Hopeisms, and, to drop this ism-ism, later additions of Don Rickles, Don Adams, Dean Martin, and a large dose of Jonathan Winters. Here and there are touches of both Allens, Fred and Steve. Fred Allen had a department called "The Mighty Allen Art Players," a witty adaptation of Stanislavsky's name for his company, and Steve Allen's Answer Man went into swami drag and became Johnny's Carnac. Also, Johnny's appropriation of Oliver Hardy's look of dismay into the lens was a shrewd choice for television.

Constant exposure has made the resultant image Johnny's own. It should be added that he has, showing through all this accretion, enormous personal charm and *un*borrowed wit of his own, and a high degree of professionalism.

The interesting contrast between him and Paar is Paar's willingness to commit emotional hara-kiri on camera and Johnny's reserve. This has resulted in each one's being compared unfavorably to the other precisely for the opposite qualities. Johnny is locked up tight and Jack is refreshingly honest and spontaneous. Or, conversely, Johnny has admirable reserve and Jack is an emotional spill-it-all. I remember an argument among friends shortly after Johnny took over the *Tonight Show* in which Pro-Paar said, "Carson's a drag. If he's on for ten years, he will never have an emotional outburst." In reply, Pro-Carson said, "For which I will be profoundly grateful to him." There you have it.

CP: Now that you've had some experience of the rigors of a daily show, are you impressed that Carson has kept at the grind all these years?

DC: I remember thinking Johnny would quit the *Tonight Show* years ago, but then I decided that he is one of those true performers who is, whether he will admit it or not, capable of a kind of happiness in his work that he doesn't find anywhere else. I think it would be genuinely painful for him to stop working on a regular basis. I, on the other hand, might be sorry if they passed a law that I couldn't perform again, but it wouldn't do me in. Johnny must be bored with the sameness of it all, and I think it would be good for him to do something else before he convinces himself he can't, but he and I are drastically different in this regard.

CP: In the fall of 1963, you went out to Hollywood to write for the short-lived Jerry Lewis TV show, an experience that you've often said was the equivalent in your profession of having been on the *Hindenburg*. Could you give some account of that disaster?

DC: That whole episode of my life seems unreal. I was out of work, having quit Carson (I later rejoined him for another year or so). I had a summer house on Long Island and was happily basking in my accrued savings. Then this offer from Lewis came through, probably because I had worked well with him when he took over the *Tonight Show* for a week. The offer was for three times what I had ever earned before —twelve hundred and fifty dollars a week. Suddenly I was uprooted, winging to the Coast, as they say, getting an apartment in Bel Air, haunting the Paramount lot, watching rehearsals of the Lewis show, then watching broadcasts of the Lewis show that looked like rehearsals, driving to Santa Barbara on weekends, overeating in Polynesian restaurants, staying up late with Mort Sahl, surviving the Kennedy assassination, which seemed even less credible in Hollywood, seeing the show canceled, disposing of my California accouterments (apartment, leased car, sunglasses, and a six-pack of Sea & Ski), and winging back to New York on a near-empty plane on Christmas Day.

The show was an ill-conceived idea from start to early finish. Because of Jerry's ability, as a guest on other shows, to break things up, somebody had thought it would be a great idea to give him his own show, and somebody else had thought it would be an even greater idea if his own show were two hours long and, on top of everything, literally live-as-it-happens, not taped or filmed.

The point everyone overlooked was that Jerry had been hilarious partly because he was a guest. It may be funny to see a man tear up someone else's place, but it is embarrassing to see him tear up his own. It was bizarre and funny to see Jerry go on Ed Sullivan's show, push Ed into the wings, and pull the TelePrompTer apart and rip the paper out of it. But when he did that kind of thing on his own show it wasn't funny so much as it was puzzling. I went around pointing this out to people on the production staff, and was told to sharpen some pencils and stay out of the direct sun. But the fact was that Jerry's comic definition—God, how do you avoid such phrases?—was taken away.

CP: Thus the show's heavy-handed gestures toward decorum—everybody in black tie, Clifton Fadiman on the panel?

DC: Right. At that precise point in his life, Jerry reached a stage where he was too dignified to play the fool constantly and too aware of his comic urges to play the professor for very long. Consequently he played both, in numbing alternation.

CP: Did you try telling him that?

DC: I don't know what good it would have done. If he'd said, "You're right, so what do we do now?," I wouldn't have known what to say. Besides, ours was not the sort of relationship, while perfectly friendly, that would lead me to give him advice. By then he was too far gone into an overwhelmingly misdirected enterprise for anyone to reform it. It was strange working for a man who would drop out of sight for several days after doing a show, and would still be gone on a boat somewhere when it was well past the time to be getting on with the next one. Perry Cross, the producer, had to have his hands tied to his sides to restrain him from removing large clumps of hair from his own head. Still, Jerry is a huge raw talent. Someday he may surrender himself totally to a genius director, and the result could be a masterpiece.

CP: Aside from the Lewis show itself, how did you find life in Hollywood? Did you sink into a languid, pleasure-loving existence on sun-splashed, hibiscus-rimmed patios, talking to producers on white poolside extension telephones while bikinied starlets tickled your feet with peacock feathers and out-of-work Oriental actors in white jackets served you exotic dark-green potions?

DC: That's uncanny. They used turkey feathers, but everything else is absolutely correct.

I did get to like Hollywood. I liked the redolence of cheap glamour that hadn't totally worn off the place. Once when Woody Allen visited we strolled around Beverly Hills and admitted to each other that each of us was reveling in childhood memories. As we passed Jack Benny's house one Sunday Woody said, "So that's where they're planning tonight's show, and Rochester is brushing off Mr. Benny's suit, and Don Wilson is using the pay phone, and . . ." One evening we tracked down W. C. Fields's old house on De Mille Drive, and gazed longingly at it as the sun set and fantasized being invited in by the late host himself for a game of billiards and some essence of grape.

I found it pleasant to drive aimlessly in Beverly Hills and Bel Air, marveling at the beauty and ugliness compatibly blended everywhere. The only houses that are truly appropriate architecturally, of course, are the Spanish-style ones, and amid these will be an English manor house clashing with the palm and banana trees (which are floodlighted crimson and green and yellow at night, something nature somehow never thought of).

I did feel myself sinking pleasantly into the poolside malaise. It's something akin to what they tell us freezing to death is like. You know it's bad for you, but there is something soothing about giving in to it for just a little longer, and, presto, it's Oblivion City. Except, instead of freezing, you are beside a pool being warmed to death.

CP: But you did take in some of the Beverly Hills cultural attractions, like the Beverly Hills Hotel?

DC: Yes, and its swimming pool, which is one of the funniest things in Hollywood. Since the hotel is a stopping place of the famous, there is naturally a lot of paging of biggies at poolside. You can sit there and hear, "Paging Mr. Van Johnson, Mr. Van Johnson," and two seconds later, "Paging Mr. Otto Preminger, Mr. Otto Preminger," and so on. You quickly notice that the famous person is usually absent. It dawned on me one day that several things were probably happening. Aside from legitimate pagings, people were *having* themselves paged there. It's good exposure, since the poolsiders are often a who's who of show business. It draws attention to the fact that you are in town, if you are, and in some cases, perhaps, establishes an alibi if you are not. It may put your name in the mind of a director or producer who is sitting there wrestling with a casting problem. If you are down and out, it suggests to a segment of the film community that you can still afford to stay at the Hills, or at least that someone (the caller) thinks you can. (You can pay a small entrance fee to sit there when you are not a guest.) By refusing to respond to a page if you *are* there, you can create the impression of being too busy to bother.

I wonder why no one has done a television series that begins at the side of the Beverly Hills pool each week with someone being paged. It would be a less interesting version of that old series in New York. Its tag line would be "There are eleven million stories in this city, all of them approximately the same."

CP: What was the tag line for you and the Jerry Lewis show? How did that end?

DC: If it were a script, the closing scene would be criticized as too contrived. On the last day, I went to the bank to withdraw my savings, rounded the corner of Hollywood and Vine to take a last look at the theater Jerry had had done over in his image (it was formerly the El Capitan), and was just in time to see a giant pulley lowering the "Jerry Lewis Theater" sign to the street. On the sidewalk in front of the theater a workman was chiseling away the caricature of Jerry's face that had been embedded in pseudomarble pavement. He was up to the eye when I walked up. For the benefit of the unseen camera I muttered, *"Sic transit gloria mundi."*

CP: Don't tell me the workman asked you who Gloria Mundi was.

DC: No, he just assumed I was a foreigner, gave me a fishy eye, and returned to removing Jerry's.

From there, this little history descends to pathos, or bathos, once I flew back to New York on Christmas Day. Carrie Nye was out of town with a show, so I went to the Automat at Forty-second Street and Third Avenue for Christmas dinner. Don't ask me why; it does sound a bit self-consciously poignant. Anyway, there I was, having my lonely little meal of leather pork chops and drowned spinach, and across from me was sitting a guy with an ear-flaps hat muttering a sort of chant that went roughly, "It's the niggers. That's who, the niggers. It's the niggers that fuck up everything. The fuckin' niggers . . ." He was just sitting there shoveling in mashed potatoes and talking to himself.

At the very next table, facing about forty-five degrees away from him and totally unaware of him, was a snaggle-toothed old crone with her stockings rolled down and a fur coat that looked like parts of it had been eaten away by an animal. She was saying, "Fuckin' Jews. It's the fuckin' Jews that are doin' it to us. Look at the grease the fuckin' Jew bastard gimme on this meat. Fuckin' Jew bastard . . ."

It was a kind of litany. Christmas Day, those two figures, their two voices rising and falling rhythmically, the snow twinkling down outside by lamplight. When I finished eating I remember getting up and saying, as if there were an invisible camera, "Why don't you two get married?" Then I walked out, regretting that there was nobody to appreciate my line.

CP: So it was all over—the pools, the pastel-lighted palm trees, the twelve-fifty a week?

DC: Not the twelve-fifty a week. Although the show folded after thirteen weeks, I had a contract for twenty. This interesting discrepancy led to an experience with one of the warmer sides of television, the proposed settlement.

This is one of the most preposterous phenomena in a business full of them. It takes the form of an appeal to the human qualities, in an industry noticeably lacking in them. To be blunt, you are asked to forgo money that is rightfully yours. Word drifted down to me somehow that I would be expected to take less than my contract guaranteed—in other words, settle. I said I didn't want to. I was told that the show was going off and it was hardly fair of me to expect to be paid for not working. I reminded them that guarantees are a sensible and acceptable part of such deals, that one turns down other shows in order to take the one that failed, that guarantees are an inducement offered early on, when everyone has visions of El Dorado—in other words, that they work both ways. And once the worm that looked so delicious to you, the fish, turns out to contain a hook, once you are pulled from the water and gasping on the shore, you should not be asked to give back part of the worm, as it were.

It makes me giggle that in a cutthroat industry, where lives and fortunes and sensibilities are trampled on as a matter of course, where people are discarded like Lily cups, when there is a failure of an enterprise that set out to destroy competition and make millions for the already fat—when it fails, suddenly they start acting like it is a church social that got rained out, and would you mind not asking for your fifty-cents admission fee back, even though you didn't get to come, because the money is for the orphans.

When you laugh at the suggestion that you not be paid in full, and when you tell them that since *you* had not asked to be let out of anything in the contract, you see no reason why you should release *them*—that's when they get dirty.

CP: How does it go—the dirty part, I mean?

DC: Before the end of the show's run, I was sitting in my little Beverly Hills office one day and got a call from a guy in the ABC knuckle-breaking department in New York. As near as I can remember, the following dialogue took place.

VOICE: Hi, Dick, this is Jerry Crum [name changed to protect the guilty] at ABC. How's it going, fella?

ME (*wondering at intimacy*): Fine. Do I know you?

CRUM: Oh, we might have met in a corridor somewhere. Why? (*Still friendly sounding*)

ME: I just wondered.

CRUM: How you liking that wonderful California sunshine? Sure wish I was out there in it.

ME: I like it fine. Look, I'm a little busy . . .

CRUM: Okay, I won't keep you. I was just wondering how our little problem is coming.

ME: What problem is that?

CRUM: The little money problem.

ME: I guess you'll have to tell me what the problem is.

CRUM: Didn't anyone talk to you about this?

ME: Yes, I'm a little confused. What is it exactly you want?

CRUM: Well, Dick, the thing is, the network has taken kind of a bath on this Lewis thing.

ME: I expect.

CRUM: And what we're looking for here is a little help, sort of the way you would from us if the situation were the other way around. Do you get what I mean?

ME: I'm trying to think of how I could be in a situation parallel to that of a giant television network.

CRUM: Well, I'll get right down to it. The thing is, we're talking about settlement, and we were wondering just how much help you could give us on this.

ME: None.

CRUM: Aw, come on, Dick. Don't make my job difficult.

ME: *My* job is difficult.

CRUM: I'm sure it is. I couldn't write a joke if you paid me.

ME: Well, I could, and that's why I expect you to pay me.

CRUM: Aw, come on, Dick. We all want to work again together, don't we?

ME: Tell me your full name again?

CRUM: (*Does*) Why?

ME: Because I want to be able to tell the Writers Guild exactly who threatened me.

CRUM: Aw, come on. Who's talking threats? This is a friendly conversation.

ME: I can bring this call to a close right now. I have a contract, and I want to be paid every cent that it calls for. I do not feel sorry for you or for ABC. I have never met either of you. I feel sorry for myself. I have a leased apartment, a leased car, another apartment in New York, and I am faced with unemployment, moving, and the threat you just made. Your threat that I will never work for ABC again is based on two assumptions: one, that I want to, and, two, that I won't report your threat. At the moment you are wrong about both. Do you have anything else to say, Mr. Crum?

CRUM: Look, Dick, don't go running to the Writers Guild. We can work this thing out.

ME: I am an old-fashioned, patriotic American, Mr. Crum, who feels that a contract is a contract and a threat is a threat. Good day.

I hung up, reached for the smelling salts, called the Writers Guild, got all my money without a further peep, and never ever worked for ABC again—for almost two years.

CP: I know you love to do dialogue like that. How come you haven't gone the way of most comedy writers and tried a play or a movie script?

DC: I *have* had the urge, but it's a small one and carries me through only as many lines of dialogue as I just did.

CP: You've often told me that comedy writing for you was a form of ventriloquism. Whatever performer you were writing for, you simply turned on his voice in your head, so to speak, and wrote down the gags that came to you in his style. Can you demonstrate right now, using different styles?

DC: There's a sense in which, say, three comedians wouldn't *do* the same joke. Their style or form being different, and form and content being inseparable, they would each require a different content. But let's try it with some incident that might give rise to various jokes—say, a newspaper item about a woman walking down Fifth Avenue with no clothes on.

Groucho Marx might say, "Well, it's certainly a way of beating the heat. It's also a way of creating it." It would mean the same if he said, "I guess its a way to beat the heat—and to create it too." But if your ear is good it will tell you that Groucho would be incapable of wording it that way, incapable of delivering it if worded that way. I grew up on his voice and phrasing, and I can just hear the line in his voice. I know I hear it right, because he never changed a word of the lines I wrote for him when he was an interim host of the *Tonight Show*.

Bob Hope would start out, "Hey, how about that lady on Fifth Avenue?" Then he would go on to something like, "One manhole cover turned to the other and said, 'This is better than Social Security.'" That's almost not a joke, which is part of the point. The sound of the line is as important as the joke it contains, at least with the great comics, whose style is in our collective ear. Of course, if Hope weren't on television he might say, "I'm so innocent that when they said, 'Did you hear about the snatch on Fifth Avenue?,' I thought they meant a robbery, but I wanta tell ya . . ." (Long laugh as Bob stares directly at audience, then shifts weight to other leg to start next line.)

Jack Benny would tell a story, giving his peculiar emphasis to certain words: "I wanna *say* something about that woman who walked down *Fifth Avenue* the other day with *no* clothes on. . . . I'll *tell* you something about that that will surprise you. . . . It *made me jealous.* (*Laugh*) I'm *serious* about that, and I'll *tell* you what I mean. I've been a *big* star for *fifty* years, I'm known *all over* the world, and *I* came to town that day and there was *no mention* of it in *any* of the papers. But an *unknown woman*, who's *never* had a radio show, *never* had a television show, *never* made a picture, *takes* off her clothes and *walks* down Fifth Avenue, and *she* hits the front pages. It *made me sore.* You know what I did? The *next* day, I took off my clothes, *left* my hotel, and *started to walk* down Fifth Avenue . . . and do you *know* what happened? *Nothing!* Not a DAMN THING! I walked for *five blocks* . . . *nobody* batted an eye . . . and *finally a cop* came over and said, 'Aren't you afraid you might catch a *cold*, lady?'"

Believe me, I wouldn't hand in anything like this to these comedians. I'm just trying to get at what you asked.

CP: You keep emphasizing the sound and rhythm over the substance, or idea, of the joke.

DC: Well, you need funny ideas, of course, but I think there is something about the great comics' voices and styles that has a lot to do with their success. It isn't just that the sound became familiar because they became successful; the sound *has to do* with their success, just as it does with a singer or musician. Sound style is part of the reason that so many great comics were stars in radio. Had they been born with nondescript voices, they wouldn't have made it. You can spot the sound of Groucho, Benny, Burns, Hope from the first word, the way your eye can spot a Picasso across the street in a window, or the way a musician can tell from a recording in another room whether it's Rubinstein or Horowitz at the piano.

I, and, I should add, most comedy writers, could take a transcript of Jack Benny talking and underline every word he would have emphasized and score a hundred per cent. You should be able to do this with every famous comedian in order to write usable material for him. Maybe you have to have a musical ear. I can ad-lib pentameter verse and rhyme it in couplets. I can't imagine a more obnoxious talent, and I confess it here only because it's relevant to my ability to write for comics in their style. Not all comedy writers have that talent, by any means, and a comic doesn't always sense what's wrong with the jokes he's given when they are not cast in his rhythm. His ear tells him something is wrong, but his brain doesn't tell him what. I've seen it happen.

I once wrote a heckler line for the late Jack E. Leonard that went, "Why don't you walk into a parking meter and violate yourself?" If it had been handed in as "Why don't you go take a walk until you bump into a parking meter and get violated?" he would have thrown it in the wastebasket. That contains the germ of a good gag, but if the writer doesn't have the right rhythm it's wasted. I've worked with writers whose ear was just that bad, and they can never figure out why their jokes aren't used. The old-time gag men with good ears might not know what iambic and dactyl mean, and might think anapest is a Scandinavian opera star, but instinctively they'd hear the metric difference between "There once was a lady from Wheeling" and "Roses are red, violets are blue."

CP: I've spent most of my working life writing under deadline pressure, but I've never seen anything like the speed with which you used to write jokes for Paar, Carson, and so on. You seemed to work in short, intense eruptions, and, if I'm not mistaken, the ideas that came the quickest, right at the beginning, were usually the best.

DC: I did write fast, to the dismay of some of my colleagues when it was felt that getting the jokes in early gained points with the star. Sometimes I would fill a page in what, to someone listening, sounded like a fairly rapid typist copying a page of something already written. But I was actually inventing and typing the jokes at that speed.

And, in the case of most gag writers I know, it is dangerous to rewrite a gag. It almost always comes to you first in its proper wording. The fatal error is to start to consider possible objections to the wording that first occurred to you. I used to do this in my act. One night I thought of a joke that Woody felt ranked with the best he'd heard, an appraisal that made me proud to be its parent. I had a routine about a wedding reception I went to once, which was staged lavishly but on the cheap. I spoke of the catered food with this line: "Somehow I don't think the caviar was the finest—I don't know much about caviar, but I do know you're not supposed to get pictures of ballplayers with it." The last sentence is worded right. Even after getting big laughs with it, one night I said, "I don't know much about caviar, but I suspected something when I noticed that this caviar came with pictures of ballplayers." It's not only flatter, but the punch is moved a fatal foot and a half farther from the subject, and the consequent laugh was there but smaller. Another night, I decided the line needed a reference to bubble-gum cards a few sentences earlier to make sure they'd get the joke when it came. Wrong. A safe rule is, the first wording is *always* the best. The only exception is if you can think of a more *juste mot*, that is, "garbage" might make a stronger punch line than "trash."

I used to get high from writing jokes. It was very exciting when they started to flow. Paar would say, "Let's do something on the Chinese New Year," and I would run upstairs, and the ideas would be forming in my mind before I got to the typewriter. It is sort of a sensual experience. I've talked to other writers and they feel the same way, although as far as I know none of them has ever reached orgasm.

CP: There were times when your facility depressed me. I recall visiting you in June, 1963, at the summer house you rented in East Hampton. I was getting ready to take a master's exam at Columbia, and one morning I settled in the living room with *Ulysses*. You went out into the yard, dressed only in bathing trunks and a baseball cap, and sat down with a portable typewriter at a picnic table. You were writing a night-club routine for some comedian. Two hours later you bounded back into the house, where I was still making intricate linkages in *Ulysses*, waved your complete routine, and announced cheerily, "Well, I just made twelve hundred dollars." It ruined my day. Of course you were merely spinning out variations on standard psychiatrist jokes ("I was so paranoid I lay *under* the couch"), and I realize you felt some uneasiness that you weren't engaged in something "serious," as I was. What you may not have realized was that I, having just got through a year in which my wife had to support me while I went to graduate school, felt some uneasiness about not being engaged in something productive, as you were.

DC: How about that?

CP: You have such a gift for summing things up.

DC: I know.

CP: At any rate, your joke-writing facility deserted you when you began working up material for yourself to perform.

DC: And how. Woody used to talk about what a backbreaking job it was for him to sit down and write his own jokes. I thought he was sort of romanticizing it, playing up the creative agony. But then, when I tried it, I found I went neurotically through the whole gamut of contortions to avoid the writing: oversleeping day after day, going through an elaborate ritual of writing out on a slip of paper at night "I will not oversleep." Then morning would come, the alarm would go off, and I'd think to myself that this note-writing business was silly—a symptom, in fact, of my need for more sleep. Finally I'd get up and say to myself that I'd sit down to write just as soon as I read the paper. Around 2:00 P.M., when I still hadn't written a word, I'd set the alarm for a half hour later and tell myself it was okay to do anything I wanted for the next half hour.

I really envy Woody. He has great concentration. He's supposed to be neurotic; *he* goes to an analyst. But he functions. I'm supposed not to be neurotic. But I have all the symptoms.

Sometimes I would actually begin writing. And when it was going well I can remember literally jumping up and down with excitement, thinking to myself how easy it was. Then the next day the battle would start all over.' Sometimes I actually managed to lose some of the stuff I wrote—lose the paper it was written on, forever, right in my apartment. There's nothing as seductive as the will to fail. But the saddest thing was to go over the stuff later and find that only a third or a sixth of it worked—that something you ad-libbed onstage had worked much better. When I began performing, each of my punch lines was separated by two minutes of excess verbiage, rambling narration, needless build-up.

CP: And what about some of those punch lines? Like the one about the little theater that did integrated productions of fairy tales—*Snow Black and the Seven Dwarfs*.

DC: Please, I can't stand it.

CP: The difficulty wasn't only with the mechanics of writing, was it? Weren't you also struggling with the broader question of—to use that phrase you hate—your comic definition?

DC: Coming up against the problem was one of the greatest shocks of my career. I had always assumed that if I ever decided to do an act I would set aside a few hours, write it, and then perform it. Because I could turn out three or four pages of good jokes for someone else in twenty minutes, it never occurred to me that I couldn't do it for myself. In fact, the first time I performed for Jack Rollins, my manager, I stitched together about thirty monologue jokes I'd written for various comics and recited them in his office, changing a word or two here and there to make them pertain to me. It was simply awful. Jack pointed out that, whereas the individual jokes were good, there was nothing holding them together. He gave me a talk on the rigors and horrors of a performing career, citing the anxiety Woody was going through at that time. I returned for a while to the warm womb of writing for others, and didn't have another go at writing for myself for about a year.

When I did finally face it I realized that my writing talent was largely imitative—which is fine and, as I've said, essential to writing for known comics. But when I was faced with writing for me I had no known quantity to imitate. What, as they say in belles-lettres, was my *voice?* And what did it talk about when I found it?

Woody's advice was, don't get paralyzed with this thought, but go to the typewriter whenever possible and put down anything I thought was funny. This unblocked me. The two things I had had going for me as a gag writer were a knowledge of the comic and his particular rhythmic style plus a knowledge of the assigned subjects. But in my case I wasn't sure of either of these. Woody based a lot of his humor on his unheroic appearance, on his looking like a victim, but I found I couldn't make my appearance the basis for jokes. And I wasn't rural enough to play the hick, nor authentically urban enough to play the city slicker. I thought of dying my hair green, then thought better of it. I felt normal, in a nondescript, goyish sort of way that seemed to leave me nowhere comedywise.

Convinced that my act had to be based somehow on my

own experience, I had the dawning realization that my having come to the East from a farm state held some promise as a comic equation.

Suddenly I had a workable premise, and the log jam began to loosen. A Nebraska Yankee at Yale and in New York became my comic persona. The jokes began to flow, viscously but noticeably. It was still hell. I could not adjust to the fact that for the first time I had to think for minutes, and sometimes hours, for the right joke. When Woody had told me that he sometimes spent a day getting a joke right, I couldn't imagine what he was talking about. He said you can't just accept the first thing that comes into your head; you have to keep thinking until you know you've got the best possible joke on the subject at hand. Woody certainly put this principle into practice. I think his albums show the finest sustained level of joke-writing genius in the history of stand-up comedy. But to me, at the time, this was a discouragement. After a couple of weeks, I had about nine jokes I felt were worth using. When I realized how hard Woody worked, how disciplined he was, and how many brilliant jokes he had already and how many more he intended to have, I had to lie down with an ice bag on my forehead.

There were times when the writing of a night-club act assumed the proportions of a personal crisis. I would decide that the reason I didn't know what to write about was that I *had* no personality. I decided that everything I said in real life was merely an imitation of people and things I had heard or read, and that down deep I was shallow, a cipher, a collection of imitated sounds and borrowed thoughts floating in front of a *tabula rasa* of a personality. At times this feeling got so intense that I would get up and look in the mirror to see if I would reflect.

CP: And did you?

DC: Only when I had a tan.
Sometime later I took this problem to Groucho, and he said it is bad to worry too much about your image. His advice

was to keep working and to appear on television as frequently as possible; eventually, he said, what I was would become my image.

CP: Has it?

DC: In the sense that my image contains a good bit of what I am, yes. Writing comedy for yourself is a fascinating personal confrontation. It contains the ultimately insoluble twin dilemmas of how much do you want your act to be an act, a mask, and how much of your life is itself an act, a mask. And, oh yes, a third dilemma: how relevant they are one to the other.

CP: When can we expect your monograph on this subject?

DC: Never, if then. I defer to wiser heads. Shake Mr. Bergson there and see if he's awake.

CP: Let's digress.

DC: If you ask me, this whole book has been a digression.

CP: True, but I was going to suggest that we digress on some subject other than yourself.

DC: In that case, you're fired.

CP: It's a subject you like and in which you're deeply concerned—the great old comedians. I know that you've been interested, naturally, in the comedians roughly of our own generation, from Caesar and Sahl and Bruce and Nichols and May right through Woody Allen. But I would say that none of these people seems as important to you as the great figures of a generation or more ago—Groucho, Hope, Benny, Burns, Laurel and Hardy, W. C. Fields.

DC: The older group has a kind of mythic importance. They are the great comedians of my time and also another time. They were all there before I became aware of them, so they're part of comic history, and they're also the comedians of my childhood, so they loom as the giants of one's formative years.

CP: Meeting some of them during your early years in television and comedy writing must have been like having your personal pantheon come alive.

DC: When I was a kid they were to me like the characters in a book or the figures in a painting. They dwelt in a far-off world. The idea that in later years they could walk into a room that also contained me was unthinkable. I wouldn't mind growing out of that kind of childish disbelief that these mythic figures actually exist and that their existence can be confirmed by the shock of meeting them, but some of it is still there. I remember the first moments I clapped eyes on Bob Hope, Jack Benny, and the others, with a special vividness, like scenes that stand out in memory from a movie. By now I've been around all of them a lot—in their homes, in limousines, chance meetings at airports, in dressing rooms, at benefits, in European restaurants, even a subway ride with Danny Kaye—but it never wears off entirely. When my secretary buzzes me on the intercom and says, "Jack Benny is calling on line four," something in me reels slightly for a second.

Even when I finally reached the point of having my own show, I couldn't accept the idea of my existence being recognized by these titans. A few months after my morning show started, Mort Lachman, who writes and produces for Bob Hope, took me to a dinner Hope was emceeing at the Waldorf. We were at a front table, and as Hope walked on, during his entrance applause, he recognized me and reached down for a quick handshake. I thought he wanted a glass of water, and I started to hand him one. He laughed, and I tried to act unflustered and pretended it was an intentional joke on my part. Later *Hope* introduced *me* to the audience. I had a woozy sensation that something was awry in the scheme of things.

CP: Earlier you talked about being with Johnny Carson on

the day Stan Laurel died, about having rather special feelings about Laurel. How did it come about that you met him?

DC: During my copyboy period at *Time*, I was working late one night, poking among the files they keep on famous people, and happened on LAUREL, STAN. At that moment I wasn't sure he was alive, but since the latest clip in the folder was not an obit, I assumed he was. I resolved to meet him someday, and meanwhile I dropped him a short letter of appreciation. I got an immediate answer, and remember bounding up the stairs with the letter from him, postmarked Santa Monica. He wrote, in an almost courtly manner, "Dear Dick Cavett, Thank you for your letter, containing such kind sentiments, so graciously expressed. . . ."

When I went to Hollywood a year or so later, with the Paar show, I resolved to meet Laurel if it was the only thing I did. One night after a taping I told Paar that I had met Laurel that day, and I must have been so enthusiastic about it that Jack caught the bug and said, "Let's do a tribute to him. Work something up, kid, and we'll do it on the show." I did, and Jack read it beautifully, with a picture of Laurel dissolving in. Stan (he asked me to call him that) was deeply touched by it.

CP: Asking somebody why he thinks Stan Laurel was funny is like asking him why he thinks the ocean is wet, but I'm curious about the particulars. What was it especially that appealed to you in his work?

DC: It's almost too precerebration to analyze. There's a special appeal to Stan, even though I adored both him and Hardy when I was a kid. He's the more sympathetic of the two. I have had to agree with Woody that Hardy is probably superior from an artistic point of view—the finer screen comedian. Laurel came from a broader stage tradition, and his gestures and reactions are sometimes a bit too large for the screen, whereas Hardy's are precise to the fingertips, scaled perfectly to the distance of the camera. But somehow this is an admission

I make only reluctantly. There is some kind of affectionate edge to Laurel. I suppose you could evolve a theory that we all feel picked on as kids and that, since Stan seems more picked on than Ollie, we identify more with him. But, as they say in college English seminars, I wouldn't insist on this.

CP: What happened when you first met him, the time that led to the Paar tribute?

DC: I just couldn't believe it. I kept walking around in my hotel room thinking that it was not possible that I was actually to meet the man who helped the fat man get that piano up that long flight of stairs in *The Music Box*. For the first time in my life, I was ready an hour before the appointment. I drove slowly to Santa Monica, savoring every moment, found the Oceana apartment house, and got a kick from seeing the name "Oceana" in the same style as on the envelopes of Stan's letters to me.

I asked the desk clerk, "Where is Mr. Laurel's apartment?" He said, "One flight up," in a way that struck me as too objective. I remember taking a beat or two before ringing the bell. He came to the door himself, saying, "Hello, lad. It sure is nice to see you." There was a note of disappointment. Although the bilateral S identified him as Stan, the appearance was not quite right. He had only a small amount of gray hair, combed flat, and was a bit thick around the middle in a way that seemed wrong for him. But the ears and eyes were unmistakable, and after a while for me he became Laurel completely. He was wearing slippers, trousers with suspenders, and a white shirt. He had no jacket, but had put on a tie, which I found charming.

The apartment, a small three-roomer where he lived with his wife, was furnished in modern style, with a picture window overlooking the sea. There was an autographed picture of John Kennedy on the wall. Stan's honorary Oscar was on top of the TV set. There was one photo of him with Hardy, but the room was otherwise bare of mementos.

He seemed to enjoy being asked about specific scenes from

his films and how they were done. I asked him if he ever got hurt during all the slapstick stuff. He said only once, when he was talking to someone between takes on a street set and he stepped backward off the curb and twisted his ankle.

CP: You do a very good imitation of him, but I assume you had the good taste not to demonstrate it.

DC: I'm not sure whether it was good taste, modesty, or naked fear, but I did refrain. I asked if he liked imitations of himself, though, and he said he did up to a point. He got a kick out of Chuck McCann, but said he was humiliated by a guy who came to the apartment once and spoke as Laurel the entire time. "It was so goddamned embarrassin' I didn't know where to look." As he said this line laughter overtook him. By the end of it his voice had risen about an octave, in a moderated version of the funny cry he used to do in films, where he would start a sentence in his normal voice and end up talking in a squeak so high it was barely audible.

CP: What did he say about Hardy?

DC: He obviously had great affection for "Babe," as he called Hardy, and knew that it was not entirely requited. He told me how he took a Christmas present to Babe, whom he virtually never saw off movie sets, and it was evident immediately that Hardy had not gotten *him* anything. It was Christmas morning, and Hardy spied, standing among the opened presents on his living-room floor, an expensive bottle of bourbon, a gift from an admirer, and picked it up and held it out to Stan. As he did he apparently realized that it was indeed a very fine bottle of bourbon, and said, "Look at that. It's hard to find this brand in Los Angeles," and put it back where it had been. Laurel was more amused than hurt by this and told it to me to illustrate his friend's eccentricity.

CP: One always hears that Laurel took the films more seriously than Hardy did.

DC: That's true. He said he would stay around half the

night helping to edit, whereas Hardy was out the door to the golf course before "Print it" had stopped resonating in the studio. In the sequences Stan directed, he said he would save all of Hardy's "burns" until last, when Hardy was beginning to fear the light was failing on the golf course, so that those great fuming close-ups contain a lot of genuine irritation.

CP: Did Laurel feel forgotten?

DC: Thanks to television, no. Neither he nor Hardy received a penny of the millions that were made off the TV use of their films, and both could have used the money. It killed Stan to see the films cut so badly for TV, and he told me, touchingly, that he had made an offer to the distributor to recut them for nothing, but had not had the courtesy of a reply.

His appraisal of current comedians was fascinating, and it was shrewd and harsh in many cases. He arrived in this country on the same boat with Chaplin, as a member of the Karno troupe. But from Chaplin's redundantly titled *My Autobiography* you would never even know that Laurel and he had met. There was no mention of their arriving together, just a caption identifying Stan somewhere in the picture section. I mentioned to Stan how this irritated me, but he waved it aside. He said, "I don't belong in the same category with Charlie."

He told me of the time when he and Hardy toured Europe, toward the end of their partnership. "We had worked so long and hard I guess we never gave a thought to fame or how many people knew us," he said. "When the boat anchored offshore from the town of Dundee in Scotland and the church bells played the cuckoo song, our theme, we looked at each other and bawled like a couple of babies."

I have one lasting visual memory of him in his apartment. It had been a clear day, and the sun was setting into the Pacific. Stan was sitting at his desk, oscillating slightly in a swivel chair, while taking a phone call. His back was to me, and I was suddenly struck by how he looked completely like the screen Laurel for the moment. The voice was unmistakable, except for the courtly, well-phrased conversation, which resembled only one thing he did on the screen—the part in *Chumps at Oxford* where a bump on the head sends the character back to an earlier stage of his life, when he was an upper-class English gentleman. I thought about his telling me how Stanley Kramer offered him a tempting (and needed) amount of money to do just a few shots in *Mad, Mad, Mad, Mad World*. But he didn't want to, because "the way I look would disappoint the kids." I visited him four or five times. He died about three weeks after the last time I saw him.

cp: Going from the sublime to the sublime, Groucho Marx is another giant who stands out in all your reminiscences. You've mentioned growing up on his voice and phrasing, writing for him, and going to him for advice on your career. Also, your conversation is shot through with his verbal wit, which is a good caliber of wit to be shot through with.

I have here a letter that you wrote to me in July, 1964, soon after Groucho came on as an interim host of the *Tonight Show*. Relax; I'm not going to read any of the filthy passages. Here is how you described a lunch that you and Woody Allen had with Groucho in a back booth at Lindy's: "For several hours we plied him with questions and listened to anecdotes and opinions and kept fearing we would wake up and it would all turn out to be a dream (cliché but sincere). He spoke of Kaufman and the comedies in detail, and Chaplin and Perelman, and it was all purest gold. He said he needed a date for the theater that night and was doing poorly with the chambermaids at the Plaza. Woody was working, so I volunteered. At intermission we ran into Marc Connelly. Standing in a theater hearing Groucho and Connelly mention Dorothy Parker, etc., made me feel I had stepped into some sort of time machine. I went home that night and made voluminous notes on the day so I could recall it all at future times."

Now I have a couple of questions about that. First, knowing your efficiency, I'd be curious as to where those notes are now.

DC: I don't know what you're implying, but I know precisely where they are. They're in the upper left-hand drawer of a desk that I sold at Parke-Bernet in 1968 to a family that subsequently moved to the Seychelle Islands and suffered a flash fire.

CP: I see. But you do recall the Groucho episode, I suspect because it was the classic encounter between a young man and something like his idol.

DC: His idle *what?* Sorry, but when you mention Groucho that's what you get.

Actually the story of my encounter with Groucho goes back earlier than that, to 1961. It was the day after I had met Woody at the Blue Angel, the day of George S. Kaufman's funeral. Woody and I discussed going; neither of us had met Kaufman, but we felt a kinship of loss, having been great fans of his. Woody had to be elsewhere, it turned out, so I put on a suit and walked across Central Park to Frank E. Campbell's funeral home. It was a gorgeous Sunday, clear and sunny. When I arrived Campbell's was full and the rites were under way; I was seated in a small overflow room near the door. Moss Hart began a eulogy to his old partner, and as he took the pages from his pocket he said, "I can almost hear George saying, over my shoulder, 'It needs cutting.'"

About halfway through the eulogy, I happened to notice that the man across from me was holding an unlit cigar, and at the other end of the arm holding the cigar was Groucho Marx. I sat there numbly staring at him. He suddenly did a characteristic lip-moistening mannerism that I'd seen a million times on *You Bet Your Life,* and I had that thrill you get when there is nothing but air between you and, yes, an idol.

Later, on the sidewalk, I stood near him, and heard a woman say, "Hello, Groucho. I'm Edna Ferber." I could hear the famous voice respond, but missed the words. My mind flashed back to a time twenty years earlier when I was visiting relatives in California. While touring Farmers Market in Hollywood, I bought a fried chicken leg, and the woman who sold it to me said, "You should have been here five minutes ago. I just sold one to Groucho Marx." I asked her if he had said anything, and she said, "Oh, yeah, you know Groucho." I cursed her mentally for not remembering what he said, and the fates for making me miss him by five minutes. It took me days to get over it.

Now flash forward again to the funeral. Groucho was joined on the sidewalk at Eighty-first and Madison by Brooks Atkinson and Abe Burrows. I watched them stroll toward Fifth Avenue, wishing I was someone in show business so I could join them. Then I decided, "To hell with it. I will anyway. I write for the *Tonight Show*, don't I?" As I neared the corner, with too-contrived timing Atkinson and Burrows both left Groucho alone. I approached and said, with the genius for originality that has put me where I am today, "Hello, Groucho. I'm a big fan of yours." Groucho said, "If it gets any hotter I could *use* a big fan," and we were off.

We walked down Fifth. After a few blocks I figured I should turn off and say good-bye, feeling I had already had three blocks with Groucho and now my life had meaning. He made me feel comfortable and welcome, and when he said he was going to walk all the way to the Plaza Hotel I remember thinking, "If I take shorter steps, maybe he'll slow up and it will last longer." He insulted every doorman along the way, and interviewed several astonished Puerto Ricans, who were having their yearly parade up Fifth as we were strolling down it. One Puerto Rican man, extremely well dressed and prosperous looking, found himself face to face with Groucho, who said, "Tell me, is it true that only a year ago you were cutting sugar cane?" We left the startled gentleman blinking and grinning confusedly, and reached the Plaza. I said good-bye, and Groucho said, "You're a very nice young man (echoes of the quiz show), and I'd like you to join me for lunch."

I was on a cloud. We went into the Oak Room, where

Groucho asked the waiter, "Do you have any fruit? I mean *besides* the head waiter?" He was alternately serious and hilarious for an hour and a half. He had just met T. S. Eliot in England and was amused that Eliot had offered to send *him* an autographed picture, without Groucho's asking for it. In a moment of inexcusable pedantry, I told Groucho I liked the epigraph he had chosen for his latest book, a maxim of La Rochefoucauld's that is a favorite of mine, and I quoted the original in French. Groucho said, "You speak very good French. In fact, it's so good you could only have learned it in a whorehouse."

The Groucho pronunciations were delightful to hear. His "learned" is closer to "lined" phonetically than to "loined." It always amuses me when people are struck by the fact that a person whom they have seen talking on television or in the movies actually has that same voice in real life. People who recognize me will say, "You sound just like yourself," and when I want to say, "Who doesn't?," I have to remind myself that is almost what I said to Groucho.

I did eventually manage to say good-bye, and I walked back through Central Park at about treetop level, realizing I would have to amend the part of my diary about meeting Howard Westgate having been the greatest day of my life.

CP: So the lunch at Lindy's, the one you took notes about, was more in the nature of a reunion.

DC: Unfortunately my notes—I really do have them—are disappointing. The stuff was so vivid in my mind that I was sure I'd remember it. Thus I abbreviated a great deal of it, to an extent that, today, is cryptic, for example, "Kaufman and seduction in car," or "Harry Ruby's envelopes." I can no longer recall the stories that these ciphers refer to.

I do recall that there was a constant stream of people to the table in Lindy's. Groucho and Woody would sign autographs (no one knew me, a fact I resented), and Groucho would insult them, and they would laugh and go back to their tables to repeat their verbal souvenirs. Later, when walking down the sidewalk with Groucho, I was amused by people's takes. Some were genuinely nonplused, and a couple of them just stopped in their tracks as he passed and made a sort of prayerlike gesture of gratitude with their hands. He was generally oblivious to this.

Occasionally he would say, with genuine wonder, "You know, the college kids line up to see our movies now; they write to me," in a way that meant he did not realize how loved and great he is. A few days earlier, an old Jewish woman had come up to him and said, "Don't die. Just keep on living." He was moved by it.

CP: He wasn't moved by everything old Jewish ladies said to him, apparently.

DC: The airport incident? I know. When he told me this, I laughed so hard I hurt my larynx. He had gotten on a plane in New York, which for some ungodly reason sat in position on the runway for *four* hours. All sharp instruments had to be removed, because the passengers were becoming suicidal. Finally the plane took off and then was delayed another hour, stacked over Los Angeles. He said, "We finally landed from this ten-hour nightmare, and while I was waiting for my bag and considering cutting my throat, so I'd never have to go through anything like that again, an old Jewish woman came over and said, 'You're Groucho Marx, aren't you?' I said, 'Yes.' She said, 'You know, you weren't very funny on the plane.' And I said, 'Go fuck yourself.'"

His genuine irritation is part of the humor in so many little moments with him that I recall so fondly. Once a couple came over and interrupted a story he was telling me in a theater during intermission, saying, "Groucho, my wife and I want to tell you how much we admire you." He said, "You'll have to get in line," and went back to his story.

CP: Yet somehow people never seem offended by his barbs, as they might be by an ordinary "insult comedian." I remember a story you told me once about riding down in an elevator with Groucho, I think in the St. Regis Hotel. Two Catholic priests got on at a lower floor. They recognized Groucho, and one of them said his mother was a tremendous fan of his. "Oh, really?" said Groucho. "I didn't know you fellows were allowed to have mothers." The priests loved that as much as you did.

DC: True, but there are lines of his that so devastatingly sum up someone's prominent failings that they would be offensive to that person. One day a well-known columnist had, as usual, mangled one of Groucho's jokes in his column. I laughingly told Groucho about it, amazed that it was possible to get a line wrong that was so perfectly constructed. Groucho said, "I know. In order to get him to print a joke right, you have to *tell* it to him wrong."

I treasure certain asides he has made to me on and off the air, partly because I can tell myself, "I'm the only one hearing this." Once he came on my show with Shelley Winters and the kids from the musical play about the Marx Brothers. Shelley was center stage, by the piano, getting ready to sing a song, explaining how nervous she was when she sang this song to audition and how her singing of it clinched her getting the part. She launched into it, and Groucho leaned over to me and whispered, "If they hear this, they'll take the part back again."

CP: By the time Groucho was appearing on your show, and you and he were, in a sense, just two comedians together, weren't you able to become more matter-of-fact about him, less awed by his presence and his humor?

DC: Sure, but I never got over the kick of thinking, "Here is Groucho Marx, and I'm getting paid to sit here with him." I remember one of his lines on my morning show that was widely quoted, and stolen by unknown comedians and by one or two well-known ones. We had discussed the musical *Hair* for a moment. It had just opened, and because it contained Broadway's first frontal nude scene with both sexes there was a lot of talk about it. I asked Groucho if he had seen it, and I knew he did not have a prepared answer. I saw the machinery whir for a split second, and he said, "No. I was going to see it, but I went home, took off my clothes, looked at myself in the mirror, and saved seven dollars." The audience roared, and the line sped round the country and into several night-club acts. Sitting that close, I could see that the suddenness of the line and the laugh surprised *him* for a tenth of a second. Then he calmly put his cigar in his mouth and waited out the laugh. The figure he chose for the price of an orchestra seat was of course not the correct figure, but it had the right number of syllables for the joke.

CP: The right number of syllables?

DC: This goes back to what I was saying about the importance of rhythm in a joke. People will think an old comedian is crazy when he tells a young writer to change a line from "There are twelve chickens on the lawn" to "There are fifteen chickens on the lawn," but he's right. Because of the rhythm, fifteen is a funny number and twelve is not.

CP: I'll remember that. You mentioned that Groucho didn't know what his answer was going to be, and when it came it surprised even him. Did you ever talk to him about this phenomenon?

DC: No, and this is something that bothers me. I always feel a kind of duty to let an artist know what he has done to and for me, yet it often can't be conveyed, partly because the artist himself isn't aware of what it is he does. My wife, at her best, is a genuinely brilliant actress who can be heartbreakingly moving, as you know. She says that although you can know a lot about acting, there is still some mystery at the heart of great acting that has to do with being temporarily *possessed*. I know she is right. It is also at the heart of great comedy, and explains why the performer can never know just how deeply he has affected you, because he is not entirely in control of what has happened. It is akin to what spiritualists call automatic writing.

I have experienced a few of these moments myself in my occasional acting experiences. I would sometimes sight-read a difficult role in a way that moved those around me, and even me. It would be enough to get me the part, but then I could never quite get it back in rehearsal or performance. Or, if I could, it would only be once or twice; I could never keep it. But when it came, the other actors would say, "You really *scared* me in that scene." And I had scared myself. This all makes me think I could act effectively in films, with the right director, where this kind of temporary visitation could be caught.

But to get back to Groucho, because of this phenomenon there is no way to convince a genius of how great he is. How do you convey to Van Gogh his Van Goghness? You spend so much time telling third-through-eighth-rate people that they are "great," a word that by misuse has been worn thin to the point of transparency, that there is no way left to tell the truly great how truly great they are. The third-raters you can convince. There is a frustrating sense in which Groucho is not convinced of his greatness and is in need of proof that he is adored, and this should not be.

I remember an odd experience I had once in Central Park. I had gone alone to a W. C. Fields movie at the New Yorker Theater and laughed my head off. On my way home I sat on a bench just inside the park and thought about Fields, and how he was dead, and what a master he was, and how I would never meet him, and how he could never conceive of how great he was and what he meant to me and to all the other people who appreciate his genius, some of which remains with you in a sort of afterglow when the laughter has faded —and tears began to well up. It had to do with this thing I am talking about, this frustration that such people can never see what they are, just once, plain, and be forever satisfied.

CP: But if they could, might it not spoil them? Aren't some of them right to say, when asked how they managed to bring off some superb performance, "I don't know, and I don't want to know"?

DC: Sure. That mystery, that visitation, is the thing they fear losing, because they don't know why they have it, what causes it. That's why so many great artists are superstitious about discussing it, for fear it will vanish, like what's-her-name in the myth if glimpsed. It gets us back to the age-old, tiresome question of should the artist risk psychoanalysis, for fear of dissolving his talent. After batting this question back and forth for years, on the air and off, I've found that most artists fear treatment for that reason. I think they're wrong. The assumption they make is that their neurosis is somehow the *cause* of their talent, which is nonsense. They say, "If I were content, I wouldn't act (paint, sing, dance, write, whatever). I do it to escape my misery." They might be right that they wouldn't, but they're wrong that they *couldn't*, which is what they fear. If neurosis causes talent, why are so many people neurotic and so few talented? Well?

CP: Don't look at me. I only came in for the free sandwiches.

DC: At least Groucho's talent doesn't spring from neurosis. All of his insanity is inspired—blessed, you could almost say. I got a great sample of it one night after my wife and I had had dinner with Groucho and one of his oldest friends, the songwriter Harry Ruby, who was one of the most delightful men in the world. We were driving them home through Beverly Hills. Groucho and Harry were in the back seat, and their conversation contained a hundred gems of *non sequitur* brilliance, of which I can remember only one. We passed a high-rise apartment building.

GROUCHO: That's the building your son lives in.

HARRY: No it isn't.

GROUCHO: Yes it is. He lives in that building.

HARRY: No he doesn't, Groucho. The building he lives in is two blocks off Beverly Boulevard.

GROUCHO: He doesn't live in that building?

HARRY: No.

GROUCHO: That's funny. I ran into him on the street the other day, and he didn't mention not living there.

CP: As a result of your friendship with Groucho, you possess a treasure that has also been vouchsafed to the likes of Harry Truman, T. S. Eliot, and Howard Hughes. Namely, a bundle of letters from Groucho. What did he write to you about, if that isn't prying, and even if it is?

DC: The usual things people write to each other about: sex, nuclear physics, Blackstone on contracts. It isn't so much what he wrote about, in most cases, but the way he writes a letter. He is a master of the effortlessly funny letter. Even his openings and closings are good, and usually novel—signing off with "Goodbye forever," or opening with "Dear Dick, this is the dirtiest opening for a letter I ever wrote."

Once he wrote me a letter in draft form and appended a little note that broke me up. It said, "I would have had my secretary do this letter over, but it's raining outside." Sometimes I'd ask him about himself or about people he'd known, and he would write back a long, conscientious, factual, zany, and hilarious reply. One time he merely sent me a short note asking if I had noticed that Peter O'Toole had a double phallic name. Another time I got a two-page, single-spaced account, minutiae abounding, in response to a query from me on how he spent his day. It was full of remarks like "I won't describe lunch, because if I did it would remind me of what I ate."

The thing about the letters I value most, looking back through them, is that Groucho took a kind of paternal interest in my career, and would watch me on television in my early days as a guest and take the trouble to give me advice. The idea that *Groucho Marx* did this, believed in me in some personal way, gets me.

*July 19, 1965*

*Dear Dick,*
    *. . . Per your instructions I watched you on the Merv Griffin show and you came off very well. I think you could now take a chance and stop writing jokes for other people. Write them for yourself. . . .*
    *I notice you seem to be adopting some of [Woody Allen's] mannerisms. Forget it. Be yourself or you'll never get anywhere.*
    *You spoke about college the other night. It's a good subject and no one else is doing it. Make up stuff if you have to. It's a field that no one is working. This doesn't mean you have to wear a beany and wave a pennant. . . .*

                    *Regards,*
                    *Groucho*

*September 2, 1965*

*Dear Richard or better yet, Poor Richard:*
    *I would have answered you sooner but my secretary, formerly a resident of Mississippi, has been reading about the segregation problem in her home town and is going back to rejoin the Klan. This means a whole new set of white sheets, a can of tar and feathers and a knout.*
    *I liked your routine about the kosher restaurants but perhaps I wrote you that in my previous letter. Well, no one objects to being complimented twice for the same thing, unless you are an extremely elderly man and in bed with your ex-wife. . . .*
    *I think you have struck a motherlode in the country yokel, starry eyed in the big city. Stick to it. Nobody has done it since*

*Will Rogers. It might even be a good idea to use a small town, perhaps a mythical one, but make that a base for the jokes. . . .*

*Sincerely,*

*Groucho*

*December 10, 1965*

*Dear Richard, Sir:*

*I received your insincere complimentary one page missive and I will answer in kind. That is the kind of language Titus Moody used to talk to Fred Allen of Allen's Alley.*

*When are you going to be in Frisco? If it is around any date that would fit in with my plans, I would fly up to see you. This is my wife's idea. Frankly, she isn't particularly interested in seeing you but she would like to get the hell out of town, any town. She has what is called a sombatchin. I don't guarantee the authenticity of the spelling but it is a kind of restlessness coupled with boredom. I could solve this sickness for her. In fact I suggested the ideal way of overcoming this, to wit: get a job in a 10¢ store.*

*I heard you tell my joke on the Merv Griffin Show. Got a big laugh. Blasphemy always does, it is what is known as a nervous titter, of which my secretary has two.*

*Hoping this finds you, I beg to remain your obedient correspondent.*

*Groucho*

*May 25, 1966*

*Dear Dick,*

*. . . I saw you the other evening on the Carson Show and got that old feeling. That, in case you don't know, is part of an old song. You were very funny. You even made Carson laugh and this isn't easy when you have been an ex-employee. Thanks for the plug and if you see Carson thank him for the Houdini*

*story and it won't be long before he has a letter from my attorney, who will sue him for every nickel he has.*

*I can't write more because the girl taking this dictation has a very good pair of legs and the whole thing is just too distracting. . . .*

Groucho

October 6, 1966

*Dear Dick,*

*. . . I received your wire and, as instructed, watched you in action. Maybe my standards are low, but I rather liked what I saw.*

*You say . . . how much farther is the top? It's when people say, "Don't I know you from somewhere?," and you answer, "You must have me confused with someone else." Be sure there's a taxi handy to hop into, even if it's occupied. Don't worry about the top. There's comparative fame and fortune if you never get there. . . .*

*Goodbye until hell freezes over.*

Groucho

January 10, 1967

*Dear Dick,*

*. . . I think your stuff is sly and you look too neutral. If you're going to discuss life in the universities, I think you should identify yourself in some way. . . . You don't have a big mustache, or a beard or funny hair and I think you have to notify the audience that you're supposed to make them laugh. At present, I think it takes too long for them to catch on that you're out there to amuse them. . . . I know I'm not telling this clearly, but my feeling is you either have to broaden your personality or broaden your jokes. . . .*

*I hope the New Year does more for you than you claim the last one did, but you must realize that you're still an ex-*

*tremely young man and offhand . . . I would guess that you're better off than you were a year earlier.*

*My best to you and whoever you're shacking up with. . . .*

*·/no signature/*

August 23, 1967

*Dear Dick:*

*I will make this letter so brief that you can read it with one eye. I envied you your sojourn at the [Hefner mansion in Chicago]. I hope you didn't also have the nerve to ask for money after living there like King Edward VII. . . .*

*You say you have rented a summer house in East Hampton that would take your breath away. If it did that to me, I might move there. . . . I am doing a show for the Kraft Cheese people and I am going to be the big cheese. We were talking yesterday about you being in it. The idea is the first half of the show would be kind of a review of old style vaudeville and its many peculiarities and mannerisms and the second half would be with show business as it is today and you would be one of the bright young comedians, assuming you are still young after the week you spent at Hefner's stable. . . .*

Regards,
Groucho

November 25, 1968

*Dear Dick,*

*Since time is hanging heavy on my hands, I thought I would write you a short note to inform you that I was almost in New York next week. It was for the Bobby Morse Show and it was only three days rehearsal and I'm at the age where I need three weeks. At any rate, I watched you this morning with Susskind, the cooking lesson and that daffy blonde who you are either enamored of or trying to be. You're doing a fine* job. I hear rumors you may replace Carson. I don't know who started these rumors—was it you or that hoodlum who handles you? I have a lot of people on the Coast now who watch you, namely because they too are out of work. Because of the hour you are on [10:30 A.M. to 12:00], it's what I call a desperation show. It's looked at by angry housewives and people who are unemployable.

I could write you a lot more but, frankly, I can't think of anything to say. . . .

Kiss your girlfriend for me—the one who's been a constant disappointment to me for some time. It was fun while it lasted, but we never really got started because we only had a single bed, and I get restless when the defense is too strong.

Goodbye forever.

Groucho

/undated/

Dick Cavett Sir:

I haven't written to you for two reasons: it's been so long since you wrote me I forgot what you said and if I did answer you I forgot what I said. . . .

It's no disgrace any more to be bounced from TV. If they continue to put big movies that are fairly recent against these piddling half hour shows, it'll be the end of TV. I'm sure I haven't told you anything you don't know . . . except about my sex life. I don't want anyone to know about that—not even my wife! But sometimes when I'm alone in my bedroom I have a good hearty laugh thinking about it.

I hope you are working and, if not, there's always the Johnny Carson show. . . .

Groucho

CP: Your performing career as a stand-up comedian began in 1964, on what used to be known as tryout night at a Greenwich Village club called the Bitter End. Considering the results of your tryout, did you consider the name of the club to be prophetic?

DC: *Au contraire.* The name was all wrong. It was a bitter beginning. I made two bad mistakes. I asked for the wrong kind of introduction, and I failed to be funny. I didn't want the audience to expect a harsh one-line comic typé, so I told the emcee to tell them there was a young man backstage who would like to talk to them. That is precisely what I did for twenty suffocating minutes. I remember I followed a noisy folk-music act, and I managed to re-establish complete silence in the room within seconds. Sweat dammed up over my eyebrows, then overflowed into my eyes, and dark patches appeared in the armpits of my jacket as I droned on. The audience looked up at me like carp in a pool, and I wondered desperately how I would get off. Somehow I did, after thanking them for remaining quiet during the dramatic passages.

The thing that struck me as funny some days later, when I

could bring myself to leave my apartment—I dreaded running into a member of the audience, who would say, "What was *that* all about?"—was that it wasn't a case of fearing that I would bomb and then bombing. I had expected to be good. I thought I would amaze my manager and everyone else with the ease with which I stepped into the comic's role. I'm still surprised that it turned out otherwise. I had stood before plenty of audiences before and made them laugh, but that night was a pisser. Part of it was the intro, but not all of it. I called Woody in Washington, or wherever he was playing, to tell him of my problem. He pointed out that you have to insist on an intro that makes two things clear: that you are a comedian, and that the audience is expected to laugh. His other advice was to do another show soon, which I did, and which worked out well. From then on it was alternating ups and downs. But I can still raise a dew on my brow on a cold day by thinking of that night at the Bitter End.

CP: When you speak of alternating ups and downs, do you mean between being booked and being idle, or do you mean the quality of your bookings, or do you mean the quality of your performances?

DC: All of the above. Except possibly the quality of my bookings, which gradually improved, from other Village spots, like the Duplex, to a national circuit that included the hungry i in San Francisco, Mr. Kelly's in Chicago, and the Bon Soir in New York.

CP: While your bookings may have been improving, the range of possible showcases was narrowing all the time. But we'll pass over the interesting coincidence that night clubs took a terrific nose dive at about the time you entered the field.

DC: I would just like to say that I was not even in the neighborhood when the night-club business died. I was playing cards with a friend at the time.

CP: It was a death unmourned by you, though, wasn't it?

You would never have gone into most of those places if you hadn't been paid to.

DC: And sometimes even then. It's true, I always had a lurking suspicion that the sort of person who would voluntarily pay money for overpriced booze and the *possibility* of being entertained, and whose idea of fun was to sit in a noisy, crowded room full of foul air and drunks, was not the sort of person I would like to stand up in front of unarmed.

CP: Still, you were good at dealing with hecklers.

DC: Up to a point. I remember one duel at the Bon Soir that went on for fully ten minutes with what can only be described, with charity, as a drunken broad. She had on a kind of Carmen Miranda hat. I kept topping her with line after line, but she was too drunk or too stupid to quit. At one point she said, "I pay your salary, buddy, with my hard-earned money." And I said, "And I'm tempted to guess at your profession." That doesn't sound like much here, but there it produced an avalanche of laughter. Still, she kept it up, until finally somebody shoved something in her mouth or she passed out.

It all produced a glorious feeling. I was high, exhilarated from the combat; the audience was in stitches; and it ruined my act. I couldn't make the transition back to the prepared stuff. I should have gone off in triumph after I finished with her, but I was too green to know this. Everything dwindled. I got off to what *Variety* might call torpid mitting. (Translation: lukewarm applause.)

CP: There's a story that at the hungry i in San Francisco you once got so mad that you invited the audience to leave the room—and it did. Is this true?

DC: That night there were nine hostile people in the audience, that is, nine people in the audience, all of them hostile, and their antagonism finally got to me, so that I invited them all to "get the hell out of here." Two people started for the door. I said, "There are no refunds," and a woman turned and said,

"We'll take a chance." And *she* got a laugh—the first and last of the evening.

cp: Your distaste for night clubs was based on more than the atmosphere of the places and the mood of the patrons, wasn't it? I remember seeing you at Mr. Kelly's in Chicago in 1965, and you were hating the whole rhythm of the job, the nightly grind, the life on the road—all that.

dc: If life were going to be a series of night-club engagements, I would, like the chap in the Russian novel, just as soon give back the ticket. Mr. Kelly's was one of the better spots too. It was well run, it had a nice atmosphere, and you got your money's worth. But even there, I'd sit in my dreary digs on Dearborn Street on a cold, snowy night, eating my TV dinner, and thinking, "Oh God, everybody in the world who does not have to go to the club and do a show—three a night—they're so lucky. They can sit in the bathtub with a lot of warm water in it, read all evening, watch television. Whatever they do during the day, they don't have to go to this goddam club tonight." And I'd dress and drag myself over there and sit in the dressing room and wait for the introduction and go on, and the show would start to go well and gradually I'd get so exhilarated that I'd think, "Gee, this is a great way to make a living, and I was crazy earlier. Nobody has this much fun. I feel sorry for people who don't do this."

But that feeling also can disappear rather suddenly. Sometimes it was terrible to think I'd have to come back the next night and go through the same crap all over again. And it could be almost as depressing to do a good show as it was to do a bad one. I'd come off the stage and think, "What have I got? It's not on film or on tape. Only a couple of hundred people saw it. Yeah, they laughed; but now they're talking about other things, and soon they're going to file out and a whole new group is going to come in, and I'll have to start the whole goddam thing all over again." Then, if the second show didn't do as well as the first, I'd think, "How can I prove to these people that I really was funny an hour ago?"

CP: If that's what it was like on one of your better gigs, dare I ask what it was like on one of your drearier ones?

DC: You mean the hungry i in San Francisco. I went out there alone, had no friends in town, the weather was dreary, and the minute my feet touched the ground I was hit with "How do you love San Francisco?" I suppose it is possible to love San Francisco, if the devotees would stop smothering you with sentences you are expected to complete about how great it is. Occasionally I did enjoy myself. I played billiards alone in a wonderful Barbary Coast billiard hall that was carpeted and had hanging Tiffany-style lamps over the tables and oil paintings of Persian scenes on the walls. I expected Mark Twain to walk in at any moment. I also rented a Mustang—the Jaguar of the Geritol set—and drove to Muir Woods, where the redwoods brought me close to a mystical vision. The redwoods are one of the last of the great transcendent experiences available to the common man without a prescription. But I saw most of San Francisco's charms through a thick curtain of depression, and generally felt a tremendous compulsion to whimper myself to sleep. That is, when I was able to get into my hotel room.

The Sir Francis Drake kept harassing me about payment, and once the management locked me out of my room. I hit the ornate ceiling. The functionary in charge of locking people out was a pale and willowy fellow with an indeterminate accent. He either was English or had worked in a boutique too long. I pointed out to him politely that I was employed, highly paid, and likable in the extreme, and if my bill for the previous week had not been paid it was due to a slip-up on my accountant's part. I said that, since they had locked me out without the grace of a warning, if they did not open the door in five minutes I would remove the fire ax from the wall in my corridor and open not only my door, but also several others of my choosing. This, plus a collect call to my bank in New York, turned the trick. When the functionary smarmily allowed as how he was "only doing his job," I said, "That's under 'Eichmann, Adolf' in Bartlett's *Quotations*, isn't it?"

CP: It was San Francisco, then, that was so awful, more than the hungry i?

DC: The hungry i could have been any old club in the Midwest or the Village. The actual onstage experiences were not that unpleasant, in the same way that the dentist is not as bad as the anticipation. The audiences generally liked me, occasionally adored me, and, except for the war party of nine hostiles I mentioned earlier, and except for another night when there was no one in the house but a couple of spaced-out Haight-Ashburyniks who seemed unaware that they were not facing the stage, and a brace of surly dykes who glared stonily at me, my moments as a clown were tolerable.

CP: At least you met Lenny Bruce while you were out there.

DC: That was one of the highlights of my visit, if there can be said to be highlights in gloom. I had seen Bruce twice before, and I thought he was lousy and overrated and depressing. Since all the best people liked him, I decided to try again, so one night I went to a concert by him. Then I saw what they were talking about. He was quicksilver brilliant, funny, versatile, and likable. I met him for a moment afterward and said, for want of anything else to say, "Are you going to do any more concerts?" He flexed his fingers like a pianist and said, "No, my hands won't permit it." It made me laugh.

In the list of adjectives I would append to him, I would leave out profound. All the "only worthy successor to Swift" jazz is, I feel, crapola. He was a dazzling performer at his best, and I don't know why that isn't enough for people. I think the intellectuals who sucked onto him like lampreys, and told him it was beneath him to play any room but the Pantheon, contributed to his already dangerous delusions and his tragic end. I can't prove it, but there it is. Anyway, he was greatly gifted. All the cruddy little establishment comics, and some of the big ones, who said he was nothing "because if you have to say 'shit' to be funny, et cetera," were themselves full of it.

He was of course hounded to death by Nixonlike mentalities in a way that I suspect, with enormous presumption here, he somehow fatally enjoyed. I liked him and wish I had known him better (we met again, briefly), but most of what has been written about him is a waste of good ink, and his most zealous adherents and hardest-core devotees are to be avoided, even if it means working your way around the world in the hold of a goat transport.

CP: The perilous shoals of a young comedian's career, or of any career in show business, are usually navigated with the aid and comfort of a manager. I believe that to most laymen a manager is a shadowy, mysterious figure. Just what does he do?

DC: A manager is someone with a derby and a cigar who spots an anthropoid specimen fresh from a backwoods area who will be an overnight millionaire rock star and invites him to a swank (borrowed) hotel room, where the bedazzled bumpkin downs a pint of tequila and signs a contract promising to give the fat man with the derby and cigar the lion's share of his income for the rest of his life. Whereupon the manager hires an out-of-work actor to pose as the star's accountant and appear once every six weeks with some official-looking papers under his arm, say, "Everything's going great dollarwise, kid," and exit. Meanwhile the manager hires a real accountant for himself, girds himself with hamburger drive-in chains, chicken farms, and a company in Arkansas that manufactures faulty parachutes, and spends his weekends in Vegas gambling and straining to perform diverse sexual acrobatics.

When the rustic's popularity fades and he awakens to find that he is broke, his capped teeth are disintegrating, his groupies have gotten married, and he owes money to everyone he ever met and several who are not born yet, his manager sends him a small check each week out of the profits gleaned from his other acts and goes around saying, "The kid just couldn't handle being a celebrity." Then the manager sits quietly for a moment to recover from the exertion of using a four-syllable word.

CP: Fortunately you've altered enough details so that only those who know your manager well will recognize him in that description. You signed on with Woody Allen's manager, Jack Rollins, who has at various times handled Harry Belafonte, Nichols and May, and Joan Rivers, and whose parachute factory in Arkansas I know for a fact has never turned out a faulty parachute. What did he do for you when you were playing the night-club circuit?

DC: One thing he did was sit patiently with me afterward in a back room, or a café, or a parked car, and talk about my act. Sometimes we'd sit up until 3:00 A.M. discussing that night's show and what I could learn from it and what I could dispense with. I guess his main chore was to keep me from getting discouraged. Jack had a convincing way of telling you that although you had both noticed that the show was a bomb from the audience's point of view (as indicated by the fact that the majority of them went home during it), it was not from his own view. He would say, "It was bad in a way that has value," and then point out that although it was short on laughter, I was working well, learning to survive, and had gotten some of the excess verbiage out of the jokes—probably in a desire to get the thing over with as soon as possible.

He also made decisions on where I should appear and where not, on which work would help me to grow professionally and which would increase my price.

CP: Sometimes it was a question of which *refusals* of work would increase your price, wasn't it?

DC: Yes. It took me a while to get used to the idea of turning down work, or, rather, of having it turned down for me by Jack. As an actor you're forced to accept anything that pays. To one who has worked his head off in summer stock for eighty-five dollars a week, it's a bit of a shock to hear a manager say into a phone, "My client doesn't work for a thousand a week," and then hang up. You say to yourself, "That's right. I don't work for a thousand a week. I work for eighty-five. Get them back!" When they call back saying, "You win. Twelve-fifty it is," you reach for the smelling salts. Before long, you're paying more taxes than you *made* in the previous year, and suddenly it's never-never land.

I had an advantage because Woody was also Jack's client. Jack had asked people to take a chance on Woody that had paid off, and now they were willing to take a chance on me. I was repeatedly told, "I wouldn't have booked you for anybody but Rollins, but if he says you're good, you're good." I was glad for them that they were relieved of the necessity of deciding for themselves—no small favor in our business.

Sometimes Jack would watch out for my interests by calling some comedian who had appropriated one of my jokes. Getting a line that worked was like finding a nugget, and having it stolen by someone who was already in the big time was infuriating.

CP: Did that happen often?

DC: Too often for me. I had only six biggies at that point and couldn't afford to loan any of them out.

I remember once I wrote what I consider one of my best jokes, or, he said modestly, anybody's. You know when you've hit an absolute gem, and you can't wait to get it in front of an audience. It would be fascinating to trace the process of the birth of a joke in your mind, but I can never remember what led to what. I needed a joke about eating out in New York, and somehow I hit on the idea of a Chinese-German restaurant. The punch was, "The food is delicious. The only problem is, an hour later you're hungry for power." I told it to Rollins, who howled and said I had a biggie there. That night it was a smash, and from then on it never failed, even when everything else did. Three days later, I was flipping through the daily papers, and my joke leaped out at me from Earl Wilson's column. Except it was attributed to Rip Taylor at the Copa.

Naïvely and furiously, I called Taylor and asked him to stop doing my line. He said, "Oh, did I say that?," and laughed heartily at the joke. I didn't realize that the witty things attributed to celebrities in those columns are rarely said by them. Often they are phoned in by a guy who gets a hundred dollars a week to plant funny sayings for that person, and when he doesn't have any he steals them.

From that point on, my best jokes would appear in Earl Wilson or elsewhere, attributed to Pat Henry or Jackie Vernon or London Lee, and once even to Woody, who had himself been the victim of this pernicious practice. We both had a good laugh over his getting one of mine. But the situation continued to gall me, and I would look out over the audience at the club some nights wondering which was the creep who was making more than I was off my material.

The print thievery didn't hurt as bad as seeing and hearing your joke on *Laugh In*, television's Niagara Falls of plagiarism, or on the *Red Skelton Show*, which survived for a year on Woody's best jokes, or in the mouth of some crap comic on the *Ed Sullivan Show*, where it would stand out like a jewel in his otherwise vomitorious act and get a hand. I had to walk the streets and have a couple of beers to get over my anger at the thought that the next night's audience at the club would think I got my jokes off other people's TV shows, when in fact it was the other way around.

Sometimes I would call Woody to report the latest theft of one of his jokes. He finally asked me to stop, because, number one, it pained him and if he didn't know about it he would feel better, and, number two, it didn't matter because the crap comics would always be crap comics, and although it hurts to have your jokes stolen, something about you puts you forever in another category and world from them, or at least that is what you tell yourself. He was right.

It hurt so bad, though, that for a time I considered taking all my good jokes out of my act until I got big and famous and could do them *myself* on Ed Sullivan. I suppose it's best to take Woody's advice. The depressing thing is that the vast majority of folks out there don't care, don't notice, or assume that a good joke is a good joke and they like hearing you do it, just as they liked hearing Jackie Vernon do it last week, if they remember hearing it at all, and couldn't care less who thought of it.

But they ought to. People should see the difference between the Marx Brothers and the Three Stooges, and they should sense that a brilliant joke of Mort Sahl's doesn't belong in the act of a schlock comic. When you're a struggling, working comic, you feel a law oughta be passed. In the cold light of day, you realize that, ludicrously, you are asking people to get seriously concerned over something they consider light entertainment. The mote in one's eye can feel like a mountain.

CP: At about this point in your career you began working in a sort of subculture of show business—radio and TV commercials, doing voice-overs for Dutch Master cigars, Coca-Cola, Excedrin, and Nair hair remover, among others. Could you see yourself becoming one of those actors who make a lucrative career out of commercials ?

DC: I can see how I could have been happy doing it. There are certain satisfactions that come from getting the rather precise timing right, being a quick study, and having the facility to do various voices and sounds. There is a shallow mastery of craft involved, or a mastery of a shallow craft. And the variety, the possibility of scheduling, in a single day, several high-paying jobs that may continue to pay for years, while you're writing your novel, basking in the sun, or enduring the gout—that can be enjoyable. A certain amount of your energy, though, would go into convincing yourself that you were just as happy as you would have been if you had succeeded as an actor.

CP: I was always amused by your stories of how the directors and the ad agency men would approach a thirty-second pitchman's spiel with an analytical solemnity worthy of a scene in *Hamlet*. And how you used to call their esthetic bluffs. Once you said a director asked you to shade a line reading a different way, and for the hell of it you read the line precisely as you had before. "*Now* you've got it," the director said. "That's much better."

DC: I hope I did that deliberately. I *would* run into the most astonishing ignorance of how to handle talent. At times it made me want to be a director. I knew the director of certain commercials was never going to get out of the actors what he wanted, because he bullied them or scared them or tried some transparent trick on them, or just couldn't express himself beyond "Could you make that a little brighter this time?," without being able to explain whether he meant faster, happier, more intelligent, or what. Once a guy said, "That's fine. Now could you color it a little?" I said, "Red or green?" He laughed, because these guys laugh at anything that sounds as if it were intended as humor.

Once I got fed up with a schmuck who was "directing" some improvised commercials a group of us were doing, because I knew that his every insensitive move was making it harder for all of us, and he had wrung us all out far sooner than necessary. Then he got mad and said, from the control room, "I don't know why nothing's coming out of the studio we can use." I said, into my mike, "The trouble's on your side of the glass window, dear friend. Your job is easy, and our job is hard and takes a certain talent, and you're doing yours lousy, and we've done ours well for longer than you deserve. I for one have had it for today, and I'm going home." The other actors looked both shocked and grateful. There was a conference in the booth, and we were politely dismissed. The next day we had a new director. What can we learn from this?

CP: I suppose the most rewarding thing you did in commercials was a series of improvised comic interviews with Mel Brooks that were later scissored into Ballantine Beer commercials.

DC: Those recording sessions, when they were soaring along, were intoxicating; it took several hours for me to come down from them, I was so exhausted from laughing at Mel. He would achieve a sort of hypermanic comic inventiveness that would explode in all directions, like an aerial bomb.

CP: Why is it so many writers and performers admire Brooks extravagantly, yet he never seems to reach a large public?

DC: There's no way of packaging his genius, which is improvised; it's inspired comic insanity on a grand scale.

He's another one of those people in our business, by the way, who have a great gift and at times are a little abashed by it. Mel is a different but similar case of what Eddie Albert, Jr., described in Marlon Brando: "It's as if somebody had put an angel inside of him, and he's aware of it, and it's more than he can contain." Mel will suddenly snap out of his inspired hilarity and make a point about a passage in *The Brothers Karamazov*, as if he had to dose himself with scholarly wisdom in order to maintain his self-respect.

This is the same kind of schizoid feeling within which Jerry Lewis constantly ricochets. Jerry can make you laugh by sticking the entire mouth of a glass in his mouth, and then he suddenly realizes he is an adult, taxpaying father of six and discourses on Descartes for a moment.

CP: Is there a moral lurking in all this?

DC: I thought you'd never ask. A person ought to accept his gifts, without searching for their sources, and stop worrying about them. A failure to do this usually results from the idea that everything valuable has to be solemnly analyzable. Where did we get this obsession that exegesis saves? God forgive that pun.

CP: Speaking of accepting gifts, you spoke earlier of show business as a field in which people sometimes have foisted on them "all the free booze and sex they can carry." Has this happened to you?

DC: Which? The booze or the sex?

CP: Take them in any order you like.

DC: If only I could. Booze would come last, at any rate. I think I've gotten drunk, really drunk, only once in my life.

It was while I was in Hollywood working as a writer for the Jerry Lewis show. I came back to my little apartment in Bel Air one night, had some Chicken Delight (a misnomer if ever there was one), and for no reason in particular decided just to drink tumblers of Scotch till I got as drunk as I could get. And I did. Then I went outside and took a walk.

Suddenly I realized I couldn't get back to the apartment, even though I could still see it from where I was. I couldn't even seem to collect my faculties enough to get off the split-rail fence I was sitting on. I just kept saying to myself, "Boy, I'm really drunk." Finally I made my way to the swimming pool outside the apartment building and took a dip with my clothes on. I had the presence of mind to take my watch off first. I carefully put it in my pocket and then plopped into the water.

Next morning I went over to the UCLA campus and sat on a bench for a while thinking, "Now I know the feeling of sin, and of the gods' vengeance on it." I had the Kingsley Amis hang-over, the one where it feels as if small animals have spent the night in your mouth. It was awful enough to have kept me from ever getting really drunk again.

CP: Have you tried other drugs besides alcohol? What about marijuana?

DC: During that awful time in San Francisco there was a girl who came to the club, a model, who, having failed to lure Noel Harrison, settled for me. She took me to a few parties, which resembled every dreary, overcrowded party I have ever been to, and gave me my first joint. I was scared to death, felt as though I had a loaded revolver in my pocket, and was sure I would be pounced on by the fuzz on my way back to the hotel. I double-locked the door, then locked myself in the bathroom, put a towel underneath the door, and lit up. I smoked it as best I knew how. Then I sat on the edge of the tub and took a dollar bill out of my pocket, laid it beside a tube of toothpaste, and sat back to enjoy color-heightening hallucinations and whatever other novelties of the senses might choose to appear. The spirits failed to materialize, and I went to bed disappointed, as I had been by so much else in that city.

cp: Did you ever get to like San Francisco, or marijuana, or both?

dc: Repeated exposure to both under different circumstances has given me a certain fondness for one but not the other. Is that clear enough?

cp: Yes, and don't move. You're under arrest.

dc: I have probably toked up, as we heads say, or, if you will, blown the gage, ventilated the weed, dealt myself an ace, copped a bomber, quaffed a dubee, called on Miss Mary, paused for a joy stick, nudged the mighty mezz, sucked a kick stick, consumed a muggle, dug the root, taken a thumb break, done a number, balled Mary Warner, done a twist, and received an air mail from Mazatlán about eight times.

cp: Where did you acquire the vernacular?

dc: I had a hip Sunday-school teacher.

cp: Did anything surpass the San Francisco experiment?

dc: Everything did. The second time was in the Village. I got totally high, laughed hysterically at the idea of a clock, convulsed myself over the fact that carpets were rectangular, saw the deep and cosmic humor in fingernails, and had to gasp for air from hilarity induced by thinking of the alphabet and the fact that it contained only one *n*. I had the total-time-warp sensation that makes you start a sentence and forget on the fourth word what the point of it was—and not care, because you started the sentence at least fourteen years earlier and a lifetime of experiences and thoughts had intervened. I walked home, still giddy, through the rain, smelling like a brush fire in Sonora, and wondering if I would be behind bars before dawn.

The last time I made moocah, or dug sweet Lucy, was with Janis Joplin, who gave me one that must have been rolled by Montezuma himself. I saw my thoughts in clear letters, and they both felt and looked like a double strike on a coin: appearing twice, a little to one side of each other but overlapping. I wanted to be let down and had no desire to turn on again, which so far has been the case.

CP: Nobody since Janis has been able to proselytize you?

DC: The people who do the proselytizing are part of the problem. I can't abide potheads as company. Their languid, listless, predictable conversation goes something like—make that exactly like—this.

POTHEAD: Hey, man, I dig your show.

ME: Really?

PH: Yea, some beautiful things go down on your show, man.

ME: Why is that?

PH: Why? 'Cause you got a beautiful head, man.

ME: On what subjects?

PH: Whatever's going down, you groove on it.

ME: You left out "man."

PH: Right, man. See what I mean? You're beautiful, man.

ME: What have you liked on the show?

PH: The whole scene, man.

ME: Who, specifically?

PH: Hendrix.

ME: What did he say that you liked?

PH: He was, like, with it, together, man.

ME: Knew where it was at? Knew what bag his head was in?

PH: Right, man. Hey, I'd dig rapping to ya sometime.

ME: Fine. Here's my card.

I have had that literal conversation, except for the last line, too many times. They are nice people, and it is true they are not hitting you over the head with a pissellum club, but I would almost rather talk to Al Capp. Underscore the "almost," in case he gets any ideas about ringing me up.

CP: So you don't like pot any more than you like alcohol, and perhaps less?

DC: I dislike being "gone" and resent not being able to get my thoughts in order, which is hard enough anyway. It does give you an insight into what mental illness must feel like—being conscious that your mind is out of order.

I guess there is a place for marijuana in the world. I know it has renewed some people's sex lives, restored potency to the forlorn and heightened the pleasure for women. I fear the long-term consequences of relying on this. Let's face it, I would prefer some mental discipline that would provide the same things that people turn to pot for. My puritan streak finds it reprehensible, yet my bohemian streak—a narrower streak, to be sure—refuses to proscribe it. Have a pot orgasm twice a year, would be the limit in my book. There is something to be said, howsoever dull, for the norm. I forget what, but something.

CP: That clears the way for us to get back to the subject of sex.

DC: Again?

CP: Force yourself. Looking back over your career, can you recount some of the highlights of your wild slalom through a carnival of casting couches?

DC: Remember Forster's remark about the young man who sat around looking modest when he had nothing to be modest about? With that in mind, I won't be modest; but the fact is that ever since about the eighth grade I have been burdened with the conviction that sex, like basketball and dancing, was an area in which I was not destined to shine. In later years it has struck me that I am attractive to the fairer sex. Should we alter that to *some* of the fairer sex, before denials pour in? At some point I began to get secondhand reports that ladies of my acquaintance, and acquaintance is almost too strong a word, wished I was more aggressive, or even a little aggressive, toward them. I was oblivious to this in each case, and not only to this, but also to what it later struck me were distinct aggressions on their parts that I had utterly missed. To put it succinctly, I had to be hit over the head. I was just on the cusp of perhaps the last generation, I hope, that felt that physical lust was not part of the make-up of ladies of quality.

CP: Can you spare an example?

DC: Let me just flip through my collection of examples a moment. Ah, yes, here's one you may enjoy. At what seems now an incredibly advanced age—let's place this, with blurred precision, in the late fifties—I found myself in a circumstance that evolved quite logically into staying overnight in the apartment of a young woman of my acquaintance.

I conducted myself as a gentleman right up to beddy-bye, at which point I politely retired to the second of the two beds in the one-and-a-half-room flat, satisfied with the naughty excitement of merely spending the night away from home, as 'twere. Conversation continued after lights out in a manner that still would have given no Boy Scout cause to blush, when I allowed as how this was sort of fun and we should do it again sometime. There was a pause, and the voice from the other side of the room said, in a suddenly altered tone, "Maybe next time you won't be such a disappointment."

' I felt the room drop fifty feet. "Did I hear right?" I thought. "Maybe it's some sort of aural hallucination. Maybe I've fallen asleep and am dreaming. Could she be speaking to someone else? Could there be more than one meaning to this remark?" The sensation was a little like discovering you are color-blind. "My God," I thought. "You mean all these years this kind of thing has been going on?" It was a kind of turning point for me, altering forever my image of myself. Although I continued to have similar experiences, there was never the shocked surprise of that night, when I was to discover, in what was surely the first and most memorable of a number of similar happenstances, that what I assumed was the subject at hand, specifically, whatever was being discussed, was not, in fact, the subject at hand.

CP: Are you going to leave that incident hanging there on the edge of the cliff?

DC: Yes, but not out of a sense of propriety. More out of an inability to shift literary tone abruptly from the almost Henry Jamesian circumlocutions of the narration so far to the bawdy Boswellian tone that would be required to convey what followed. Anyone so craven as to be seriously concerned with the details can either send a self-addressed, stamped envelope or, better still, for a pallid-by-comparison but similar account of what followed, see Boswell's *London Journal*, the Lady Louisa incident.

CP: Anyway, the point is, you instantly perceived yourself as the satyr you had always been but had not suspected until this obliging damsel helped you to see your reflection in the pond?

DC: Dig it. Actually, it didn't work that way precisely. I

continued to drop easy pop flies, and realized that a few line drives had whizzed past my head that I hadn't even seen and was only told of later through frustrated confessions delivered to third persons. This is beginning to sound like some serious delusion, I'm sure.

Once, in Hollywood, a girl I worked with invited me to a party at her house in the valley. When I arrived there the party was me, although I failed to realize this and continued to make harmless assumptions about the nonappearance of the other guests. Then another lady arrived and further dispelled any doubt. The various reasons given for the failure of the rest of the guests to materialize seemed reasonable. I felt I was in particularly good form conversationally, and decided that what now and again resembled suppressed yawns on the part of the ladies were merely oddly similar facial tics. We drank wine, and I rattled on until what must have been nearly dawn, when suddenly (again that shift of tone) one of my hostesses said, "How long are you going to keep this up?"

I thought she meant my current profession, and I began to discourse on my career plans, until I noticed exasperating glances being exchanged, and she said, "*Dick!*" I stopped in midword, and she said softly, "Have you been to bed with two girls?" I said, "You mean altogether? In my life?" Neither of them cared for my joke, if it was a joke, and I realized it had happened again, only this time I was outnumbered. I suddenly saw myself in the most humiliating light—the victim, you might say, of the opposite of salacious gossip. I thought, "All over town I have been judged innocent behind my back. It's grossly unfair. They assume my closet is devoid of skeletons. Perhaps a femur or two and that's it." It was embarrassing beyond belief.

CP: And? And?

DC: Oh, stop that panting! Here I am engaged in an act of self-analysis, and you're grubbing for smut.

CP: I am merely a trained journalist seeking fullness of detail.

DC: Oh, well, all right. You might have guessed from my reluctance that I blew it. I don't know why. Would it sound absurd if I said that in some sense I recoiled at the idea of being a sex object? It certainly would to me. But I swear there was an element of that. There must also have been an element of uncertainty and inexperience over the precise details of making the beast with *three* backs, if the author of *Othello* will forgive me.

I'm not really clear on this, but whatever I did must have seemed decisive, because I remember a sudden picking up of empty glasses and emptying of ash trays and purposeful clicking of heels across kitchen tiles, and my noticing for the first time that the door to the bedroom was agape, had been all evening, and that there in the center—in a seductive pool of blue light, mind you—was the article of furniture itself. The stage on which the proposed drama of the evening went unplayed, the central actor (I *assumed* central; again, my unfamiliarity with the proper mechanics) having proved a dud.

I will add that the evening did not turn out to be a *total* loss. Again, I'm afraid, it's stamped-envelope time. The details, not unremarkable in themselves, would add little to the core of our discussion.

CP: Can one assume that your pursuers were mostly of one sex?

DC: By no means. I have broken hearts on both sides of the sexual equator. A friend of mine, who is, I have always assumed, bisexual, was sitting with me under a tree one night in Stratford, Connecticut, after a rehearsal for the Shakespeare Festival. We were discussing the previous summer, when we had both been in the Shakespeare company at Ashland, Oregon. After some laughs over recalled goof-ups onstage of the kind that inevitably plague repertory, there was one of those pauses, and he said, "You were sort of the star of the season." I thought he was making a mocking reference to the roles I landed—2nd Murderer, 3rd Lord, and so on—and he said, "I mean your body. There wasn't anybody in the company who didn't want to go to bed with you."

I was aware that certain people of all sexes had wanted to, but some of the names he mentioned suddenly cast whole murky areas of that somewhat socially baffling summer into a new light.

CP: Such as?

DC: Oh, you know. One guy, whose company I enjoyed, suddenly turned on me mysteriously one night with a series of statements that included "I know you and Art [another actor] have brought girls into your rooms at night." I couldn't figure out why this was included in a list of things he found reprehensible and decided that he was secretly some sort of rigid moralist. I completely missed the point until that night a year later under the tree in Stratford. I liked the guy; he was one of the wittiest people I've ever met. I wish I still knew him, and I feel discriminated against sexually—curious reversal there.

The funny part was, my under-the-tree friend, after revealing to me that I had been the cynosure of the company's collective libido that summer, said, "Nobody believed me when I told them I *had* gone to bed with you." The fact is, he had, and I had forgotten about it. Do I have to explain that too?

CP: It might add a certain symmetry to your having finished the other tantalizing anecdotes.

DC: Very well—solely in the interests of symmetry. There was a party at the rooming house where he and other members of the company lived. I lived in a barracks on the edge of town. The party lasted till about three. I had been told there was a bed for me there, and no need to go home, since there was rehearsal the next morning and the theater was three blocks away. When it came time to retire I learned there was *half* a bed for me. Suspecting and fearing nothing, I got in. My friend was a perfect gentleman. At one point, the bed being rather narrow, he said, "This seems to be the right place for my arm," and placed it across my back. I suppose I could have thrust it away, but I was tired, and, as someone once said, "It didn't hurt me and it seemed to give him a lot of pleasure." And when Rosie fingered the dawn, I awoke, innocence intact. He gallantly had not *claimed* a conquest to other members of the company, but merely indulged in an occasional "Hey, Dick, you got make-up on my pillow the night we slept together!" shouted across a restaurant.

CP: Are you telling me that you've gone through all these years in show business and remained virtually deaf to sexual overtones?

DC: No. Although I'm still not totally cured, I have, with work, come a long way. (Say, whatever these drinks are, they're making it much easier to talk.) I was even showing marked progress on occasions as early as our undergraduate years at Yale. Such as the time, one cold November Sunday, when I was on one of my lone pilgrimages to New York and decided to visit the Cloisters.

Amidst the medieval structures I wandered, a wintry orange sun setting in the chill gray sky beyond the Hudson. (The river, not the car.) I met a vaguely whorish-looking blonde, complete with chewing gum and a strident laugh, incongruous among the tapestries, *prie-dieux*, and statuary, who had chosen that particular day to satisfy her curiosity as to "just what this old place was, anyhow." It was cold outdoors, warm in the Cloisters, there was that kind of panicky malaise and loneliness that Sunday afternoon brings, she had an insouciant air, I liked the way she had her hands thrust into her loden-coat pockets, and I wanted to marry her.

I took her to Downey's, where I bought her the most lavish dinner I could afford (chopped steak) and had a Manhattan to screw up my courage—which it did, badly—and then another one, which had the desired inhibition-dissolving effect. I invited her to my small but cozy (four dollars) single in the Hotel Times Square, where, as Walker Percy says in one of his novels, "I gave her the merriest time a girl could imagine."

As we stepped gingerly into the corridor on the morrow (Monday, 7:00 A.M.) the incubus of puritan guilt materialized before me in the person of a low-comedy maid complete with long-handled dustpan and broom. She looked at me and then at my Lady of the Cloisters and emitted a sort of guttural snort. If she had said, "I oughta turn the both of yiz over my knee," it would not have surprised me. Or, perhaps, "And your parents schoolteachers!" (How could she know?)

I could feel her eyes on the back of my neck as we proceeded, with assumed nonchalance on my part, to the elevator. My companion bore it with an amused dignity that is part of the indubitable superiority of women. Dostoevskian fear and guilt wracked me as I paid my bill to the pencil-mustached desk clerk with the sun-lamp tan, expecting him to say, "That'll be double, sonny," and wondering if I would have the gall to carry off an outraged refusal.

Having somehow endured the year that it took to cross the lobby, I began to get my pulse under control. Outside, in the gray, misty dawn of a thousand short stories, I suddenly felt the kind of cleansed feeling that sometimes comes from the right combination of drink, too little sleep, and the rest of it.

She told me I was sweet and vanished gradually down the subway steps, waving over her shoulder without looking back, like Simone Signoret in *Room at the Top*, and I headed for Grand Central feeling *mature*. I decided that the really delicious move would be not to make my roommates jealous with this yeasty yarn, but to keep it as my own savored secret, merely saying yes with an air of *significance* when asked if I had had a good weekend.

What I really wished was that I was in the Daily Themes course, so I could write up my weekend Experience and hand it in as my casual daily offering. Later that year, I asked a young instructor-reader in that course what daily theme he got sickest of getting over and over, and he told my story, give or take a detail, almost to a T. I swallowed and chuckled knowingly.

cp: But such incidents, then or later, never entangled you in those webs or conspiracies of sex that we're always hearing about in show business?

dc: I'm not sure I even had any knowledge of those supposed webs or conspiracies. The London theater, you know, was said to be dominated by a sort of homosexual cartel for decades, to the extent that there was virtually a heterosexual black list. I've heard on good authority, from people of all sexes, that this was literally and sinisterly true in London, and I find it intriguing that it might be true in New York, but I doubt it.

I have known of cases where absolute no-talents have been cast because a producer or director was smitten with their charms, but then, the same has happened with women cast by heterosexual producers and directors. I can't believe that it's true in the good old U.S.A. It may appear that way simply because of the large number of people who, as they say, happen to be homosexual and are also greatly talented. Other homosexuals may have a slight edge socially in meeting those people, and it might *appear* that there is a conspiracy. But I think mainly such talk is a rationalization after the fact on the part of people who are long on heterosexuality but short on talent. It also helps explain the vast number of untalented, undeserving people who infest the theater and all of show business.

The real explanation for the teeming hordes of no-talents is simply that there are more jobs than there are good people, more people with the neurotic urge than the talent, plus a hell of a lot of people putting other people into those jobs who don't know good from bad, plus a vast segment of the public that doesn't see the difference between crap and quality anyway. So some people who are talented do get left out. But it's more than just, as a discouraged actor friend of mine said before he quit, "who you know and who you blow." Forgive me; I realize that phrase is ungrammatical.

CP: And your career has been neither advanced nor retarded by sexual activity?

DC: Not by my own, although once it was temporarily delayed by somebody else's. I was appearing on a well-known television panel show years ago and hoping that if I did well it might net me a permanent job on the show. I did so well and got so many laughs that I fully expected the producer to make me a fat offer afterward, I had been such a smash. I went backstage, and he stretched out his hand lethargically and said, "Thanks, Dick," and drifted away. Later, I asked someone who had been in the viewing room with him why he hadn't liked me better, and was told that he had been pitching a blonde so openly and heavily that neither he nor anyone else in the viewing room had been able to watch the show.

CP: You did quite a lot of work on panel and game shows in that period of, say, 1966 to 1968. As I recall, your first guest appearance was on *What's My Line?*

DC: Wow, *that* was the time machine. I remember lying on the couch in my basement in Nebraska when I was in *eighth* grade and watching *What's My Line?* It was really disorienting, almost fifteen years later, to find myself backstage waiting to go on it. And there were three of the same people I used to watch—John Daly, Bennett Cerf, and Arlene Francis. On the air, when we were all blindfolded for the famous mystery guest and it came my turn for a question, I said, "I have a feeling the mystery guest is trying to figure out who *I* am." It got an enormous laugh.

CP: From there you went to guest appearances on the talk shows, starting, I believe, with Merv Griffin's.

DC: That's right. The producer of the *Tonight Show* had seen me in the Village and decided I wasn't ready yet, so my manager put me on Griffin. My first appearance went smashingly, and I got my first good notice from Jack O'Brian, who headed his column "Dick's a Fine Calmic," which was his way of describing my low-key style. I must have done a half-dozen Griffin appearances before I moved over to the Carson show.

CP: Do you want to take this opportunity to deal with the mischievous rumor that on the day after your first appearance with Griffin you walked the streets to see if you'd be recognized?

DC: Yes. That rumor is completely true. And the worst of it was, I *wasn't* recognized. Wait, I was, but it was days later. I passed an oil truck, and the guy on top of it looked at me strangely. I pretended I had forgotten something and turned and walked past him the other way, and he got down off the truck, took off his glove, and said, "Hey, you're the guy on Merv Griffin." I said I was. He asked what my name was, and when I said "Dick Cavett" he agreed and repeated a couple of my jokes, so that we would both know that that was in fact who I was. I thanked him and nearly invited him and his wife to dinner.

CP: Another time-machine experience for you was cracking the Ed Sullivan show. I remember your telling me that when you were a kid in Lincoln, every time a comedian came on the Sullivan show you used to think, "I know how he feels. Someday that'll be me. But I'm glad it isn't this week, because I'm not ready." One day it *was* you. Were you ready?

DC: Reasonably ready. I'd been doing my act for some time by then. When I had watched the show as a kid in Lincoln, I had wondered whether, when I finally stood on the same stage, I'd feel thrilled, transformed, in a world of magic, and whether the sensations shooting through me would be so overwhelming that they would make it impossible for me to speak. When it finally happened I didn't feel much of anything. I wasn't particularly scared. There was a sort of sadness that I was actually living through what had been a specific dream of mine and that by living through it I would end it.

As I stood in the wings waiting to go on I looked out at the shiny glass floor they had put down for a dance number, and I could see *dust* on it. And there was a bored-looking stagehand leaning against the wall sneaking a cigarette. I had come through the looking glass and found it mundane. From the inside, it was not glittering and the atmosphere was not heady. Just crowded.

When Sullivan introduced me I walked out thinking, "I'm now walking onto our TV screen out in Lincoln," but I felt mortal and surprisingly calm. It went well enough, and when I had finished my first and only appearance Ed gripped my hand, the way I had seen him with a thousand other people, and said, "Nice to have you back." My head swirled slightly at that; then I realized it was Ed who was confused and not me. I went backstage, got congratulated, washed up, and went home. I had not been transformed. I still had to push on a door to make it open, my feet touched the ground when I walked, I fixed some supper, and the sun came up the next day as usual.

CP: How did you make the transition from doing guest spots on TV to being a star?

DC: My first starring assignment was on a show for NBC that was never seen on the air. It was called *The Star and the Story,* and it was conceived as a cross between *This Is Your Life* and a talk show, with a well-known actor or personality as the guest. We made a pilot with Van Johnson. Whereas most pilots are "in the can," this one went down it. Years later, when I hosted an Emmy award show on NBC, I was caught on camera running upstage to examine the celluloid streamers festooning the set. I thought they might be my pilot for *The Star and the Story.*

CP: You did star in a couple of specials for ABC that actually got on the air.

DC: And one of them, a new-talent, youth-oriented show called *Where It's At,* turned out reasonably well. When the show was brewing my manager heard that I was being considered as the star, or, more modestly, host. The producers,

With Groucho Marx on the *Kraft Music Hall* TV show, 1967

Getting a dancing lesson from Fred Astaire on the *Dick Cavett Show,* 1971

Joking during a taping with
Katharine Hepburn, 1973

*(Right)* Interviewing Orson Welles
in London, 1973

*(Right)* Making peace
with Lester Maddox, 1972

Watching Marlon Brando
demonstrate a point, 1973

*Ann Limongello, © 1973 by American Broadcasting Compan*

David Redfern, © 1973 by American Broadcasting Companies, Inc.

Ann Limongello, © 1972 by American Broadcasting Companies, Inc.

The Bergen News, *Palisades Park, N.J.*

*(Above)* At home on Long Island with Carrie Nye

*(Opposite page)* With Robert Redford at Lake Powell, Utah, 1972, and with Woody Allen in New York, 1970

On the porch and swimming
near his home on Long Island
*Michael Mauney*, Life, © *Time Inc.*

Yorkin and Lear, had heard of me but never seen me, I believe. Jack Rollins felt it was a good enough possibility that it would be worth flying to Los Angeles to meet Yorkin and Lear. Something in me left over from the Ivy League affliction of fearing to be caught trying too hard made me shrink from such obvious job seeking, but I consented to the dreary ten hours of skying back and forth to the coast.

We arrived at LA airport clutching two kinescopes of me on the Merv Griffin show. Hopping a cab, we pulled up in front of Y & L's business digs, paid the cab driver, and strode to the door, where we both noticed that each of us had both hands free. After a simultaneous exchange of "I thought *you* had the kinescopes" and a mirthless laugh, I suggested we get the next flight back, before anyone saw us. Miraculously, an hour or so later the cab driver noticed the two cans of film being chauffeured around Los Angeles and brought them to us. We laid a ten on the cabbie, and I got the job.

CP: And didn't that in turn lead to the morning show?

DC: I guess it led ABC to feel they already had some money invested in me. The special had gotten some good reviews, and when ABC dreamed up the notion of a morning talk show it was decided that my fresh face, nimble wit, and succulent body might appeal to the laundry-and-baby-imprisoned housewife. Thus was born *This Morning*, starring your humble servant, soon changed to *Dick,* et cetera.

CP: So you had made it, you had your own show, and you could relax and be happy.

DC: Relax? Happy? I know you're jesting, because you must have seen the ghastly, gaunt, pale, rigid wreck that passed for myself in the early days of that show. The agony of starting a new show is unimaginable. Your nerves are on the point of snapping, taut as a violin string, and everything is an irritation, a pain, an interruption, and there is no fun in life. You constantly ask yourself, "What in hell did I want this for?"

I remember once staring into the sink in my dressing room and thinking, "So this is success. I make a five-figure salary per week, I'm not doing anything well, my guts are knotted with tension, I have a headache half the time, the network is on my back to get the ratings up and has no idea how I should go about it, and if I go on like this another week I'll have an ulcer and a nervous breakdown."

When I pulled out of this I said, "Never again." I came out of it with a clear idea that none of it was worth that kind of suffering, that it was pointless not to enjoy what I was doing. I decided that if I ever felt that tension building up again I'd just say, "Screw it. So it's air time and I'm not ready. Even if it comes off lousy, the sun will still come up tomorrow."

CP: Did that work?

DC: No. Shortly thereafter, I did one show that was such a bomb that the sun did *not* come up the next day, and I've been in a funk ever since.

# PART FOUR
# INSIDE THE MONSTER

*In midafternoon, a taxi pulls up to the corner of Fifty-eighth Street and Seventh Avenue in Manhattan. Out steps a slim, smallish, rather tousled-looking man wearing corduroys, a pull-over, sunglasses, and an army-surplus jungle fatigue hat, and clutching an untidy bundle of papers and books. Head down, he walks quickly west along Fifty-eighth Street toward the Elysee Theater, a onetime legitimate playhouse now converted into a TV studio.*

*A few knots of people are gathered under the marquee, mostly young, many of them women or girls, some hunched cross-legged on blankets spread on the sidewalk or sitting in ponchos with their backs against the glass doors of the theater. The man says nothing as he walks past them, barely glances sideways, but still they begin stirring and murmuring. They have penetrated his disguise, for it is a disguise of sorts, and just before he darts behind the stage door, a few steps down the sidewalk, one or two of them call out, "Dick Cavett!"*

Thus Dick begins the countdown to the taping of his TV show.

It's a countdown of considerable tension—tension that has been coiled all day and now will start winding tighter with every twist of the second hand on the clock. The tension is part of the reason he has no greeting for the early queuers outside the theater, why he has, in fact, few words for anybody from now until they are supposed to start flowing from him on the air.

In his apprentice days, Dick used to wonder sometimes why stars, especially his onetime employers Jack Paar and Johnny Carson, couldn't take more time to be civil, to talk a bit. It didn't seem to be asking too much. Now that he's in their shoes he knows it *is* too much. "Nobody has any idea what it's like to do such a show," he says. "There is a sense in which you carry it around with you for hours beforehand like four plates spinning at the end of sticks, and even a momentary interruption or distraction is more than you can afford. A civil hello is an accomplishment."

Later in the evening, if things go well, the approximately five million viewers at home won't see much of that tension when the show is broadcast by some one hundred and sixty-five ABC affiliate stations around the country—usually at 10:30 or 11:30 P.M. Perhaps only a brow or upper lip beaded with sweat, a stammer or two, a brief clenched silence. Mostly they will see a self-possessed-looking young man sitting in a chair chatting and laughing, with seeming casualness, with guests seated around him. The calculated, slightly absurd illusion of people who have come together almost at random in a living room will be achieved. It will look easy.

Even to the studio audience it may be deceptive, although they can see a good many more of the complications and distractions that are involved. They can see that the carpeted area where Dick and the guests are sitting is really a small arc-shaped platform that forms a lonely island in the center of the stage, its position marked by scraps of tape. They can see the flies and ropes and brick wall behind the set; the tiers of lights that glare down in a white-hot blaze; the three cameras that nose around the edge of the pool of light like futuristic creatures, with TelePrompters (for commercials) clamped to their brows.

A platoon of shadowy figures slouches out of camera range gesturing, shifting equipment, bending and moving to unheard commands. At stage left, orchestra leader Bob Rosengarden cues his sixteen musicians with whispers and waves of his drumsticks. At stage right, the stage manager, the producer, and, at times, the announcer stand and watch, occasionally talking to the control room on an internal phone, often making hand signals or holding up signs to Dick as he asks questions of his guests, listens, cues commercials.

Only Dick can really know what it feels like to sit in that chair and try to conduct a show in the middle of all this.

"I know it looks as if all you have to do is follow the conversation," he says. "But you're also thinking ahead, wondering whether to change the subject or pursue it, trying to decide whether there's time in this segment to start something new, dying inside when the guest launches into a long story and you know that there's less than a minute left before the station break and that the guest will be thrown and the story ruined if you interrupt, thinking that his last story may involve the show in a lawsuit and wondering if you should say something that might help or let it pass, knowing that an upcoming guest has said, 'If that schmuck is still out there when I come on, I'll leave,' trying to remember what it was he told you not to forget to ask him and trying to decide, of five things you wanted to get to, which two to leave out, since time is running out, and wondering why the audience seems restless and what signal the stage manager just gave you that you missed. Usually these things all come together about the time you've just decided your fly is open and that's what the ladies in Row E are whispering about and why the stage manager signaled. It's a wonderful job for people who have never had a nervous breakdown but have always wanted one. Trying to have a real conversation with all those imposed time limits is like getting someone's life story on a subway platform just as your train is coming in."

As if all this frantic mental juggling weren't enough, there is something else that confronts him: the constant icy edge of dread at what may happen next. More than most TV shows, a talk show is a leap into the unknown. Despite all the massed technology, all the formulated procedures, all the research and planning, there is simply no way of anticipating what the guests are going to say or do.

Dick has had guests fail to show up at the studio. He has had guests lurch onstage drunk, and he has had guests turn out to be all too sober, their promised conversational torrents evaporating under the lights and leaving a residue of parched monosyllables. He has had guests say slanderous things, blasphemous things, cryptic and incoherent things, inaccurate things, and *non sequiturs*. He has had a guest walk off the show in a fit of temper—former Georgia Governor Lester Maddox— and he has had one guest get up and make for another as if to punch him in the nose—Norman Mailer versus Gore Vidal. He has even had a guest die of a heart attack while taping a show— J. I. Rodale, the publisher and advocate of organic foods and farming. (This, of course, was not seen on the air; a previously taped show was substituted.)

How does Dick prepare himself for such an ordeal? How does he arrange a typical workday, and what does he feel as air time draws near?

When Dick and I were at Yale we used to speculate about famous people whose private lives remained obscure, at least to us. How did they spend their time? we would ask. What, for example, did Orson Welles do after breakfast? In a similar spirit, I followed Dick through several working days some months ago, during the period when he was on the air five nights a week. The object was to see what *he* did after breakfast. Since no single example would be typical, what follows is an amalgam of those days, as representative as I can make it.

*10:00 a.m.* Dick pads downstairs in his seven-room duplex in a converted town house on Manhattan's East Side. He is wearing old trousers, a sweater, socks, but no shoes. He hasn't shaved or combed his hair. He seems to compensate at home for being so kempt-looking on his show. In the dining room, the Cavetts' golden-crested cockatoo, Serena, has gotten out of its cage again—apparently no latch has been devised that it can't undo—and is strutting on the floor between an eighty-five-pound black poodle named Louis and a five-pound, honey-colored Yorkshire-cairn named Daphne.

"Bird thinks it's a dog," Dick mutters. The only other pet, a moody Persian cat named Charles, is skulking in the kitchen.

Breakfast is fruit and tea, perhaps, or Soy-O and raisins. This is the only meal of the day that Dick and Carrie Nye fix for themselves. Lunch and dinner are prepared by a Bermudian cook who comes in for about five hours every day and who is one of the two Cavett household servants, the other being an Irish housekeeper.

As he eats Dick reads through a manila folder full of material on tonight's guests—a breakfast ritual. There are biographical sketches, suggested introductions, and page after page of notes drafted by the writers or talent co-ordinators who have interviewed the prospective guests. For some unknown reason, they are customarily typed up in question-and-answer format, complete with fanciful colloquialisms like "DICK: That's interesting . . ." or "GUEST: I'm so glad you asked, because . . ."

Dick pushes them aside with a sigh. "I don't like the notes on R—— very much. They don't tell me whether the co-ordinator has even talked to him, or which questions supposedly elicit the good responses. I don't know—they don't give me a very good *feel*."

*10:50 a.m.* Out on the street with Louis for a walk. The Cavetts use a dog-walking agency to cover the frequent occasions when they're busy or away, but Dick enjoys exercising Louis when he can. He stops at a newsstand on Lexington Avenue a block from his apartment.

"Hiya, Mr. Cavett. What'll it be today?"

"A *Times*. Oh, and give me a London *Observer* too."

"There were some girls here asking for you."

"Tell them they can't have me."

"Hey, that's good."

Dick has no newspaper delivery to his door, no regular regimen for keeping informed (though he does keep well informed). This is partly in reaction to his early days as a writer of topical monologues for the *Tonight Show*, when he had to scan half a dozen papers daily in search of possible subjects for jokes—the Chinese New Year, freakish weather, hijackings, quintuplets, political chicanery.

*11:15 a.m.* Back home, Dick goes upstairs to his study, a large front room furnished with armchairs, a sofa, two walls of floor-to-ceiling bookshelves, a TV set equipped with an automatic video tape recorder, and, lying loose on a counter, four Japanese samurai swords. In one corner is a large glass case crammed with artifacts of the northern Plains Indians—Crow moccasins, Cheyenne saddlebags, Sioux hair ornaments and pipe tomahawks, and so on. In another corner is a six-foot oak desk, where Dick, having cleared away papers, books, the typewriter, a teacup left over from yesterday, and a wadded-up pair of brown corduroy trousers, sits and reads the *Times*. His personal effects are perpetually in a state of benign chaos. He knows, for example, that folded into the pages of a book somewhere in his bookshelves is a rather valuable autograph letter of Oscar Wilde's, but he hasn't been able to find it for years.

This apartment used to belong to Woody Allen. The decor during Woody's residence was Early Warehouse, featuring pool table, jukebox, and packing crates. Now, under Carrie Nye's supervision, it has been transformed into Old Edith Wharton-*cum*-Indian Museum. All is dark wood, rich draperies, gleaming chandeliers, and plant fronds. It is very warm and comfortable, yet the Cavetts get out of it whenever they can.

Their real home, their spiritual center of gravity, is near the eastern tip of Long Island, three hours from New York by train or car. There, on a bleakly beautiful heath overlooking the Atlantic, they have a slightly eccentric white clapboard house with blue trim wrought—almost overwrought—in 1890, by Stanford White, with a flourish of dormers, belfries, and rambling galleries. Carrie Nye says it is a house of "blown sand, lost bees, musty old sofas, books like *Willoughby's Tracts,* and pajamas that have been there since the 1880s." That is unfair to her redecorating, but it catches the solicitous affection they feel for the place.

Dick goes out almost every weekend while he's working; whenever possible he stays for weeks at a time. Company is at hand if he wants it. Andy Warhol has a compound of houses just over the hill, where Dick occasionally stops for lunch with, say, Truman Capote and Lee Radziwill. The writer Jean Stafford, a good friend of Dick's and Carrie Nye's, lives a half hour away, in Springs, East Hampton. Dick keeps a horse—a roan gelding quarter horse named Twilight Time—and a twenty-four-foot motorboat nearby. In warm weather he swims and snorkels. In all seasons he spends long hours reading, gazing out to sea through binoculars, poking through the gorse, or prowling the beach below. He has never for a moment felt bored there, and it pains him every time he has to leave.

*11:25 a.m.* The phone next to the desk rings. It is Dick's secretary, Doris Mikesell, checking in. "I don't have enough on R——," he tells her. "Could you get somebody to put together some more stuff, some articles or something . . ."

Doris will be calling back two or three times today. In the next hour Dick also gets several other calls. His producer, John Gilroy, phones to confirm the order of battle for tonight's show. His lawyer, Alfred Geller, reports the results of negotiations with ABC for extra promotion on an upcoming show (moderately successful). His manager, Jack Rollins, passes along a request for Dick to emcee an advertising-awards dinner next month. "I don't think I want to get into that," Dick says. "Who'd they have last year? Oh. Yeah, let's blow that one."

At this point, he isn't consciously working on tonight's show, but he isn't forgetting about it either. It buzzes at the back of his mind like a fly at a windowpane, keeping him from concentrating on much else. About the only things he will schedule during these hours are a doctor's appointment, a trip to a museum, maybe lunch with a friend. In the early years of having his own show he couldn't even do that much. I tried several lunches with him in those days. He sat with his fists clenched under the table the whole time, and I practically had to wave my hand in front of his face to get his attention.

Now, with nothing scheduled today, no lunches, no museum jaunts, he begins to pick at the accumulated bumf on his desk. Three or four books written by people who will be guests on future shows make a formidable pile. There are several invitations to address schools, clubs, and other groups. The manager of the ABC affiliate in Des Moines wants him to record greetings to an Iowa sales club on a tape cassette, then send the cassette to Des Moines to be played to the assembled multitude. Doris has sent him a batch of letters culled from the thousand or so his show receives each week. Of these, he usually sees from twenty-five to a hundred, representing the full range of opinions expressed by viewers and including any that are from well-known people or for some other reason require a personal reply. Across the top of these, Doris, who knows Dick for the procrastinator that he is, has written, "You really ought to answer—*now.*"

*12:15 p.m.* The phone again. Dick's number is unlisted, but an awful lot of people seem to have it. Sometimes, if he wants to find out who is calling before he commits himself, he answers in a disguised voice. He has an uncanny falsetto imitation of a Puerto Rican woman that has fooled even close acquaintances into thinking it was a maid or cleaning woman, despite the fact that the Spanish is hardly authentic (*"No predos comprende . . . yo se María . . . quandos per noche . . ."*).

This time he answers straight. It is a wildlife group from whom he has requested some information. Partly at Carrie Nye's prodding, he has become a genteel crusader on conservation and wildlife. "How many western states? . . . Jesus! Where can you get that film? . . . Gee, thanks." He scribbles a few notes, trying to frame a statement he can read on the air tonight about mistreatment of mountain lions.

*12:40 p.m.* A messenger arrives from his office with more material on R———. There are several typewritten sheets, a magazine, a couple of reference books. One of the books has a scrap of note paper stuck between its pages with "Very good" scrawled on it in red grease pencil.

*12:45 p.m.* The phone. "And the fucking phone," Dick intones, as if reading from the book in front of him, "rings all the time." It is for Carrie Nye, from the costume designer for a TV play that she has agreed to do.

Summoned from the bedroom down the hall by a bellow from Dick, she peeks in, looking girlish in a floor-length dressing gown and no make-up. The girlish effect is immediately dispelled when she clasps the phone and begins talking in her deep, molasses voice. "I adore your designs and put myself completely in your hands. Do you know what I look like? Oh, no, no. What could he have been thinking of? I'm blonde and skinny. I look like an Afghan hound."

Dick, who has been accompanying the conversation with a pantomime of mincing, prissy gestures, stops and looks appraisingly at Carrie Nye. Yes, an Afghan hound is very good.

After making an appointment for a fitting, Carrie Nye hangs up and begins pacing the room, raising her arms to the ceiling and declaiming, "What do women want? I'll tell you what women want. Women want not to have to do all the dreary chores that I have to do today."

Dick tells her what the wildlife group said about mountain lions. She falls into an armchair and listens intently, chin on fists. "Are you going to do something on the air?" she asks.

He nods, then changes the subject. "You know, J——— crapped out of tomorrow's show. The office says they're probably going to have to book B——— in his place, if only by default."

Carrie Nye ponders for a moment. "That's not so good. Can't they get somebody else? How about, oh, S———, or even old E———?"

They begin a series of verbal shell games with the guest

line-up for tomorrow's show, and, indeed, for the rest of the week's shows. The usual protocol has been observed: Carrie Nye has volunteered nothing until her views are solicited, but then she has sounded off freely. Both strong-willed, independent, and occasionally stubborn people, she and Dick dance these minuets in order to avoid collisions. They dance them not only at close quarters, treading respectfully around the edge of each other's province, but also sometimes at a considerable remove, living and working apart for brief spells. The strength of their relationship seems to come from the fact that its distances are as important as its intimacies.

This equation is never clearer than when they banter about whether Carrie Nye will watch Dick's show, something she does only about half the time. "Darling, aren't you going to watch?" Dick will say.

"There's nobody on that I want to see."

"*I'm* on."

"That's what I mean."

Carrie Nye stands up now to face those dreary chores, chief among which is shopping for the ingredients of a curry dinner for their friends the Robert Redfords tomorrow night. Gliding toward the door, she assumes an air of weary sophistication and drawls a Noël Coward exit line: "Darling, you *will* try *very* hard not to be pompous at dinner, won't you?"

*1:20 p.m.* Dick turns in earnest to the notes for tonight's show. In earlier years he would have been in his office by this time, taking phone calls in a big swivel chair behind his desk, dealing with a procession of staffers, composing his features into a semblance of attentiveness and judiciousness—and inwardly seething over the valuable time he felt he was wasting. Dick loathes all administrative and personnel matters and, not surprisingly, isn't good at them. He feels alternatively like a fraud and a prisoner in the role of boss. He has a perverse tendency to be elaborately patient and polite with people or ideas he doesn't like. As he once put it to me, "What it comes down to is that I seem to be incapable of simply saying, 'No. Next?' "

Even with people or ideas he does like, he can be maddeningly inconclusive. Trying to get a firm decision from him on some routine piece of business is like trying to nail jello to a tree. He has always left the ramrodding of his office, including all hiring and firing, to his producer. When it has been the producer who was to be hired or fired (as it has, two or three times), he has left that to his manager.

In the last couple of years, he has decided that both he and his office would be better off if he worked most of the time at home and went directly to the studio before the taping. This has made him remote from his staff, which doesn't worry him, and has somewhat impeded the upward flow of ideas, which does (but not enough to send him back to the swivel chair).

Dick's office is technically the office of his company, Daphne Productions Inc., which is named after his dog. (Interviewer: "I just can't *believe* Daphne Productions is named after your *dog!*" Cavett: "I know. I guess Daphne Productions *is* a silly name for a dog.") Daphne is on the thirteenth floor of a nondescript stone building on Broadway—one of those places whose frosted-glass doors typically announce small law firms, dance studios, obscure steamship companies. The offices were once compared by L. E. Sissman, in *The New Yorker*, to the headquarters of a failing advertising agency. They are a jumble of small, raffishly decorated rooms containing twenty-two even more raffishly decorated associate producers, writers, talent co-ordinators, researchers, and secretaries.

There John Gilroy handles the calls and staff meetings, and, above all, presides over a huge bulletin board on one wall of his office. The board, divided into calendarlike columns and squares, is speckled with three-by-five cards bearing the names of guests for upcoming shows—scheduled, under consideration, and in reserve—along with their salient professional and conversational traits. The whole operation of course revolves around the booking, interviewing, and care and feeding of these guests.

*2:35 p.m.* Time to get ready to go to the studio. Dick stuffs papers into manila envelopes, snatches up books and then sets some aside, ransacks drawers, pats his pockets, runs up and down the stairs, and opens and shuts closet doors, all the while mumbling and swearing to himself. He gets to the door once, remembers a forgotten item upstairs, dashes up to retrieve it, then, back at the door again, stops and gazes with seeming bemusement into the dining room, where Serena is sitting complacently atop her cage, instead of inside it. "What's wrong with this picture?" he asks in a lecturer's tone.

*2:45 p.m.* On the street, after putting on sunglasses, tugging the brim of his cap down, and going into an uncharacteristic slouch, Dick flags a taxi. He used to ride a limousine to the studio, but began feeling uncomfortable about it, especially whenever the drivers were what he calls "dancers in attendance"—obsequious or fussily attentive liege men. (He still rides a limo home from the studio, however.)

In the taxi, he carefully asks for a street corner near the theater, rather than the theater itself, and even alters his voice slightly. He knows from tedious experience that, if recognized, he will be subjected to one of three conversational gambits by the driver: (1) reminiscences of other notable fares ("Y'know, one time I had Durward Kirby in this cab too"); (2) presentation of the driver's own show-business credentials ("My wife, before she was my wife, used to work for Dale Evans"); or (3) rebuttal to a gag about cab drivers used by a guest on the show ("Next time you see that Joan Rivers, you can tell her from me . . .").

As the taxi winds through Central Park Dick gazes through the window at people sunning themselves on benches, strolling aimlessly, lying in the grass. "I envy all those people. What are they doing right, that they can lie out in the sun while I have to go to work and worry about ratings, contend with the network, and do a show?" He sighs. "To think I used to be one of them, when I was a comedy writer and before. I used to think nobody should have to work on a day like this, even if they needed the money and faced dire consequences if they didn't work, as was the case with me. Of course those people probably have worries that I no longer have—like paying the rent. That's my rationalization, anyway. That the guy who looks so content under the tree over there is actually contemplating suicide. Or is already dead."

He frowns at the envelopes piled on his lap, then pulls a sheet of paper from one of them. It is a typed memo from his lawyer, with the words "Read this" written in ink across the top. "What else am I going to do with it?" he murmurs. A few weeks ago, one of his guests committed a howler about United States citizenship laws, drawing several dozen letters to ABC. The memo is a draft of a correction and apology for Dick to read on the air. "If I do this, plus my bit on the mountain lions, then when am I going to do the program itself? I guess we'll have to scratch the mountain lions. Which sounds dangerous." He slides the memo back into the envelope.

"At about this point I usually begin wondering whether I've done enough preparation—or too much. And I begin thinking of all the mood changes I've got to go through tonight. I've got to get up for the monologue, get earnest for the citizenship correction, frivol—is that a word?—with T——, then be sober and responsible with R——, all the while making sure that K—— gets his due . . . Jesus! The show is overbooked! How did this happen? I probably won't get to K—— until the last half hour, when the show is practically over. It really is. Once that clock gets past twelve-thirty [during the taping, the studio clocks run from 11:30 to 1:00, for easier reference to the actual times when most viewers will be seeing the show], it just seems to go faster than in other half hours. I swear I can see not only the minute hand but also the hour hand racing along. It's something to do with where the commercials fall, or the psychology of the end approaching. Shit-oh-dear."

*3:05 p.m.* The taxi pulls up at the appointed corner. Dick

adds a big tip to the fare (maybe he was recognized, after all) and makes his quasi-incognito way to the stage entrance. After he slips inside and begins striding up a kind of stone runway that leads backstage, the guard has trouble latching the door behind him. Without stopping, Dick calls out, with a borscht-belt comedian's inflection, "Either get it fixed or get a welcome mat," then adds to himself, rather glumly, "Funny."

The theater, still only semilit, is deserted except for a couple of Dick's staffers and a few stagehands, the latter lounging in lordly fashion in the chairs designed for Dick and his guests. The stagehands are having a different kind of conversation from the one that is soon to be broadcast from this set. "So we took a taxi back to my place," one of them is saying, "and she spent the night there."

"Did you do anything?" asks one of the others.

"What do you want, a film of it?"

With merely a cursory glance around, and a few abstracted "hi"s and nods, Dick bounds up a white-brick stair well to his dressing room. He is going into phase two of his preshow nerves. In phase one he had a vaguely preoccupied air. Now he has a definitely preoccupied air.

His dressing room is on the first landing of the stairs. On the mustard-colored door, no glittering star à la backstage movie musicals, just a small black and white plastic sign saying PRIVATE. Inside, a tiny room that looks more like a combination sitting room and office—paneled walls, thick gold carpeting, TV set, typewriter perched on a coffee table in front of a sofa, a clutter of books and papers. Another door opens into a narrow dressing alcove leading to a bathroom.

3:15 p.m. A girl from Dick's staff comes to the door with a green mimeographed sheet called a rundown. This is a sort of agenda of tonight's show, divided into three half-hour segments and itemizing each of the guest appearances, commercials, station breaks, and so on. It graphically illustrates why a talk show is in some ways not a favorable climate for good talk. In all, there are seventeen interruptions for commercials, not counting station breaks. The longest continuous period of conversation is about ten minutes; the shortest, about two.

"Oh, damn," Dick says, scanning the sheet. "They've got everybody in two segments, which isn't what I said at all. Look where K——— comes on. That's too late for him. We're trying to do too much on this show." Then, a traitor to his own calling: "Why, why didn't we just dump the comic?"

He calls Doris with instructions for revising the rundown.

*3:20 p.m.* Sitting on the sofa, Dick becomes aware of a cool draft blowing through a gap between the bottom of the door and the carpet. For a latent hypochondriac like him, as fastidious about his throat as an operatic tenor, a draft is more than an affront; it is a danger. He fetches a towel from the bathroom and wedges it under the door. "There. Now I'll just get my coat and muffler, and we'll get on with this."

He stomps back to the sofa as if through deep snow, hugging his arms and huffing exaggeratedly. Now for more work on the notes. He gets them in two versions, regular and abbreviated. Having digested the regular ones, he attacks the abbreviated ones with a pen, further abbreviating them. This process, he says, "helps get the material into my head."

From his earliest days on TV, when he bolstered himself with stacks of material and as many prepared questions as he could devise, he has made a steady effort to streamline his research, to pare it down, at least by air time, to a few key points and questions. "I hate to go out there with twenty, thirty questions," he says. "It makes my mind stop functioning. I think, 'I've got all these to get through. Why bother with what *I'm* interested in?' Sometimes the hardest thing is to think of the simple, obvious question that any intelligent person would have if he met the guest. That's why I try to say to myself, 'Never mind the research. What do I *really* want to know about so-and-so?'"

As an exercise, he begins typing a summary of what he

already knows or wants to know about tonight's guests, further compressing his by now superabbreviated notes. He uses any form that comes to mind—letter, essay, memo. His typing is very rapid and very inaccurate, and is accompanied by a running commentary: "What a mess . . . goddam thing . . . oh, frap . . ."

He stops and reads aloud from the notes in a David Brinkley voice: "From *night* clubs, you went into the *the*ater. But while *you* were ready for the *the*ater, the *the*ater was not *ready* for *you*." His voice modulates upward into his nose; he purses his lips more, and without any pause or transition he is doing Don Adams: "Then you killed the king. Then you told Nora . . ."

He breaks off and leans back in the sofa. "What's bad is when you get into the mood for a show two hours too early. You peak, and then you inevitably start declining. When Godfrey was taping his old radio show, he used to warm up with the musicians and just start whenever the mood was right, but never until it was right. Sometimes he kept people waiting for hours."

A long stare at the ceiling. "I'm going into a slump. Do I take a drink or not? Or maybe a nap? Strange as it seems, I could easily take a nap right before a show, and sometimes during."

*3:55 p.m.* The girl from his staff returns with the new rundown, this time on a pink sheet. He opens the door a crack and asks her to pass it through. "I'd invite you in, but there's a towel stuck under the door." Her expression indicates that she doesn't understand, but that she's used to this sort of thing from him.

Dick nods as he reads the new rundown, which limits most of the guests to less time. "Now the guests will get pissed off because they've seen on the first rundown how much time they would've had without this change. Their managers will go grousing around about what we're trying to do to their boys."

*4:00 p.m.* A buzz from the intercom on the wall, which connects with the console backstage, where the stage manager stands.

"Yes?"

"Commercial time, Dick."

"Oh . . . [silently mouths a string of obscenities] . . . all right." He goes downstairs to rehearse a dog-food commercial.

From its earlier atmosphere of a late-night bus depot, the theater has erupted into what looks like a lively street fair. The lights are up. Dozens of people are milling around, onstage as well as backstage. The band has arrived and is rehearsing a bristling, pulsating rhythm number for one of tonight's station breaks. In time with the music, two stagehands are doing a shambling buck and wing across the set. Ex-chorus boys, from their swagger. On monitors overhead commercials are being run off silently. A voice booms from an unseen loud-speaker, "Strike chips, please. Could we have the color girl?"

Dick takes his place behind a waist-high counter on which a bloodbound is brooding. "Its name," says somebody nearby, "is the Hermitage Absalom. Why couldn't they call it Sam or something?"

As a camera dollies into position Dick tonelessly reads his spiel from the TelePrompter. Standing next to him, the girl from the agency that provided the dog harangues him about some horse farm that seems shady in more ways than one: ". . . so they take partly broken horses out back, abuse the hell out of them, then bring them in and sell them as well-broken horses . . ." Dick, looking a little glassy-eyed, is obviously restless to get back upstairs.

*4:10 p.m.* From his dressing room, Dick calls Doris and asks her to order him a turkey sandwich and a chocolate milk shake. The star syndrome at work: it doesn't seem to occur to him that in the time it takes to call Doris he could call the restaurant directly.

*4:12 p.m.* A stocky, smiling man with wavy gray hair looks

in. Michael Scrittorale, Dick's dresser. He wants to consult about which of the three hundred outfits in the wardrobe Dick will wear tonight. Part of Michael's art lies in discovering in advance what color scheme will be formed by the guests' clothes, then dressing Dick in contrasting colors, so that he will stand out. Dark blues and browns will dominate tonight, Michael announces; *ergo*, light gray for Dick.

*4:20 p.m.* Dick's writer, Dave Lloyd, pokes his head in. His face is thinner, almost younger looking than it was at Yale, but the top of his head is now almost completely bald, leaving a monklike fringe on the sides and back. "What do you want to do up front?" he asks Dick. "Some monologue? Some blue cards?" Blue cards are those circulated in the theater, before the show, on which the audience can address questions to Dick. When he reads a sampling of them on the air his answers are almost as spontaneous as they seem; but Lloyd usually writes some gags and phrases for him to fall back on.

Today Dick wants to do a monologue, but he wants to keep it short enough to allow for his citizenship correction. As standard procedure, Lloyd has already drafted a sheaf of suggested jokes, which he now hands over. "Hey," he says, "did you see the typo in the New York *Times* clipping about your citation from Yeshiva University—given to people for their contributions to the farts, the sciences, and public affairs? I guess we know where that leaves you."

"No. Why was this kept from me?"

"It was in last week's mail report."

"Oh." Another bit of paper work neglected.

*4:25 p.m.* Dick's food arrives. While munching and sipping, he reads through Lloyd's jokes, picks out the ones he likes, rewrites some, adds one or two of his own. Then he reduces each to a few choppy phrases, which will be transcribed on large cardboard cue cards and held up for him to see while delivering his monologue. He feels that reading word for word from cue cards throws off the rhythm of his delivery, so the phrases he selects with which to prompt himself are the merest highlights of the joke, cryptic in themselves. For example, for one cue card all he has written is:

Good news/Bad/Balcony . . .
Good is . . . flames reach.

The joke as he will deliver it on the air goes like this:

I have some good news and some bad news for the balcony. I'm not going to tell you the bad news, but here's the good news. It will take several minutes for the flames to reach you.

Dick has asked himself for years why he should start his show with a monologue. While he has never found a satisfactory answer, he has never found a better way to start the show either. "I realize that everybody does it because Jack Paar did one," he says. "It's a convention that I'm sort of stuck with. At the same time, I think it's important in some way that I'm not sure of, because when it works it gets the show off to a good start. The looks on the faces of the audience are gratifying, as if I were doing something right. But it's a terrible pain in the ass to have to come up with it every day."

*4:55 p.m.* A quick shave.

*5:00 p.m.* John Gilroy, the producer, stops by. The only man in the theater wearing a suit and tie. Thin-lipped, gray-haired, rather handsome, but severe looking—perhaps because of the imminence of air time. "I saw the new rundown. How do you feel about it now?"

"I still think we've got too much," Dick says. "I guess we better let some of these people know they're only going to get so much time." Gilroy nods. "Also, could we have somebody fix this door someday when we're off? There's a gale-force wind coming in underneath it. It blows papers off the coffee table and makes it impossible to work in here." Gilroy gives him a look. "*You* know."

"Okay, Dick." Gilroy too is used to this sort of thing.

*5:05 p.m.* Dick returns yet again to the notes, crossing things out and scrawling over them, inserting lines, drawing boxes and arrows. The notes are beginning to look like a menu from the old Lindy's.

*5:25 p.m.* A talent co-ordinator comes in to reassure Dick about the preparation on R——. "Everything is all set. He's going to be fine. He just has one request. When he comes out, he'd like to be seated to your left."

Dick narrows his eyes suspiciously. "I hope that's merely vanity about his left profile and not bad hearing in his left ear."

"No, he's fine, really. He's marvelous. I want to hug him."

"You have my permission. Jesus!"

"What?"

"Sorry. I just remembered the goddam citizenship thing I've got to read tonight."

As the talent co-ordinator withdraws Dick paws furiously through papers and other paraphernalia until he finds the envelope containing his lawyer's memo. Pen in hand, he begins hastily editing the memo from legalese into colloquial English.

*5:30 p.m.* A knock at the door. Dick, still editing, shouts, "Who is it?"

"Make-up."

"How do you expect me to do a show if you people keep interrupting me?" He admits a willowy black girl, who goes straight into the dressing alcove. Her name—"and her function," Dick sometimes adds, with a Grouchoesque eyebrow waggle—is Toy.

In a T-shirt, seated at his dressing table, Dick squints and grimaces at himself in the mirror. "I'm all right . . . I'm all right . . ."

As Toy dabs on make-up, a man enters the dressing room without knocking, says "Cue cards," snatches up Dick's coded jokes, and exits.

"Were you through with those?" Toy asks.

"No, but I'm afraid of that guy."

5:35 *p.m.* Toy gathers up her kit and leaves, saying over her shoulder, "Good show."

"Zengyou." Even with his make-up, Dick is looking somehow pale. The skin on his forehead and cheekbones is stretched tight, almost translucent. He begins to pace the room and talk to himself. Phase three.

"Tension is the enemy. It's the most undesirable thing you can have. It contributes nothing. Energy is all right. I'm not pissing on energy, as Ruth Gordon would say. She once said to Carrie Nye, 'Don't piss on Lady Macbeth.' And Carrie Nye didn't."

He launches into a song called "The Girl in My Dreams," from the 1957 Yale undergraduate musical, *The Great Gatsby.* Characteristically, he remembers every line of it.

A pause to slip on the shirt and suit Michael has laid out. Then, pacing again, he shifts his gait into the springy saunter of Bob Hope. "Hi, this is Bob Join-the-Peace-Corps Hope! Hey, how about those short skirts?"

5:45 *p.m.* The intercom buzzes. "Yeah?"

"Fifteen."

"Where does my day go?"

Michael comes in to finish dressing him. Dick sits at his dressing table while Michael rubs his shoulders and neck. He does a couple of voice exercises, sounding like a little boy imitating a dive bomber.

"Do your breathing," Michael says.

"God, I just hyperventilated."

A man hurries in and pins a tiny microphone to Dick's tie. Dick gives no indication of even noticing him, but recites in a singsong voice, as if admonishing a child, "There's no reason to be tense. How many times have I done this? Certainly more than . . . six. The folks at home aren't tense. They'll wonder why *you* are. . . ."

"Drop your head," Michael says, massaging. "Inhale real good, through your nose, up in your nasal passages."

"I just realized—I have to go on *television* in a minute.

I think I also have to pee for the third time in a half hour. Do you think they'd understand if I took a catheter onstage?"

5:50 *p.m.* Another buzz. "Ten."

Michael combs Dick's hair.

"I don't want that Julie Andrews look over the ears."

Michael recombs.

"Oh, balls. I've got dry mouth." To Michael, in a Mayfair accent: "Could you put a lemon on the set for me, there's a dear." Michael dashes out.

Dick bolts for the bathroom.

5:55 *p.m.* The buzzer. "Five."

Sound of Dick brushing his teeth and gargling in the bathroom.

Doris comes in. A tallish blonde, in sweater and slacks, she manages to combine the three potentially conflicting qualities of efficiency, wholesomeness, and attractiveness.

"Need anything?" Doris calls.

"Mnnnn. Ghaaaaaaaaaaaaa."

She begins to tidy up the dressing room, throwing away Dick's unfinished sandwich and milk shake, gathering up the scattered fragments of his notes. In accordance with union regulations, she will hand the notes to a stagehand, who will then put them on the table next to Dick's chair onstage.

Dick catapults out of the bathroom, motioning toward the litter surrounding the sofa. "Doris, there are little scraps that go with things, like and all. Wait. I tore off a little chunk I wanted to attach to that—not this; why did you force this into my hand?"

Doris, absently, without looking up from her search: "Testy, testy."

Michael dashes back in. "They went out to buy your lemon."

5:58 *p.m.* Downstairs to say a quick hello to the guests before going on. On most days, Dick has no time for any more than a quick hello. Occasionally, too, he may deliberately avoid chatting beforehand, in order to capitalize on whatever spontaneous reaction he and the guest have to each other when they meet before the cameras. From the stage comes the voice of band leader Bob Rosengarden doing the audience warm-up: ". . . and when Dick comes out, please, let's have waves of love coming up from the audience . . ."

At the word "love" Dick freezes on the bottom step with a stricken look on his face. "Doris! Can we get a five-minute delay? I've got to pee again. I *really* do."

Doris looks at the stage manager. The stage manager says, "*Three* minutes." Dick turns and disappears.

*6:01 p.m.* Back downstairs, he ducks into the green room, which isn't green and isn't really a room. It is a windowless wooden shed constructed slightly behind the set, painted black on the outside and furnished on the inside with paneling, leather-and-chrome furniture, and scores of color photos of celebrities who have appeared on the show. Here the guests, along with visitors and members of Dick's staff, watch the show on a monitor while awaiting their time. There is a similar, smaller room in the basement for sponsors, where Sidney Tamber watches and takes notes. Tamber is a program editor for ABC's department of broadcast standards and practices: in other words, a censor.

Greeting the guests, Dick is so taut he almost vibrates. (The theme music strikes up.) His smile is little more than a baring of teeth. His features seem stretched downward, as if his whole frame were straining to burst through the top of his skull. He manages some small talk nonetheless: "How are you? . . . Nice to meet you, now that I know all about you . . . Hi, B——, how's it going? . . . Sorry about the time squeeze tonight. [Announcer Fred Foy booms out the opening credits.] . . . Somehow we've got enough for three shows . . ."

Then out to stand, alone, for a moment behind the flat. Head down, jaw muscles working, hands unconsciously tugging at the tail of his jacket.

*6:03 p.m.* A fanfare. "Ladies and gentlemen . . . *DICK CAVETT!*"

A wait of two or three seconds. Then, straightening and brightening, "Hey, that's me!" And on.

*7:38 p.m.* It's over. Dick has got up for the monologue and been earnest for the citizenship correction. He has frivoled with T——, been sober and responsible with R—— (after seating him on his left), brought on the comic, and given K—— his due.

There were some good moments and some flat ones, several laughs and a few fumbles. Dick tellingly made use of his research on some occasions; on other occasions, he trusted to wayward, fitfully crackling spontaneity. It was neither his best show nor his worst. It was a show.

The guests are clustered at the back of the set saying their good-byes, exchanging invitations, following up abandoned lines of argument from the show. Dick joins them briefly. As he relaxes his professional, on-camera cool he becomes agitated again. His conversation is desultory, half-finished. His gaze jumps around the group restlessly, never quite focusing. He isn't down yet.

John Gilroy comes up behind him and whispers a few words about tomorrow's show. Dick moves off from the guests, waves, starts upstairs.

*7:45 p.m.* In his dressing room, he exhales explosively. "God, I feel like I've just ridden four horses simultaneously in four different directions. This job can't be good for you."

Doris follows him in. As he settles at his dressing table to remove his make-up she leans against the wall and opens a stenographer's notebook. A few final details. "Sidney [the censor] is looking at that part with K——," she says.

"Of course. I expected that. Call me if there's a problem."

"Remember I told you about S——, the lawyer for W——?"

"Yeah. Tell him I can't do it. Hope he understands, et cetera."

"And a journalist called from —— Magazine. He said they

were doing a question column on famous people and wanted to include you. The question is, 'Who are you tired of hearing about, and why?' "

"Leslie Fahrquahr. The reason? I forget." Doris carefully sets this down for transmission to the journalist.

As she leaves an ABC page comes through the door with an armload of autograph books sent up by members of the audience for Dick to sign.

*7:55 p.m.* Back in his scruffy clothes now, heading down the runway toward the stage door, Dick quickens his pace, hunching his shoulders like a halfback about to hit the line. The guard swings the door open. Applause. Squeals. Shouts of "There he is!" A small crowd of thirty or forty people, mostly female, presses in on him. He nods, smiles, but above all keeps moving toward the limo waiting at the curb a few feet away.

A tangle of arms and hands reaches out to touch, pat, clutch him; some of the hands proffer gifts. From behind a candy-bar-shaped object wrapped in tissue, a voice says, "Want to take this from the jelly-bean kid?"

"Is it ticking?" he asks. Without quite accepting anything, he seems to accrete packages and slips of paper while furrowing through the crowd.

Finally he reaches the car and dives into the back seat. As he rolls the window up a girl thrusts a postcard inside, almost getting her fingers mashed. Hands wave; fingernails drum on the window. A face swims into view and shouts faintly, "You look cute without your clothes on." Dick smiles wanly. The car pulls away.

Dick slumps down in the seat, looking at once drained and tense, like someone trying to master pain. He loves applause, attention, recognition as much as any performer; but not this kind. "Once," he says, "I came out that door, and a girl dropped to the sidewalk when she saw me. At first I thought she'd fainted, but actually she'd had an epileptic seizure. A friend was with her who knew how to give her first aid, but somehow I felt obligated to stay there until help arrived. All the so-called excitement of my appearance drained away. The whole artificial relationship of fan and star evaporated, and all of us, me and my public, were just a bunch of people standing around, awkwardly making conversation. It was strange."

He sorts through some of the flotsam from his progress through the crowd. The candy-bar-shaped object in tissue paper turns out to be a candy bar. The postcard from the girl who almost got her fingers mashed is a handwritten request to make a short speech for a charity. There is a box containing a tie with hand-stitched caricatures of Laurel and Hardy on it. Enclosed is a note: "We like you a lot and we know you like Stan and Ollie so we made this for you. Hope you'll wear it."

Dick tosses the tie aside wearily. "If they understood *anything* about me, just from watching the show, they'd know that I'd never wear something like that. Sweet, though."

No matter; home soon. He has nothing ahead of him this evening—no meetings, no socializing—just dinner with Carrie Nye, maybe a look at the show, some reading and puttering, then bed.

As his car rolls north through Central Park a taxi overtakes it and careens ahead. In the taxi's window a flash of grinning faces and waving arms. Dick's driver says, "There they are, Mr. Cavett."

Dick claps his hand over his eyes and groans. He hasn't completely run the gantlet yet. In the taxi are his most devoted, not to say fanatical, admirers—two young girls who send him gifts, haunt his haunts, wear Oliver caps because he has been photographed wearing them, and (so their letters inform him) even own a black poodle like his. Lately, after watching him leave the studio, they have taken to tipping a taxi driver to beat Dick's limousine uptown, so they can watch him enter his apartment too. These tributes only embarrass and depress him.

"My God, isn't that dumb," he says, watching their taxi gun out of sight around the next curve. "Look at that. Don't they have anything to do?" He goes into a plummy Queen Victoria accent: "We are not amused."

A snort of appreciation for his own line. As if reminded of something, he rummages around in his gear and pulls out a paperback biography of Oscar Wilde. He switches on the overhead light. Then, shutting out the girls, the day, the TV show and all its works, he resolutely begins to read.

*In early evening, a limousine pulls up near a corner on the upper East Side of Manhattan. Out steps a slim, smallish, rather tousled-looking man wearing corduroys and a pull-over and clutching an untidy bundle of papers and books. He has no need for sunglasses at this hour, but an army-surplus jungle fatigue hat is tugged over his eyes. Head down, he walks quickly across the sidewalk toward a onetime brownstone now converted into an apartment building.*

*Two young girls in Oliver caps hover a few yards from the entrance, while dog walkers, strollers, late-returning businessmen pass by. The man says nothing to the girls, barely glances sideways, but still they begin fidgeting and giggling. Others too have penetrated his disguise, for it is a disguise of sorts, and just before he darts through the door, to be re-enveloped by privacy, one last voice calls out from the corner, "Dick Cavett!"*

CP: What have you learned from your years on television?

DC: That quality does not necessarily insure longevity, and, perhaps more surprising, that it does not necessarily insure failure.

CP: Anything else?

DC: That everything would have been better and easier if I had developed an over-all philosophy of hanging looser sooner. I had an unfortunate combination of high standards and poor organization that created more anxiety and problems than were necessary.

CP: Why do you put that in the past tense?

DC: I know, you've just finished describing some of my current anxieties and problems. But, believe me, it was worse in the beginning. As I mentioned earlier, there was a period of my morning show, which I've almost completely repressed, that was nightmarish. I felt constantly rushed and behind, the clock was my mortal enemy, and if the weekend ever came I dreaded its ending so much that I couldn't relax—and then the whole thing started all over again. I had a kind of psychological ringing in my ears. For the first week or two, so much was going on in my head that I couldn't hear what the guests were saying. I simply couldn't put their words together. It was close to what I imagine aphasia is like.

CP: Was there some particular low point?

DC: Well, one of the most traumatic experiences of my television career took place at the very beginning of the morning show. Woody Fraser, then my producer, had wisely arranged things so that I could tape two shows before D-day (debut day). Thus if one was noticeably superior we could use it first.

Somehow the taping of the first show was gotten through. It had Gore Vidal, Muhammad Ali, and Angela Lansbury. Miraculously, working in a lousy, dirty theater, with equipment that seemed to have been salvaged from a sunken Japanese destroyer, and with all the angst and the novelty telegrams of a first show, we got through it. There were even laughs and spontaneous applause, and it ended on time. "Opening night" was over, in the can, and would never come again. I dimly remember a few people complimenting me, a lot of handshaking, and total amnesia as to what had taken place on the show.

Then an ABC executive appeared and summoned me and my producer and manager to an upstairs office, for what I assumed would be a compliment. Instead, he gave us the news that the show stank. I felt as though I had been electrocuted. I sat limp in an armchair and listened to a string of complaints about how this was "not the show we bought, bargained for, or wanted." The only complete quote I can remember is, "Nobody in the world wants to hear what Gore Vidal or Muhammad Ali thinks about the Vietnam war." Other approximate quotes would include the words "slow," "tedious," "dull," and "painful." I was told that I had made Angela Lansbury look boring and that the other guests were stiffs who shouldn't have been there anyway. I was told that the show had none of the pace, variety, and sparkle of Carson's show. Where were the fun people? The comics? The wit?

Humiliation began to set in as the network voice droned on. It all flashed before my eyes. My career, which had seemed so promising and had led so logically to network TV, was a disaster. I had failed everybody. I cringed at the condolences of friends and the jubilation of enemies that would come when I was replaced. Mentally, I was already out on my ass, and I just wanted to get out of that room and go lie down in a hole somewhere. Fraser nobly took the lion's share of the blame as I sat there mute, looking at the graven faces of my agent and manager. We all filed outside, having vowed to try to shape up, but knowing that we had just blown the chance of a lifetime.

The exec went home, and Fraser asked if anybody wanted to see the tape. It sounded like a lousy idea, and I was too tired to sit upright. But we all got a bite of unwanted food and went up to ABC to watch the awful thing, if only to depress ourselves further, so that from then on there would be nowhere to go psychologically but up.

We flopped into chairs in the viewing room, and the tape started. Surprisingly, it really looked like a TV show. The music sounded good, the set looked all right, and I got laughs in the small monologue. To make a long story less tedious than necessary, as it rolled we began to sit up and realize it was not lousy at all. Lansbury was charming, the talk was interesting, and I didn't look like the zombie I had felt like at all. It was as if it had been redone. We called the network biggie in Scarsdale and told him that frankly we thought it was good. He repeated that it was not airable, implied we were nuts, and said we should see whether we could do better in the second taping. He agreed reluctantly to take a look at the tape the following morning.

The next day's taping was a corker. Buoyed by the upness of it, and by my relief that the tape of the first show had proved it was not a disaster, I came offstage cheerful and looking forward to a career in television. Glad hands and cheerful faces greeted me. I had fewer enemies than Norman Vincent Peale. I could now have a badly needed day off. We were summoned by the executive again. I had forgiven him his aberration of the day before, and was ready to be complimented and to accept his explanation of how he had just been so wrought up he had completely misjudged the first show and how we now had two good ones in the can and all was hunky-dory. Or at least hunky.

"That was much better," he said, with more reserve than I would have liked, "but that first show is still a loser, and we're going to tape another one tomorrow and decide which one to open with." I looked around at my representatives, clad in a variety of sickly smiles, and had a pump of adrenalin that would have blown my hat off, had I had one.

I opened with *"BULLSHIT!"* I took a deep breath, my heart pounding, and explained, in as reasonable a tone as one can in a quiet rage, that I was not going to function this way, that I was not going to work from day to day on somebody's opinion of whether the show was acceptable or not, particularly someone who had been wrong so dramatically the day before, that they could tape a show the next day if they wanted to, but I was not going to be in it, and if they *were* going to panic each day, and deliver the verdict after each show, they could get themselves another boy, and if they knew so little about performers that they could come back on opening night and reduce their star to a quivering shambles, which simple intelligence should tell them was a bad *practical* move (regardless of whether they *liked* him or not), since he had more shows to do, then *they* ought to get out of the business. I think I said all that in one breath. When the network biggie opened his mouth to object I did an incredible thing. I said, "I only want to hear one thing from you, and that is—when are you going to stop being *chickenshit?*"

I don't find *that* incredible, the chickenshit part. In fact, in retrospect it sounds unduly reasonable. But when I said it— I blush to confess this—I stamped my foot.

CP: You're embellishing now.

DC: I did. I stamped my little foot, the way they do only in comic strips and amateur acting classes. This stunned me so that I turned on my heel (almost as corny) and left the tableau of pale faces, and went to my dressing room and slammed the door (a third cliché, but not in the same category with foot stamping for sheer corn). Then I put my head in my hands and began to laugh.

To wind this up, I did *not* tape the following day, they put the shows on in reverse order—with the one they had called hopeless second—and nobody bombed the network. A few reviewers even said that the second show showed real promise, as a departure from the routine talk-show style, and should have been first. What is the moral?

CP: That's a question for the network biggie. How did this incident affect your subsequent relationship with him?

DC: He never hauled me into court to prove that he wasn't chickenshit, and when, later on, I gave him a tour of Hugh Hefner's house one night, neither of us tried to push the other into the pool fully dressed, although I noticed that neither of us let the other get behind him.

Our careers have advanced simultaneously for so long that I wouldn't know what to do without him. He is now an ABC vice-president. I've decided we were made for each other. I do think a sort of bond is formed with someone you have blasted or who has blasted you. It's much healthier than the usual conniving, secret, smiling villainy that runs in the blood stream of our business.

CP: Besides those criticisms of your first effort, did you get any advice from ABC during the early days of your show?

DC: Constant and bewildering. The network's wisdom was generally summed up in the phrase "Get big names." The fact that the shows I did without big names sometimes got not only the most press and praise but also the highest ratings was brushed aside in favor of conventional wisdom. One season ABC got big names to star in various prime-time series—five of the biggest movie names—and they all bombed out in a matter of weeks. I suspect, however, that there is still a sampler on the wall of the network offices that says, "Get big names." Except that now it probably says, "Get them cheaper."

CP: What about individual stations affiliated with the network?

DC: They had their say from time to time, and it ranged all over the map, depending on the caliber of the station and its manager, which reaches from the highest (exemplified by Martin Umansky in Wichita) to the lowest (some yahoo from Texas, whose suggestion at an affiliate meeting was that the show needed a dumb-blonde side-kick and a band leader who dressed funny).

CP: In any case, you feel you're hanging looser nowadays?

DC: Relatively. Taping a show is still like being an actor in a repertory company where in one day—in one performance— you do scenes from a drama, a farce, a low comedy, and a tragedy. It's a satisfaction in one way, in that you get to use all the arrows in your quiver, or strings in your bow, or bats in your belfry. But it's also very wearing. Your transmission begins to wear out from all that shifting.

When I was on every week, and a week of shows was starting, I'd think, "Oh, my God, I'm going on for four hundred and fifty minutes, during which I may make the worst blunder anyone has ever made publicly—let alone worrying about how I'm going to get through four hundred and fifty minutes." I would be almost paralyzed by the thought of the show going on and on. It's like that Rilke story we were so struck by at Yale, in which the character begins to sense the passage of time as a wind blowing past his cheek and ends up paralyzed by it. The corresponding image, I guess, would be a flock of talk-show guests flying over me like birds.

The terror usually hit me hardest about two hours before air time, when I realized I was all knotted up about the day's show and had to get my mind off it. So I'd think about the next day's show, and that made it worse. Then it hit me that there was an endless-seeming procession of such shows, reaching God knows how far into the future, and each one presented new problems and anxieties, and, oh Christ, how did I get into this? This agonizing thought also contains its own heartsease, though, because if you hold a thought like that long enough in your mind it eventually shatters into absurdity. You realize there is so much to worry about that there is no reason to worry about anything—that you are trying to put up an umbrella against an avalanche, and you might as well let it come down on you and, like the old maid being violated, try to enjoy it. As of now, I guess I've progressed to the attitude "Suppose the worst does happen? At least then the worst will be over with."

CP: In the preceding chapter I quoted you—accurately, I trust—as saying you could take a nap right before air time. That doesn't seem to jibe with what you're saying about the tension and pressure you still feel.

DC: Paradoxically, I can take a nap just before doing something I'm extremely nervous about. Back in the days when my show wracked my nerves more than it ever has since, or ever could again, I was able to nap until fifteen minutes before going on. It's not so much that I could as that I almost had to. There are times when I need a nap the way a drunk needs a drink. I can panic over the thought of not getting one. I have leaped into cabs, raced to my apartment, and run around like a silent-film figure getting things done, all so I could squeeze in fifteen minutes of sleep.

And if I can't get to my apartment I find some other place. I once took a nap under a piano in Buffalo. I was meeting my parents in Buffalo for a cruise they were taking of the Great Lakes. I got there an hour early, and the hunger for sleep came down on me. I remembered from my magician days that hotel ballrooms were always empty during the day, so I found one. It was dark and cool and quiet. The stage curtains were drawn, and behind the curtains was a baby grand, which I crawled under. During the nap, a janitor or someone came within ten feet of me, and I had the appalling problem of whether to say hello and scare the hell out of him, or to risk letting him find me and then having to explain what I was doing under a piano.

CP: Of course, if you'd told him just what you've said here he would've understood perfectly.

DC: Of course. In any case, he moved on. Maybe he was looking for a place to take a nap too.

CP: Another thing you mentioned in the preceding section is your effort over the years to cut down your reliance on staff research and preparation for the show. That would seem to indicate that you've grown more relaxed and confident, wouldn't it?

DC:

CP: Dick? Hello?

DC: Oh, sorry. I must have dozed off there for a minute. You were saying?

CP: About your tendency to rely less on preparation.

DC: Yes. Too much preparation can inhibit the flow of a show. But I think my desire to reduce my dependence on it also has to do with a universal actor's nightmare. I keep imagining that someday my staff and all the paraphernalia of research and reference will collapse, and I'll have to go on with no preparation, knowing only the names of the guests, and wing it.

CP: That sort of appeals to you too, doesn't it? The idea of winging it—as a feat?

DC: I've done it a couple of times, and should have more often. The fact is, it's the essence of a talk show. You live by your wits and instincts from night to night. A live interview, I've decided, needs a little preparation, but a lot of guesswork and luck. It's amazing the things you get credit for. You ask one right question, and both the subject and the audience assume you really know what you're talking about. Many times, if a segment of a program had gone on one second longer I would have stepped over into the abyss of ignorance that I had been tiptoeing around for three minutes.

Then again, too much spontaneity can be as unnatural as too much preparation. Doing the show—the concentration, the synthetic curiosity when I often feel the opposite of curious— corresponds to something that occurs in real life about once every two weeks, but I have to do it, sometimes, day after day. I hear myself saying, "This is a subject I'm really fascinated by— hieroglyphics," and I think, *"Hieroglyphics!"* I suppose I should learn to admit that I'm not interested in hieroglyphics but that I'm interested enough to conduct this interview.

CP: Doesn't the selection of guests have a lot to do with whether the show works?

DC: Yes, a lot. And no, not very much. There is a kind of chemistry about a show that comes as a surprise. Whenever you try to derive a rule from it, it fails the next time. I'm not saying that, instead of the Lunts and Noël Coward, I might have done a better show with the Lunts and Moms Mabley, but almost nothing is guaranteed, so you find yourself trying to proceed methodically in a world without laws.

On another hand, the fact that you bring interesting people together does not, in real life or in TV, necessarily mean an interesting time. If the interesting people are actors and actresses, it's terribly difficult to ask them original questions.

At times the sheer number of guests can be more important than anything else about them. Once I had Robert Young on the show, along with several others. He was nice and sort of amusing. Then, just about the time when I could have gotten into the subject of alcoholism—which he knows about at first hand, and on which he's quite eloquent—it was time to move on to the next guest. So you keep laying the groundwork for your second act and never getting to it.

It's easier with just one guest, and I wonder if it isn't a relief for the audience too. The show is so fragmented by the commercial interruptions anyway. We get a high percentage of calls and letters from people who appreciate seeing a single personality emerge more fully before their eyes. Orson Welles was a good example, especially since most of the viewers had no idea what he was like. They said, "Thank you for returning Orson Welles to his American audience. Give us more people like that." Of course they don't realize there aren't many more people like *that*. There's also something about having a single guest that digs deeper into me. After a certain point, I have to come up with a lot of things that are on *my* mind, instead of what I think I ought to ask. People are always saying they want to see more of me. When Welles turned the questions on me they loved it. You never know what they want from you.

CP: But, as you mentioned in connection with guests who are actors or actresses, even if you come up with good questions, things that are on your mind, they may not get you anywhere.

DC: You can't rely on questions. I don't know how David Frost could bring himself to ask those godawful, formula-interview, what's-your-most-embarrassing-experience questions night after night when he had a talk show. The interviewer's role should consist of more than that. I don't know where I got obsessed with the idea that interviewing was simply asking questions. It's so much nicer when it's more of a dialogue; it's so much easier when you have that break-through, and you get into something that resembles actual speech as it would be spoken away from the lights and the camera. Suddenly all the pressure that you usually feel falls away, and you realize that this is happening almost—sometimes exactly—as in real life.

When that happens, I feel that I'm in it as an equal, rather than as somebody who is standing aside.

CP: How much can you, the interviewer, do to try to make that happen?

DC: One thing you can do is avoid that fascination with extremes that I guess we owe to the old *Time* magazine: What's the largest elephant you ever rode? The longest movie you ever made? The whole country seems to have that. The high school interviewer, for instance: What's the biggest number of hours you ever spent preparing for a show? Nine. What's the difference whether I spend nine or three? But it *sounds* like history. There are people who feel the day isn't going well if they haven't some peak experience that sets a record: I've just been through *the most fan-tas-tic nap!* We're a country of record breakers. There are, of course, some Extreme Questions that can be interesting; for example, who's the worst person you ever worked with?

CP: Have you developed any rules for yourself on what makes for good talk on TV?

DC: Yes—not having any rules. Do you remember my answer to a magazine questionnaire asking for "the ten rules of being a good conversationalist"? I wrote back saying that I had not known there *were* any rules, much less that they were ten in number. Then, just in case the magazine didn't get the message, I included the following list:

1. Do not place yourself in such a way that your back is to the person with whom you are speaking.
2. Be within hearing distance of the other person.
3. Do not leave the room while the other person is speaking.
4. Have at least one language in common.
5. Do not attempt to conduct the conversation in an inappropriate place, such as the center of a busy highway.
6. Do not use the word "albeit" more than four times.

7. Make an effort to be wearing clothing during the conversation.

8. Do not address letters or repair a diathermy machine during the conversation.

9. Do not light firecrackers or attempt to fish during the conversation.

10. Do not take hold of a wart on the other person's face and go "beep-beep."

CP: All right, I withdraw the question. But what about the rules of being a bad conversationalist?

DC: Well, as far as TV talk shows are concerned, there are certain lines that should be banned forever. We could dispense with "Nice to have you here"; "It's good to *be* here." Or all congratulatory sentences that begin with "I'm not just saying this because you're here." Or anything that begins with "May I just say one thing to you?" Watch out for that one! Because it is always followed with a fulsome compliment triggering fulsome applause. I have seen whole talk shows where the host had never seen a movie to equal the movie of his movie-actor guest, a play to equal that written by his playwright guest, a song sung better than by his singer, nor enjoyed a book as much as the one by his lady author. It was a night of firsts for him, and records were broken all over the place. Until the following night. An investigation of television could be launched on the sole ground that as a public medium it is being used largely to congratulate people on their performances in other media.

CP: True, but I was also thinking of bad conversation in the sense of improper or indiscreet conversation—the things one shouldn't say on TV. Do those things exert a perverse attraction, like the urge to shout an obscenity in church?

DC: Always. I have a streak of irreverence in me that wide. One night Dame Judith Anderson graced our stage—distinguished actresses invariably *grace* your stage—and as the ovation faded she looked to me for seating instructions. I had an awful urge to say, "Just park it anywhere, Judy."

CP: I wish you had.

DC: So do I, and I probably always will. But you have to obey that inner voice that tells you when to do those things and when not to.

CP: What else has that inner voice told you not to do?

DC: A great many things, my son. One time there was a famous actress on the show who, I happened to know, had had two—count 'em—two astronauts in the sack.

CP: It wasn't Judith Anderson, I take it.

DC: My lips are sealed. This was before they were allowing the astronauts to get divorces, and we were led to believe that the least virtuous astronaut was at least an eagle scout. The actress and I chatted about relatively innocent things, and I suddenly wondered what would happen if I said, "So how are Captain X and Colonel Y in the kip? Would you compare and contrast them in the light of your total experience in that line?"

I never would do something like that, of course, particularly to the astronauts, who were the victims in so many ways of the image created for them. One thing I *do* wish I had done, though, was to ask the astronauts how the hell they go to the bathroom in space. At the time they were on my show, nobody had revealed that. There were weird rumors about giant diapers and worse.

CP: Why didn't you?

DC: I was about to, but Leonard Goldenson, the head of ABC, was sitting in the front row. I was afraid the three astros would shatter before my eyes and Goldenson would press a button dropping me into the pit of alligators ABC keeps under my chair for just such an emergency.

CP: How *do* astronauts go to the bathroom in space?

DC: I don't think NASA allows them to. Anyway, the real fun of making some sizzling revelation would be to do it to one of the truly giant moral hypocrites who for years have been shamelessly marketing their wholesomeness for praise and profit.

CP: Would you care to name some names?

DC: My inner voice says no, and I think my lawyer would agree.

CP: I thought perhaps it was Al Capp time again.

DC: Capp has brought me close to literal nausea a few times on other people's shows with his cast-iron so-called satire. Like when he said, "I didn't like the parts of *Easy Rider* that the rest of the audience did—but when those two kids got their heads blown off at the end [rictus resembling laugh], I loved that part." I swore I'd never have him on my show, but I eventually did. He complimented me profusely backstage on something I had done the night before, and followed Lloyd Bucher, the captain of the *Pueblo*, who was so moving and who said that humorists "like the man backstage, Al Capp," were part of what made life endurable during his captivity in North Korea. So I didn't have the heart to go for Capp's jugular that night, nor did he give me reason. And his work was, once upon a time, amusing.

CP: Another illusion shattered. I thought Capp was your abiding hatred.

DC: I don't hate him, I guess. I have hated him at moments, but I think he is more pathetic than anything. He is even capable of a certain charm. He wrote me a letter once about how I had given pain, unintentionally, to the heirs of John P. Marquand, and presumably to Capp, who as far as I know is not a member of the family, by grinning at a slighting remark Truman Capote made about Marquand on my show, without leaping to Marquand's defense. I was smiling at Capote's audacity, and did not leap to Marquand's defense because I had not read a work of Marquand and have no present plans to. Nonetheless, it was not a bad letter. I wrote an answer, but probably didn't mail it.

CP: Would the consequences really be all that dire if one night you let slip a—what did you call it?—a sizzling revelation?

DC: How can you ask that? Everybody knows it would probably set off a chain reaction that would shake the world. The immediate victim would retaliate by revealing something about me that he or she got from, let's say, Marlon Brando (this is a hypothetical illustration). I would know the source and reveal something about Brando and the wife of a senator (still improvising). The senator's wife would reveal something about her husband and a supposedly heterosexual psychoanalyst; the pschoanalyst would then reveal everything about his famous patients, including the President, and it would take another Deluge to put the thing out. Might be good for everybody concerned. It would put the professional gossips out of business, because everything would be used up, and the world would get down to business, refreshed from this giant revelation. The FBI's files would be worthless, since they would be either duplicates or anticlimactic. I guess I'll do it. Get the ball rolling, as it were.

CP: There have been times when your inner voice was silent, haven't there?

DC: At least when it hesitated fatally, and I just took a chance on looking like a cheapass. Like the time I asked Abba Eban, the Israeli foreign minister, if he would want his daughter to marry an Arab. A lot of people were offended by that, but I really wanted to know. I usually get two kinds of reaction from viewers on that sort of thing. Some say it was the very question they had on their minds, but that they would never have had the nerve to ask. Others say it was on their minds too, but how tacky of me to ask it, depending on their own spontaneous thoughts as a criterion for tackiness.

Sometimes the doubtful thing I allow myself is not a question, but a reaction, as when I had Salvador Dali on. He was warbling on, in that completely unintelligible manner of his, about some equally unintelligible theory of art, which ended approximately, "De boice demoderen ar-r-rt ees extracteeeeeed [voice rising to shill scream on last syllable of "extracteeeeeed"] fron ayssance day simplicit*eeee* [another shriek] ahv raycrenayssance ob booterfly*eeeh* [shrillest shriek of all, punctuated by thump of gold-headed cane on floor]!" To which, on a sudden impulse, I wiggled the fingers of both hands in his face and said, "Boojie, Boojie!" A lady later told me she nearly fell out of a Washington, D.C., hospital bed with laughter and had to have part of her incision resewn. It had her, you might say, out of stitches. The audience loved it, I loved it, and Dali appeared to have turned to granite. Hate mail abounded, claiming I had offended the entire art world. So be it.

CP: A trivia question: how many viewers recognized the source of "Boojie, Boojie!"?

DC: All the Marx Brothers fans did. Groucho does it at the gypsy hag in *A Night at the Opera,* in one of the funniest quick-cut laughs in moviedom.

Another tendency of mine is illustrated by my saying to Senator McGovern, shortly after he was buried by the 1972 landslide, "I'm going to ask you a difficult question now. How did it feel when you learned you had lost Sammy Davis, Jr.?" You can see the guest tense at the first part and then laugh heartily with relief. I haven't decided if this is unethical or not. It certainly gets laughs.

CP: How important is that to you? Getting laughs?

DC: Not terribly. I feel that I go for them because there is an audience sitting there. But I think my instinct is pretty good for when not to go for one.

Howard Cosell disagreed, in his book *Cosell*. He said I was an intellectual cheapass (at times) and didn't know how to needle back when needled. How Cosell could judge such a thing as needling I don't know. He once walked around with a harpoon sticking out of him for two weeks without noticing it.

CP: Remember the time you were telling me about some guests on your show who, you said, "were stoned, or should have been"? I asked you whether, by "stoned," you meant "high" or "pelted with stones by the audience." I've always thought that your reply was typical and revealing. You said, "Which is funnier?"

DC: What is the question?

CP: Interviewers shouldn't rely too heavily on questions, somebody once said. What I'm getting at is that you'd rather amuse people than move them. I realize I'm skirting around a quibble here, in that amusing people is also a way of moving them, that is, moving them to laughter, and, furthermore, you're not faced with an either/or situation of having to choose only between amusing people and moving them, but if you did have to choose—well, you know what I mean, don't you? Say yes.

DC: Yes. A thousand times, yes. Make that eight hundred and forty times. I *would* rather be funny than heavy, given the choice. I don't think of myself as a sage, but I have, on occasion, bordered on wit.

Also I tend to suspect those so-called "moving" or "touching" moments on a show like mine, or indeed on most shows. This probably goes back to what you said before about people finding me cold in some ways. If by that they mean that much of the time I am numb and without feeling about some of the things and people I come in contact with on the air, they are hitting the nail on the head, Charlie. I am not good at hiding the fact that some of my guests and their subjects and personalities leave me as stiff as a haddock. Many times I consciously resist moments where I know I could score points as a good, warm soul with the kind of banality I have seen others exploit on the tube.

CP: *Vive la résistance.* But, just to stay in the clinical spirit, why do you hold back?

DC: I guess it's because I know that some of those people who come off as cuddlesome, sentimental, and warmhearted souls on TV are such phonies. I think they genuinely believe the sweet sentiments they mouth while they're saying them, but their truer nature is expressed during the day, when they're bestial to their underlings, lousy to their families, and kick cats.

CP: Sentimentality apart, you do have moments of strong feeling on the air. Certainly you have them off.

DC: Sometimes I get something like all-over gooseflesh from an entrance of some fabled personage. It happened when the Lunts entered together, introduced by Noël Coward, and it happened when I first introduced Orson Welles and he stepped onto the stage. Brando's entrance was dynamite; the audience greeting was like a prolonged thunderclap. So was it for Nureyev. Unfortunately the mikes neutralize extremes, so that at home you get only a flattened version of a sound like that. Watching Fred Astaire dance on the same stage I was standing on was a high-voltage moment. Seeing Groucho step out to the strains of "Captain Spalding" always gave me a charge, or Hope to "Thanks for the Memory" or Benny to "Love in Bloom." There is a moment when a flash bulb seems to go off in the nervous system, as if an enduring picture of a rare occasion were being taken by your senses. Music helps at such moments, of course, and when Bob Rosengarden was with me regularly his collection of literally the best musicians in the business was partly responsible for the effect the audience and I felt.

CP: You're criticized at times for showing excessive deference to living legends on the air, and, at the same time, for remaining too passive in the face of sallies by more aggressive and assertive types—in short, for not standing up to your guests and mixing it up with them more.

DC: Want to make something of it?

CP: Let go of my throat! I just want to know what you have to say to your critics.

DC: I can only say they are sometimes right and sometimes wrong. A bland answer, but accurate. So far as I know, I am still the only talk-show host who has said to a guest, in these precise words, "I really think you're full of crap" (to Timothy Leary, circa 1970). I have had set-tos with Elliot Roosevelt ("Perhaps you could now bring yourself to answer the question"); Lester Maddox, in which he demanded that I make an apology I felt was unnecessary or he would walk off (I didn't; he did); Jane Fonda and Mark Lane, the night Jane forgot that the French had played a role in the American Revolution; Louis Nizer, when he came on an early show of mine with an apologia for the Vietnam war that raised my hackles so much that I never got around to bringing on the other guests; and Patrick Buchanan, the Nixon assistant, who nakedly admitted the Nixon administration tried to "buy off" Daniel Schorr of CBS, who, they had decided, was an unsympathetic "clown," by offering him a job "in the Environment" (I asked, "Is that the administration's opinion of the environment, to put a cluck in there?").

CP: My own favorite occasion was your verbal scuffle with Norman Mailer on the Mailer–Gore Vidal–Janet Flanner show, when Mailer drew his chair apart from you and the others to proclaim his intellectual superiority over all of you, and you asked whether he'd like another chair to contain his giant intellect. Then he made a patronizing crack about your supposedly having to refer to your note sheet in order to come up with the next question, and you said, "Why don't you fold it five ways and put it where the moon don't shine?"

But the question of excessive deference arises, I think, more with the kinds of show-business people who, as you just said, give you gooseflesh when they enter—the Noël Cowards, the Orson Welleses.

DC: I suppose I have been too impressed by them for some people's tastes. But not for mine. The fact that I cannot be deferential or assertive at the precise times that critics want me to be is a failing I have learned to live with.

CP: And it is, after all, a genuine response on your part, not an act. A part of you is still the star-struck kid from Nebraska. I remember once, earlier in your talk-show career, when Lucille Ball invited you to dinner after being on your show, and your response was a slightly incredulous "Do you really want me to?"

DC: That was *much* earlier in my career. But yes, somehow going out to dinner with Lucille Ball didn't seem right. It was almost a sense of "If she likes me now, why should I tamper with this state of affairs by going out to dinner with her?" One evening Jack Benny and Phil Silvers were on, and they complimented me and the show. At that time it was amazing to me that Jack Benny and Phil Silvers even knew my name. I still feel, in a certain sense, I really shouldn't go out to dinner with a Lucille Ball or a Jack Benny, even though I have done so. I really want to keep some distance.

CP: Aren't there times, though, when you watch your own show and second-guess your performance wishing you had been harder or softer on this guest or that guest?

DC: Sure. And the occasions when I strike the wrong note

often come about because I'm aware that the effect I see before my eyes while doing the show is not exactly the effect that is being made on the home screen. For example, the guest who seems pushy in the studio merely seems energetic at home, and the hesitant guest may strike the home audience as being intimidated by me. The lying camera can make a guest who seems nasty in the studio appear merely animated at home. When you have embarrassed yourself a few times by a misreading of this effect you get a little gun shy.

CP: Let's come back to that phrase "the lying camera." One of the TV shibboleths of our time, especially in political campaigns, is that the camera does not lie. That in interview or debate situations, as opposed to commercials or formal appearances, the close-ups mercilessly expose the man behind the mask—or the mask behind the man.

DC: The truth is that people who are experienced with the camera, notably actors and politicians, will develop a false genuineness that is indistinguishable from the real thing. Many is the time I have sat onstage and thought, "Everybody will see through this guy's act," then sat at home and found that what I saw while doing the show had gotten lost somewhere between the man and the camera.

The camera also has a mysterious way of filtering out certain things. It fascinates me, and it has caused me to treat certain guests in a way I would not have if I had known how they were coming over.

CP: Can you give an example of, say, a guest you would have been rougher on?

DC: William Buckley's brother-in-law L. Brent Bozell. He or an organization representing him demanded air time on the show to counter some proabortion views that we had aired from time to time. I was in a pretty foul mood that day anyway, because I was irritated at having to do an entire show with four guests who, like Bozell, had either demanded "equal time" or had it demanded for them. The network had "suggested," out of a combination of a sense of fairness and a thoroughly distorted interpretation of the phrase "equal time," that I have them on.

I found Bozell's views repugnant, which I made clear enough, but I would have made it clearer if it hadn't been for the lying camera. He was articulate, but seemed highly agitated. He sweated a lot, his hand trembled enough to make his cigarette a fire hazard to those nearby, and there was a perceptible twitch in his cheek muscle. Feeling that perhaps *I* was doing this to him, I went easier in not opposing his poisonous philosophy than I might have. I felt a certain sympathy for the state of his emotions, and I felt also a fear that the audience would think I was picking on the afflicted. When I saw the show he looked shrewd and cool, the tremble didn't show, his cheek muscle was firm as Gibraltar—and it looked as though I were letting him off too easy. When I tell you that I did say, "I don't know which I find more repellent, your manner or your ideas," you can get some idea of what I was holding back.

People are so fond of the notion that the TV camera is an X-ray camera, as the cliché goes, that it will always be with us. Plenty of rogues have been seen through on TV, but plenty have not. Like any camera, which sees something different from what the human eye sees because it is not a precise duplicate of the eye, it does nothing *but* lie. It may lie in a person's favor or in his disfavor, by either missing or emphasizing something in his personality, but it will never show precisely what is there.

CP: Another complication, I assume, is that, apart from the camera's distortions, sometimes not even you can see precisely what is there. During one of Orson Welles's appearances on your show, he commented that the whole world came to you, and you said that it was a limited world, because you usually saw your guests not as they really were, but as they wanted to appear to be in order to impress people.

DC: Yes. I suppose it's possible that you could go for years on television without meeting any actual people.

CP: Don't they get any more actual during the breaks for commercials?

DC: People watching at home constantly imagine that wonderful things happen during the breaks that they are not privy to. Sometimes things happen, though how wonderful they are is another matter. I've been propositioned, for example, by both male and female guests.

CP: Just like that?

DC: Sometimes it's as blatant as "Do you ever fool around?" or "Do you want to fool around after the show?"

More frequently, however, guests just ask if the preceding segment was all right, or ask about the upcoming segment, or fix their hair, or make a crack about some girl in the second row, or silently tap their feet to the music. Some of them just sit there and watch the commercials on the monitor.

A certain speculation arises, I suppose, when viewers see a remarkable donnybrook, like the Mailer–Flanner–Vidal show, in which there is verbal violence and the threat of physical violence. What are they saying to each other during the commercials? In that case, nothing was said. The band, mercifully, played loudly, the audience buzzed with excitement, and the four of us stared straight ahead, or at some neutral corner of the carpet, until the next segment began.

Sometimes a juicy remark is uttered in the break that could never get on the air. You know, I ought to find out if our audio tape in the control room records the things the guests, who are still on mike, saying during breaks. If so, I have some highly incriminating stuff on tape. I would never release it, however, for reasons of national security.

CP: Meaning there have been juicy remarks by prominent national figures?

DC: I'm glad you asked that, as prominent national figures

can't seem to avoid saying these days. Yes. Once I was reading the writer Richard Harris's piece in *The New Yorker* on the dirty dealing that went on during the so-called May Day riots in Washington a few years back, when antiwar activists staged the demo that was supposed to bring the city to a halt. Harris detailed the illegal activities indulged in by what, in Nixon's first term, was laughingly called the Justice Department—specifically, the ways in which the young lawyers from Justice were instructed to falsify arrest records, with a contrived list of arresting officers whose names they would arbitrarily rotate, and so on. Reading it, I had that rage that an ordinary citizen gets when he thinks, "Why aren't these bastards confronted with this stuff and forced to justify themselves publicly?" A few months later I had Richard Kleindienst, then attorney general, on the show—they were changing so fast in those days that mail to the attorney general was addressed "Occupant"— and I simply read the Harris paragraph to his face, which empurpled somewhere in the middle of the last sentence. That sentence ran something like this: "This betrayal of its own young lawyers by the Department of Justice was one of the sorriest episodes of the whole sordid business." Kleindienst's response was, of course, that the article was inaccurate.

During the break, I said that I would be glad to put Harris on a show with Kliendienst, but that I doubted if he would come, because he had been asked to appear once before and he had said he was one of those writers who were constitutionally too shy to appear in public. To which, the chief law enforcement officer of America replied, "Well, *fuck him!*" Fortunately the band was playing something (presumably "It Ain't Necessarily So"), and I noticed that some people in the front rows seemed to be saying, "Did you see what it looked like he said?" I focused on the distended veins on the A.G.'s forehead and said something like, "Is that your considered legal opinion, Mr. Attorney General?"

On another show, the critic John Simon and Mort Sahl got into a murderous argument. During the break, through the sound of the band and my meaningless shuffling of papers on my table, I heard Mort say something that ended ". . . and if you don't knock it off I'm going to punch you in the mouth!" Wondering what I would do if he did, I started the next segment by introducing what I hoped would be a less inflammatory topic. But somehow it led Simon to say something to Mort like, "Speaking of intellectual sloppiness, perhaps you'd like to tell the audience the intellectual way you threatened during the commercial break to punch me in the face." I guess it was nice of Simon not to let the home audience miss anything. I suppose if he had been hosting, instead of me, during the Kleindienst episode, he would have said, "As head of the Justice Department, suppose you tell the ladies and gentlemen how during the commercial break you so judiciously suggested the fucking of Mr. Harris."

CP: All this talk of appearance and reality, of the actual and the artificial, leads to one great truth about your show.

DC: What's that?

CP: You've never had on the gabbling Gabors.

DC: At first it was because I just thought they were overexposed. Then, when I was praised specifically for not having them on, I thought, "Why spoil a good thing?"

CP: It may turn out to be your one indisputable contribution to Western culture.

DC: Well, it's something.

CP: I thought I'd lay out now, as we used to say in jazz bands, and let you take a few solo choruses.

DC: Good. As it happens, I do have a few things I'd like to get off my chest about the international balance-of-payments situation.

CP: What I had in mind was a few of your most memorable shows—backstage reminiscences of what made them memorable for you, that sort of taradiddle.

DC: I get so tired of being asked that question—and of not having the chance to really answer it. At length. In exquisite detail.

CP: Go ahead. It's your book.

DC: The one show that people seem to recall with a slight catch in the throat and hush in the voice is the one with the Lunts and Noël Coward. Jack Paar called the day afterward to say it was the best thing he'd ever seen on television. George Burns said it should be run every year, and Jack Benny mentions it nearly every time I see him. It thrilled not only the people who loved show business and who knew the Lunts and Coward, but also my youngest viewers, some of whom couldn't have told you exactly who the Lunts and Coward were the day before. I was in a kind of pothead *boite-cum*-restaurant about halfway out Long Island late one night, half-disguised, sitting alone in a dark corner of the place. A despondent-looking shaggy young male of perhaps sixteen, who appeared to have dropped even further out than he meant to, got up from the corner of the floor where he had been ruminating. He looked the type of bad apple that Spiro Agnew was suggesting we eliminate from the barrel of our society—in the days before Spiro's own worm was discovered. He ambled over and said, "Mr. Cavett, I wanted to tell you how much I enjoyed that program with Mr. Coward and the Lunts. Such fine and witty people, and everything they said was so spontaneous and yet so well spoken. They were in such clear possession of themselves. Anyway, thank you." And he returned to his corner. Sounds like one of *The New Yorker*'s "Quotes We Doubt Ever Got Quoted," but that is close to the precise wording.

On the day we taped that show, the Lunts arrived several hours early, meticulous artists that they are, to see the stage setup and to arrange their entrance. We had constructed a ramp for them to come down, and they practiced entering, checked how many steps it took to get to the bottom of the ramp, and decided where they would bow. They also wanted to know how the chairs felt. I think they were slightly disappointed that we had changed the set somewhat for them, because they had watched the show avidly, I learned, and wanted to see how it really looked.

I came upstairs to my dressing room after doing a commercial rehearsal and found them there, sitting on the couch with Coward. I had one of those light-bulb flashes. Here were the three people in that famous photograph from *Design for Living*, taken nearly forty years earlier, sitting on my couch now, rather than rollicking on theirs. There was an exquisite tea set on the table that Miss Fontanne had brought, along with her own hot plate, in order to brew tea just before air time. "I recommend tea before a performance," she said, "but only tea. Drink . . . drink is chancy."

Mr. Lunt was extremely worried that he would make a botch of the whole thing—Miss F. had told me he would be—and seemed sorry for me that I was about to be stuck with him. He was marvelous on the show, and afterward, as Miss Fontanne had assured me he would, he felt he *had* made a total botch of things. She said he had been this way all their lives as performers.

I guess I will never forget the three of them sitting there, while a kind of montage of their careers flashed through my mind and I tried to guess how many times they had sat backstage together in how many parts of the world, waiting for their curtain and enjoying themselves and worrying a little, the way they were doing now. There was an eloquent poise in the way three great professionals sat waiting to "go on." All those great instincts and talents and years of experience that would suffuse and condition every move, gesture, and word when they stepped out under the lights. And their deep friendship. Miss Fontanne called Coward "Noëly." They made the business seem so damned respectable.

During the show I succumbed to nerves only for the first few minutes with Coward, whose devastating ability to get a laugh with one syllable and thereby fire the ball back into your court got me off balance for a moment or two. But there is a kind of warm security about being onstage with a truly great professional that took over quickly and made me quite comfortable. There is a closeness for each other that you feel in such situations, a sense of "It's us against them up here—and they're liking us." This mutual dependency produces a kind of signaling to one another that you know when to come in, that you will get one another out of trouble. I had a gratifying sense that a great star was at that moment somewhat in my thrall, somewhat dependent on me, needed something from me, and knew that he or she was getting it and was grateful and doing well because of it. It's a wonderful, wonderful feeling, and I just love it when it happens. Later there is an afterglow, a sensation of having been taken aloft for a time. That night it happened over and over with the Lunts and Coward.

It was their last appearance together, the three of them. Coward died four years later. And it came about because—dare I say it?—the Lunts were fans of *mine* and had asked a mutual friend, Leueen MacGrath, to introduce us. I mustn't dwell on this, or it will eat up the remaining morsels of my modesty. What can we learn from all this?

CP: That drink is chancy?

DC: I'm beginning to see what you meant when you said you were going to lay out. Anyway, moving on, I can also reveal what Laurence Olivier has for lunch. Three green apples, which he skins expertly, spiral fashion, a wedge of sharp Cheddar one inch thick and about the size of a slice of pie, and a glass of white wine. An actor friend of mine has eaten this lunch regularly since I told him about it, but reports no marked improvement in his abilities. I learned this in London, where I went after Lord O. had agreed to do the show—I had always considered him one of the ungettables I would just have to learn to live without—and he had asked if I would have lunch with him a day or so before the taping, "if it wouldn't be any trouble." I consented.

As I was being driven to the National Theatre, of which Olivier was then the director, I pictured his office as comparable to that of an opera impresario in a Warner Brothers movie: palatial, velvety, with oil paintings and a baronial fireplace. When my driver turned in to what can only be described as an alley, and pulled up alongside a kind of barracks row, I decided he was stopping to collect on a gambling debt. When he said this semi-Dickensian setting was our destination I thought he was having me on. I got out, took four steps, looked in a window, and there, smack in front of me, was Olivier in profile. He was sitting at a desk in a tiny office, wearing half glasses and doing some paperwork. And looking like a million dollars. Undevaluated.

I gulped, went in, and found his secretary, who ushered me instantly into the cramped presence, and Olivier took my coat and made some small comment about how I must be bushed from the flight. His tone and manner were so comforting that I knew this was going to be sheer pleasure. There was a small table laid for lunch, with sandwiches for me, the aforesaid for him. There was a third plate, exactly like his, made available "in case *my* lunch makes you jealous." The poor man is probably so accustomed to people being bowled over and being tongue-tied in his presence that he has developed a light, winning, disarming style. I had an attack of something there should be a French phrase for, like *déjà vu*—perhaps *déjà connu en plusieurs personnes.* As the man at my elbow lunched and chatted amiably, I realized, by flashes, that I already knew him in movies as Henry V, Heathcliff, the man in *Rebecca*, Hamlet, Richard, Archie Rice, and—by still photo only— Oedipus. (I was startled by the fact that the man has hardly noticeable lips, and yet those characters all had prominent mouths of various styles and shapes.) It was as if characters you had known from Rembrandt, El Greco, and Holbein were somehow all there mysteriously beside you *and knew your name.* I recalled photographs of an earlier Olivier: the man who looked something like Ronald Colman in photos of Hollywood lawn parties of the thirties, the performer dressed in baby clothes doing a duet with Danny Kaye at a benefit, the husband helping the distraught Vivian Leigh from a plane after a nervous breakdown, and many others. Here he was, all of him, in a dark blue three-piece business suit, casually peeling an apple and making expert small talk. What in hell did he make of me? I wondered.

Before the taping, he said he was afraid he would be boring on the show. He paced somewhat in the wings, and after I came off from a brief warm-up talk with the audience he said how brave he thought I was to go out and speak to them like that. I have a fantasy dating back many years that someday I would be able to look into the wings and confirm that the man I was about to introduce was Laurence Olivier. Now it was about to happen. I thought back to sitting in the second balcony of a theater in Boston, where I had traveled solely to see Olivier in *The Entertainer*. Some friends had tarried too long over dinner and almost made me late. It was so close that I had to get out of the cab in a traffic jam and run the last four blocks, cursing them all the way, so that I sat in my seat puffing and sweating and trying to remember how to ward off a heart attack. I knew Olivier entered doing a combination tap and soft-shoe, and I didn't want to miss his entrance even if my life depended on it. I had gotten to my seat with a couple of minutes to spare and spent them thinking, "There are people behind that curtain *with* Olivier. They can see him leave his dressing room; they know what he's doing. What *is* he doing? Chewing gum, doing exercises, singing 'mi mi mi,' praying, drinking, laughing?" Is that a yawn you're stifling?

CP: Just scratching my nose.

DC: Olivier backstage after the taping was a wonder. He took off his jacket and tie, met my wife and our friends the Barry Fosters (he was the necktie strangler in Hitchcock's *Frenzy*), and began behaving like any actor who has been through something difficult and, now that the pressure is off, doesn't exactly want to go home, but has another kind of energy to let off and does it among his fellow actors. He seized a drink off the inevitable trolley of booze that is one of the civilized features of a British TV studio, and calculated that he had already missed his train. Almost two hours and a couple of drinks later, he had missed another train, and we were all still standing there swapping stories, but mostly listening to him tell anecdotes about his life and career. Most of them could not be told publicly, for various reasons, at least by *Lord* Olivier, a thing I realized as I hungrily calculated what a fabulous show this would make. As good as the other one, but totally different. I realized that here, with his jacket and now his tie off, relaxed and uninhibited, was *Larry* Olivier. The man his friends see. He was not awesome. Just friendly, funny, appealing, and comfortable to be with.

He has an uncanny ear. Whenever he repeated someone's conversation—famous directors, authors, whoever—for purposes of the story, he imitated the voice to perfection. Luckily I had gotten him to imitate Sam Goldwyn on the air, so people would know what I meant when I spoke of this talent.

Suddenly we realized everyone had gone home from the studio and we might be locked in. Olivier feigned a mock panic, pounding on doors and wondering aloud what would become of us all. We found an exit, and he gave thanks to God in an impeccable comic Irish accent. When I gathered up armfuls of stuff from my dressing room—wardrobe bags, loose shirts, shaving kit, all to be taken home—he changed characters again and became a kind of distracted, fussy manservant taking things from me, laying them on the floor, picking them up again, handing them back, saying, "Here, I'll take this and you carry that, and . . . no, I'll take this and you carry these, and . . . no, *you* take this, and . . . no . . ." It was much funnier than it sounds. Then we headed down a long corridor for waiting cars and shook hands, and he exited, via a Rolls limo, into the slightly foggy London night.

My other big catch overseas was the show I did in Stockholm with Ingmar Bergman, who, like Olivier, was making his first appearance ever on an American talk show. I couldn't get over his joviality. I recalled that you had told me about this, but it was a shock just the same. One expects to be ushered into a dark chamber at the end of which a brooding figure sits veiled in thought and cobwebs. I met Bergman for dinner, in front of that restaurant with the torches burning across from the Grand Hotel in Stockholm, and his energy and enthusiasm and alertness made me feel old. I don't think I've ever met a man who seemed so entirely *awake*. When Bibi Andersson joined us (late, as Bergman predicted) he jumped up, kissed her, and fussed with her chair. He then ordered for everyone and began asking me questions about the show. He had agreed to do it only after seeing a kinescope of an old show. Given a choice, he had selected one with Orson Welles. He said that the minute the kinescope started, with my brief monologue, he decided against the idea. "But then there was an interval. When it started again you were sitting down. I didn't like you standing up—but sitting and talking you were a different person. I liked you from then on and decided to do the show."

There are two physical things I remember about Bergman. He said he has an ear that lets in too much sound and that this is one reason he fears coming to New York: that the ear and other senses will be overwhelmed with impressions that will leave him shaken. He also told me that his legs get very nervous at night just before bedtime, a thing I also get—a sort of muscular anxiety in the lower legs. We described our symptoms to each other and felt a foolish kinship from the knees down. I told him I would air-mail him some Supp-Hose, but he said they only made it worse.

So there you have it. Bergman has nervous legs at night. I'm sure that information is all some cineaste needs in order to write a monograph reinterpreting Bergman's *oeuvre* as a vision of man in spiritual anxiety owing to his shaky lower limbs. The restlessness, the uncertainty about fundamental values owing to the lack of roots, of a firm grounding . . .

CP: It sounds horribly plausible. Let's move on before somebody does it.

DC: Still speaking of strong physical impressions, the most powerful one I got from a guest was from Marlon Brando. The power in him hits you the second you meet him. The day he was scheduled to do my show, I was pacing up and down in my dressing room—although there is really only room enough to pace up. We had gone through a day of hell, not knowing whether Brando was in Tahiti, in New York, or on a jet somewhere between. He was already late, and I had all but decided his existence was a fiction. There was a knock at the door. I opened it to find a crowd of people, most of whom had formed a flying wedge to get Brando in through the mob outside the theater. Suddenly he came at me through the crowd, like a tank pushing through a haystack.

If you'll pardon me while I dust off a cliché, being alone with him in a small room is like being in a cage with a large animal. It is hard to know where the effect comes from, but there is a sense of leashed violence about his presence that is exhilarating and weird. Stanley Kauffmann once said, in a review of some film of Brando's, referring to a shot from behind Brando's back, "The man's very shoulders seem to *impend*." At other times, he is as adorable as a pussycat and the impending is not there at all. If you've seen him on the screen you know all this, but for it to be there in person is unusual. Movies are full of people who project a mysterious something on the screen that is entirely absent when you meet them. I can't remember which director of Garbo's I once asked, "When you were standing there next to the camera, and she was in front of it, did you see the magic thing the camera saw in her?" He said no. But there it would be on the film. George Cukor, it was.

My time alone with Brando in the dressing room before the show was a little spooky. He sat on my couch, took off his aviator glasses, and gave me an eye-widened stare. I had read about this habit of his and stared back, thinking, "Is this the eye test he gave Maria Schneider when they met before making *Last Tango in Paris*, the one he supposedly held for thirty minutes without saying a word?" I knew I was good for at least two minutes without blinking. While I debated whether to say, "C'mon, man, I got no time for the eye bit," he turned it off and began to play with my electric typewriter. Then he got up, and began to pick up various objects in the room and examine them closely. He went into my john, took a leak, and began to examine the things on the sink—mouthwash, toothbrush, aftershave—turning them over in his hands and seeming to make Sherlock Holmesian deductions about their owner. I told him to stop picking up things that didn't belong to him. He chuckled, sat down again, and said he did not want to make an entrance on the show, but wanted to be discovered as "the man sitting on your right."

I said that this would be unfortunate, because the entrance was so effective theatrically, and that, while I knew he was not there to be theatrical, it was important to the show as a whole. He said, "Well . . ." and took an ominous pause, in which the making of *Mutiny on the Bounty* flashed through my mind and I pictured his saying, "Call me when you feel like doing it my way," and heading for the door.

Instead he said, with a grin, "I'll do whatever you say." His entrance was worth the price of admission. They always say what a shame it is Brando left the stage and that if you have not seen him there you can't imagine it. Constance Welch, the brilliant acting teacher now retired from Yale, once said to me jokingly, "I *discovered* Brando. Years ago, when *The Eagle Has Two Heads* came through New York [the show Brando was dumped from because he clashed with the star, Tallulah Bankhead], I was sitting in the audience, and suddenly this unknown young man came on the stage and I was hypnotized by him. I had never seen a man move so brilliantly. You couldn't take your eyes off him, which, with Tallulah onstage, is saying something." She said there was something incredible about his hips when he moved, animallike. I saw what she meant when I screened the tape of his entrance on my show. I had them play it back three or four times. My wife was in the audience and said there was a shock wave when he entered.

The shame is that we have not seen his Oedipus, his Hamlet, his Richard II and III, his Orestes. In some ways he is better equipped than Olivier, and the people who still cling to the notion that he can't talk are full of shit. He can master any dialect or style of speech known to man, despite the nitwits who still refer to him as "Mumbles Brando." If this were a dictatorship and I were the tyrant in charge, I would force him to be the lead actor in our national theater. That is, after I ordered the creation of a national theater.

With all this forcefulness, it strikes me that Brando also has a wonderful ingenuousness. He landed in the hospital with a bad case of human bite (*morsus humanis*) from the scuffle that took place after my show, when he slugged the photographer Ron Galella. I spent a lot of time visiting him. One day, as he lay there in blue pajama bottoms and with an Oliver Hardy-size bandage wrapping on his right hand, for some reason I told him about a silly word game I had invented that goes back and forth very fast and forces you to make up a phrase without thinking—thereby resulting in obscene, silly, and, if you believe in psychology, revealing inventions on the part of the players. He wanted to play it. We did, and fell into fits of laughter, the way you do when you're nine years old. Am I rattling on too long here? Why are you setting that alarm clock?

CP: I'm sure you have many more fascinating reminiscences, but I don't want to tire you.

DC: Think nothing of it. I'm sure I can manage one or two more, since you insist.

People ask me about the time Lester Maddox, the former governor of Georgia, walked off my show because I refused to apologize for what he saw as an insult to his constituency.

Was he right to walk off? Yes. But not because I failed to apologize. He was right because it was theatrical and well timed, and got him more attention than he had had since the old pick-handle-brandishing days of the Pickrick Restaurant. I heard that he papered the walls of his office with the congratulatory wires he got. Maddox is smart as a whip—or should I say knout?—and knows how to exploit the media as well as or better than Jerry Rubin or Abbie Hoffman ever did. As I said on the next night's show, he also knows the value of television time, walking off as he did a scant eighty-eight minutes into the show.

Truman Capote, who was also on the panel that night, says

that, of all the TV he has done, to this day people still refer to that night wherever he goes. He always chastises me for going after Maddox—I followed him to the street during a commercial break—to see if he would come back. It wasn't so much that I wanted him to come back as that I wanted to see what his real mood was.

There was a minute or so to go on the show, and I said, on the air, that I was sorry the governor left, because we had had no chance to talk about the romantic beauty of the South or some such. A guy in the audience yelled, "Don't back down!," and I responded courteously, "Shut up! I'll tell you when I'm backing down."

My feeling is that Maddox did not plan to walk off the show before he got there, although he may have. But I'm more inclined to think he saw a good opportunity when it presented itself to grab some publicity. There had been heated moments earlier in the show, but Ol' Lester was always winking at me with his up-camera eye, and during the break he would ask if it was going all right. So I was totally unprepared for what happened. I was manipulated, set up, exploited, used by a master of showmanly instinct.

A day or so later, mail began to come in like the blizzard of '88, congratulating me for my courageous refusal to apologize or chastising me for being the insulting, snotty, lily-livered fink that I am. The mail did not break down, as you might expect, between North and South. Many southerners were applauding me and apologizing that Lester was the sort of representative of Dixie who made headlines; and a lot of northerners said he was terrific and ought to be president, and that I should try swimming in the Yazoo with an anvil around my neck. One lady said that Lester had redeemed the loss of the Civil War.

I sometimes think everyone in America saw that show. His walk-off was reported on the news from coast to coast between taping and air time, so that people who had never seen a late-night show stayed up for that one. In Greenwood, Mississippi, my wife's home town, there was a country-club dance, and the guests had heard the news on their car radios on the way. When the show started, the dance floor slowly emptied as people filed into the lounge to watch. One of my wife's childhood friends reported that in the middle of the show she looked out into the formerly crowded ballroom, and it was bare except for the orchestra and my wife's uncle Ralph, a lanky, no-nonsense, six-foot-five-inch plantation owner, and his dancing partner. I think Uncle Ralph had always feared that his northern nephew-in-law would do something disgraceful on nationwide TV and had probably decided that this was the night. The crowd in the lounge watched in stony silence, although in earlier times ninety-nine per cent of them would have cheered Lester.

A year so so later Lester returned to my show. I had thought of attaching a seat belt to the guest chair and, when he sat down, reaching over and buckling him in. Instead, as a joke, I walked off on *him*, pretending to be insulted. Left alone on the stage, he calmly cued the orchestra and broke into a solo of "I Don't Know Why I Love You Like I Do." I returned and joined in the second stanza, and thus was the hatchet musically interred.

Which brings me to Katharine Hepburn—I've been saving her for last in any case. She is like a work of nature. You want to sit back and look at her as you do at a beautiful rock formation or a splendid animal—the way the chin goes with the mouth, the mouth with the cheekbones, the way the curve of the cheekbones is duplicated in the outward curve of her hair. As Jean Stafford pointed out, after watching the two shows that Hepburn did with me, you realize that that voice is the only one that could have gone with those looks. It was startling, as I watched the show on the air, to see it cut from a close-up of Hepburn's face to a commercial, and a close-up of one of the vapidly beautiful models in a hosiery or eye-shadow commercial. It was merely cutting from one beautiful woman's face to another, but it was like switching from Mozart to Muzak. The triumph of Hepburn's art is that she has been able to play the plain girl that none of the beaux wants to marry. The audience could always see what they were missing, but the young men couldn't.

Just because she is appealing in so many ways as a performer, I didn't see any reason to expect her to show all her charm, gusto, playfulness, and wit when she appeared on my show. But she did. At the end of the second show I told her I'd never enjoyed anything more. She said, "You know something? I've had a good time too. I wasn't sure I would, but I did." There was a hint of a tear and a smile when she said it, taking my hand, and I felt something inside me go over the brim. Luckily it only remained for me to say good night. Mustn't let the troops see you snuffle. And never mind reaching for that bucket; I'll get off this now.

A few days after the Hepburn shows were taped I was at Edward Albee's annual lawn party, and a striking-looking woman of a certain age, who was obviously *somebody*, suddenly grabbed my face in her two hands, held her head so close I couldn't focus on hers, and said, "You don't know me, but my name is very well known to you." Irritated, I said, "Betty Crocker?" In spite of this, we had a friendly chat. She was Irene Mayer Selznick, and a good friend of Miss H.'s, and told me she had never seen her friend Kate go through such an ordeal as the decision on whether to break her long-standing rule against appearing informally on TV by doing my show. Hepburn is the kind who will make herself pick up a snake if that is the thing she is most afraid of, and that plus the fact that some friends (and even her brother) urged her *not* to do it probably helped convince her to do it. Her dilemma was that a show like mine violated her principle of privacy, yet she hated the idea of becoming so set in her ways that she would miss out on a challenge.

She later told me that when I went to her house, in the Turtle Bay section of East Side Manhattan, for what was, in a sense, *my* audition, she was teetering on the brink. She said she realized quickly that she could talk with me and that the decision was, for all practical purposes, made. She still insisted on coming to the empty studio with a couple of changes of outfit to test for color. I had said to my producer, a week or so beforehand, "Let's have some tape ready, in case she decides to do a little something on the day of the test." At first we were going to have an hour's worth, but I had a premonition and said, "Have more." When she arrived, she taped over three hours of programing, in a virtually nonstop five-hour session.

There is, as with Brando, a physical phenomenon about Hepburn. Her incredible energy affects the people around her as if they had been given a stimulant. Somewhere deep inside her there is this dynamo racing, and if you are close you can damn near feel it. It must be hell on her. The day she taped my show, her energy seemed to increase as time went by and was still on the upswing when we quit. I had another show to do, and was beginning to feel the physical effects of the lights and of just sitting there that long. By the time we had to stop she was like a horse at the starting gate, and I know she could have gone on a few more hours at full tilt. I learned later that she went home with a couple of friends and in fact did talk for several more hours before beginning to wind down.

She was also in the studio a second time, to do some little pickup pieces—introductory bits, transitions—for editing purposes. Both times, when she left, those of us who had been enclosed in a small space with her—my dressing room—found ourselves acting stoned for a half hour or so after she left. She's like a shot of brandy.

I had vacated my dressing room for her, and I got a glimpse of her make-up supplies. They looked like Lon Chaney's equipment for making up as at least thirty of the characters he played. There must have been over a hundred individual eye liners, grease sticks, rouges, powders, lipsticks, lining brushes, pancakes, sponges, puffs, base creams, eyebrow pencils, and eye shadows covering the surface of a large dressing table about half an inch deep. Yet she wore practically no make-up on the show. Another thing: during the breaks in the taping she would stretch out on her back on the floor and converse from that position.

The lack of a studio audience was right for her. An audience naturally affects the tone and nature and intimacy of the conversation, and Hepburn's instinct was right, although wavering, on this. She had said, "Won't it be better if we just talk to each other, rather than to each other *and them?*"

I wish I had talked with Brando that way. There is a sense in which the audience are intruders on a conversation, demanding certain asides and jokes for their benefit. Viewers at home sometimes say how irritating the studio audience can become. If I had it to do over, I would still do most shows with an audience, but more without one than I have done in the past.

After her shows were broadcast, Hepburn was genuinely amazed at the effect they had. I called after the first one, and she told me about having taken a walk in Manhattan that morning. Cops on horseback yelled to her, cab drivers commented, people discovered where she lived and shoved mash notes in her mail slot. It's hard to believe that Katharine Hepburn could become even more recognizable and popular than she was, but she seemed to. She was somewhat taken aback by the peculiar power of the home screen. No other medium could have had the impact that TV had in making people feel that close to her.

A lot of this has to do with the close-up shot, which is one of the few things the medium can do well. TV begins to lose its effectiveness the minute it cuts from a close-up, single-face shot to a two-shot (two people in the same shot). Anything wider than that, and the viewer feels he is suddenly sitting in the outfield. When you're watching a talk show, notice what happens when the director cuts from a single portrait shot to a wider shot in the middle of somebody's sentence. Even though the camera cut does not at all affect the sound, you have the sensation that you can't hear as well, and you have to refocus your concentration. The only time a director should do that is when he wants to include a noteworthy action, like another guest falling asleep or undressing. This is one reason that plays and movies lose their effectiveness on TV. If I directed a play on TV it would be mostly close-ups, and there aren't many plays you can do that way. It's a lousy medium for drama.

CP: Speaking of the power and intimacy of the medium, I don't think you should leave out the show that was probably the most dramatic one you've ever had, and the one that couldn't be broadcast—the one that would've given viewers a jarring close-up view of death.

DC: That show reminded me again that one of the remarkable things about death is how *little* time we spend thinking about it—even those of us who are a bit obsessed with it. The ornery way it has of appearing at the most unthinkable times, as when a man rises at a big banquet table to accept a gift at his retirement party, or when a man dresses up as Santa Claus at the family Christmas party, proves that if there is Someone up there, He has one hell of a sense of humor. Of all my guests for whom it would have been a grim joke to kick the proverbial pail, none was more appropriate than the one who had just finished discoursing on how to achieve longevity through proper nutrition. This was precisely the guest old Nobodaddy chose to tickle his warped risibilities with.

J. I. Rodale, a charming man, who looked like an avuncular Trotsky, was the publisher of various health and organic-gardening magazines and had been the subject of a Sunday *Times Magazine* cover story two days before he came on my show. He was my second guest that night, and was amusing; he told of how he had fallen downstairs recently but was so limber and cheerful, due to good living, that he laughed all the way down. He was a hit with the audience, and I made a mental note to have him back.

At the twelve-thirty station break I introduced Pete Hammill, the journalist, and just as Hammill began to talk, Rodale, who had moved down to position two, next to Hammill, made a snoring sound. The audience laughed. I knew instantly it was trouble, but I guess the audience assumed he was going to say, "I forgot to show you how I can fall instantly asleep." Hammill said, through clenched teeth, "This is bad." My memories at this point are mixed. I remember going over to Rodale and taking his wrist, having no idea what I was doing it for, and saying, "Mr. Rodale, are you all right?" He clearly was not. I remember noticing that a stewardess in the front row, who had been laughing throughout the show, was suddenly crying. There was that ominous murmur now in the audience, the very sound that extras can never manage to get quite right in the movies—a thought that, oddly, occurred to me at the time—and as I began the sentence "Is there a doctor . . ." a little voice said, "Avoid the cliché," and I said, ". . . in the audience?" instead of "house." I puzzled about this afterward. When I told Hepburn about it she said it was an instinct telling me to avert a laugh.

By chance, there were two young interns and a nurse from a nearby hospital. Trivia flooded my mind. I thought that here was a true Pirandello situation—a man wearing make-up dying on a stage with lights and camera before an audience summoned to view his demise. Such intrusive thoughts are natural, though. Remember the guy in *The Brothers Karamazov* fixing on the prosecutor's interesting ring while his life was at stake? And I remember a time I thought I was drowning when my main concern was, "How will they get the rented car back?"

Rodale had now turned the color of a plumber's candle, and I remember the sound of his chest being struck with what sounded like a body blow in a prize fight. Someone on my staff made a tragicomic walk-on entrance with two out of the three parts of an inadequate home oxygen device, a few moments before the fire department arrived from across the street with a real one.

The scene was grotesque. People in the audience were standing and murmuring, or leaving, or crying; Rodale's shirt and pants were opened for chest massage, his eyelids fluttered occasionally, and I noticed a cameraman watching it *through* his camera.

Rodale was DOA at the hospital, and when I got upstairs to my dressing room I found I had several objects of his in my hands. Someone must have handed them to me: a watch, some vitamins, a credit card. I had an afterimage of Hammill professionally taking notes in the midst of the ugly scene.

Moments like that seem to overwhelm everything so. I remember thinking I could never do the show again in a light-hearted manner, a feeling I had also had after the assassinations of Bobby Kennedy and Martin Luther King. The next night I opened with a statement about the death, because it had been reported in all the news media, and in the next segment the guests, the audience, and I were all laughing and scratching again.

Hugh Downs and I were once crossing a street in Manhattan, and a cab nearly got us. He said, "The hard thing to take about your own death is how quickly people can adjust to it. The next day at the office someone would say, 'Isn't it too bad about Dick and Hugh? Say, have you had lunch yet?' "

CP: We started out a while ago talking about quality, which has always been a problem for you.

DC: Thanks a lot.

CP: I don't mean achieving it. I mean deciding what level of it to set for yourself. Earl Wilson, of all people, posed the problem in 1970, shortly after you started in the daily late-night slot. He wrote in one of his columns that you ought to try to make a broader appeal to the mass audience, or, as he put it so elegantly, "Dumb it up, Dick." Your response on the air was to promise to bring on a fat Columbia University professor and make him dance by shooting at his feet.

DC: That was an exaggeration, of course. I only intended to use blanks. But you're right, it is a problem, and a perennial one. Is it better to try to reveal something, to expand people's minds? Is that my goal on the program? Or is it to present a variety show? "Neither" and "both" would be equally accurate answers. Leaving aside Earl Wilson, I'm always torn between pleasing those viewers who say they're so grateful to be able to switch away from yakking starlets and the necessity of having the yakking starlets for the ratings. It would be an awful lot easier just not to give a damn. I sometimes wish I had made a clear decision that I was going to be strictly commercial or that I was going to provide a radical alternative. But either would be a false decision. I'm not all that enthralled by show business, and I'm not all that much of a highbrow.

CP: Not that much of a highbrow? You? The talk-show host who has read Henry James? Why, to a great many people out there you are intellectual the way Jack Benny is cheap or Doris Day is chaste.

DC: I have been misperceived as an intellectual. My mind rarely goes from the particular to the general of its own accord, and I sometimes think I am the *least* cerebratious—is that a word?—person I have ever met. I read fiction for the story, go to the movies to see how they come out, and believe that the essential, mystic value of sex is that it feels good. I like to read poetry for what it says to me and have learned to stop a good hundred yards this side of exegesis. If a poem raises a chill on my spine I do not need to trace its imagery patterns to know why. I had enough talk of imagery tracing, tension, ambiguity, and paradox at Yale to tide me over for a lifetime. Who was it who rejected some elaborate intellectual construct that someone had offered as the meaning of his poem by saying, "My poem means what it *says*"?

CP: I think it was Eliot.

DC: Gould?

CP: There, you see? That was an intellectual joke. Why do you protest so much?

DC: I suppose out of residing anger about the amount of trouble it has caused me in a commercial medium where "intellectual" is automatically a dirty word. And once you have been labeled it, you are expected to live up to it. Recently I got a letter from a fan saying, "I finally got my mother to stay up and watch your show because I told her it was the only intellectual show on television, and there you were singing with that appalling Spanish woman [La Lupe] and tearing your shirt off and making a fool of yourself. Well, good-bye forever, Mr. Cavett." Good-bye, dear, and don't let the door bat you in the fanny on the way out.

CP: On the other hand, you don't dumb it up either.

DC: At least not consciously. If I were really angling for mass-audience acceptance, I suppose one good rule would be: don't do a program that requires the viewer's attention. I have a theory that if you ran television for a month without broadcasting the sound—just the same shows with pictures coming from a silent set—there would not be a significant drop-off in viewership. If you've ever been in a room where a set is on but the sound is off, or at a meeting where there is a monitor in the corner turned on but tuned to a test pattern, you know that most eyes are on the screen most of the time. It's eerie. The person talking will make visual contact with the other people in the room, but before his sentence is finished even he is watching the screen.

Television is *made* hard to listen to. The attention given the graphics and the quality of the picture far exceeds that given the script and the sound. Since these things are done on the basis of research by the manufacturer, there was probably a test given somewhere that proved that most people couldn't answer a simple question about something that was said on TV, but could tell you what they saw. People are more likely to say "We got a great picture last night" than "We saw a great picture."

You could easily devise an argument that you reduce your audience in direct ratio to the amount of content, import, substance, or whatever you want to call it, that you put into a show.

Anything that arrests, disturbs, or quickens will cause people to tune in to something more innocuous. It's only a theory, but it may well be true. It is known as the depressing theory.

CP: But you deliberately, and fairly frequently, go against this theory by, say, devoting whole shows to issues like crime, alcoholism, or pornography. And although you once said to Jerry Rubin, on the air, "Politics bores my ass off," that isn't quite true either. Whenever there's a political crisis—the Christmas, 1972, resumption of bombing in Vietnam, for example, or the Indian occupation of Wounded Knee, or the Senate Watergate hearings—I hear you say, "What can I do? How can I put together a show to deal with this?"

DC: It's only natural. If something of world or national importance is going on, how can I not do a show about it? At those times I do think the show performs a real service. Or, less pretentiously, it fills a real need. At those times I have gotten a kind of fan letter that really is gratifying. People who have said, when Robert Kennedy was shot, or when there was the blood bath at Attica, or at various times in the Watergate mess, that they couldn't face the usual TV fare and just wanted to hear somebody, almost anybody, talk about what had happened. They close with a "Thank God for your show last night; I wish it had gone on another two hours." I suppose, if I'm forced to admit I've made a real contribution to television from time to time, it is on those occasions.

To give the network its due, they have recognized the value of such shows, if only because in the main they are in the business of making money, and whenever they can be praised for doing so by selling something of "quality," they welcome it.

Again, I would caution anyone from concluding that my goal at such times is to inform, educate, or enlighten a vast segment of the public because I feel it is MY DUTY to do so when others will not. It is just that I too want to hear good people talk about important things.

CP: So is there also another theory—an encouraging theory? One holding that there is at least a limit to how much you can dwindle your audience by putting import, substance or whatever, into your show?

DC: Something like that. You can, after all, reduce the reasons for watching TV to but two: to be lulled, and to be stimulated. Some people do one sometimes, the other sometimes. Some people do all of one or all of the other. (Am I going to be arrested here and sent to a home for the criminally obvious?) Fred Allen called TV chewing gum for the eyes. Although many people write me after a show and thank me for educating and stimulating them, my guess is that a larger number of people want TV to be a visual Muzak, a mind deadener. More of the masses are in search of an opiate than in search of a stimulant. And I think to the degree that I have succeeded, when I have, it is because of what Marlon Brando complimented me for on the air (some saw it as an insult, but let that pass), that is, being able to balance the sweet, the light, and the escapist stuff with the substantial, the disturbing, and the bitter.

CP: The balance you've struck has brought you generally lower ratings than your competition, and therefore has led to a few actual or threatened cancellations of your show. Is it safe to ask how you feel about ratings?

DC: Actually, I feel that the Nielsen system in general is quite diligent and even fair, in the sense that it is full of disclaimers, which are not taken much cognizance of. For instance: small samplings can be wrong. The Nielsen book contains enough of these caveats to justify folding it up into paper airplanes for the network executives to sail from their high office windows, yet they cling to it with a religiosity that suggests mental imbalance. Despite the extensive margin-of-error warnings, champagne is broken open if a show beats the other networks' shows by a tenth of a percentage point, and gloom spreads if it misses by a tenth. Also, I've spoken to a couple of people in a position to know who have told me of another fallacy in the system. Nielsen gets a high percentage of turn-downs, by people who don't want to be bothered with being a Nielsen family. The number of people approached who do not want it, the kinds of people who would see it as an inconvenience, an invasion of privacy, would also tend to be independent viewers who would prefer a certain type of TV show—that is, a high-quality program as opposed to a roller derby. Consequently there can be a "bend" in the ratings slighting the so-called quality shows.

I've seen people watch the action shows without sound. Whenever there is a chase scene or a fight, their eye is taken by it, they watch it, then continue talking or diddling with their fishing tackle or repairing their hi-fi.

I think this is why I survived at least one near cancellation. There are sponsors aware of this who made themselves known to the network—actual sponsors, the money spenders, who said, "We don't want the big dumb masses idly glomming our commercials. We want a quality audience who hears, sees, and understands. There is almost nowhere in TV for us to go for this audience. Don't dry up one of the few remaining oases."

When a program hits a high point in the ratings and holds there for a time, it is disconcerting to realize that it does so because three or four more Nielsen families are tuning in. But I've never been convinced that those ratings measure my audience, a large segment of which is college students sitting around in dormitories. Much of my mail comes from college kids. On my show I once asked young A. C. Nielsen about that, and he said something about dormitories and such requiring a special measurement that would be very expensive.

The network often admits that I've done a fine job for them, that I've had excellent reviews, and that I've brought prestige to ABC. But they like me best when those capricious three or four extra Nielsen families are on board.

CP: Do you blame the ratings system, with its lowest-common-denominator effect, for the fact that there's so much crap on TV?

DC: Only up to a point, after which it's a little like blaming the barometer for the fact that there's so much bad weather.

It could be that crappy people have put crappy things in because that's the best they were capable of, and that viewers just like the phenomenon of TV—they bought a set and they want it *on*, it takes their mind off things, and they take whatever is put on it, crappy or not. Nobody has ever proved that if better things were on the total number of viewers would drop, that they would say, "I don't like that stuff; put something crappier on."

Then there's the fact that, in most cases, the people who have tried to do quality TV are so pedantic and heavy-handed about it, and make such a point of being serious and lecturing into the camera. That's why a lot of educational TV is just punishment to watch.

Of course it's also a mistake to assume that only the dummies watch the escapist shows. Surely there's a professor at Princeton who comes home and watches *Lucy*, because he's had enough of astrophysics or whatever.

The point is, there should be seventy-five channels of television, where you could watch, among other things, lessons in any language, a man doing card manipulations, a ballet rehearsing, pornographic films, a poker game with cameras behind the players, surgery in progress, home-medical-emergency instruction, a chess game, how to tie knots, live cameras on the main streets of world capitals, lectures from major universities, someone constructing a harpsichord, plays presented by prisoners in Sing Sing, séances, yoga, lessons in juggling, a course in elementary logic, authors reading their works, a Navajo doing sand paintings, birth-control demonstrations, a Yo-Yo champion, World War II newsreels, eggs hatching, nutrition instruction, horses breeding, and, of course, *Lucy, Hawaii Five-O*, and so on.

CP: Do you have anything to say about the effect of TV on America's psyche, consciousness, or national character?

DC: Happily, no.

CP: You're not really comfortable with those orotund, Ford Foundationese questions about our contemporary TV culture, are you?

DC: Something leviathan-sized in me rolls over and goes to sleep whenever I hear the word "culture" used in any but a medical sense. Whenever somebody asks me where I think the future of television lies, or what I think the medium's message is or should be, I feel the old Cosmic Yawn coming on. I am not one for trying to define something as vast as television, and I am uncomfortable in the presence of those who think they can. The definition of TV I feel most at home with would be "Television is what you get when you turn on the set."

That desire to eschew the Big Questions is partly inborn and partly the result of too many experiences with writers of magazine articles who ask, for example, "Do you think the cult following for Mel Brooks's two-thousand-year-old-man record had to do with *where we were in the fifties?*" Depending on my mood, I answer either, "Yes. *I* was in Iowa." Or, as graciously as possible, "I don't think it's a sociohistoric matter. It has to do with Mel Brooks's intrinsic funniness. It would have been just as funny a record if it had come out in the Harding administration." At times I haven't had the sense to give such questions short shrift and have found myself caught up in long, looping sentences I have no idea how I'm going to get out of, and sound as stodgy as a freshman debater who has just learned the phrase "diametrically opposed."

CP: Unanalytical as you say you are, haven't you devoted even a smidgeon of analysis to the curious popularity of your own kind of show on TV, the talk show?

DC: I confess I've caught myself occasionally pondering the oddity of that one. Why should people pay for a machine that will show them people talking when they can get real people to talk to them and can even join in themselves? And do it all without having to see commercials? It goes back to the fact that a talking machine is company; the house is disturbingly quiet with it off. If you add to this the sound of *people* talking there is even more of an illusion of company. There is also, if you are going to listen to what they are saying—by no means a safe assumption—there is also the possibility that they will say something unexpected, startling, shocking. So there is company plus suspense. If they are saying something interesting, informative, entertaining, you have a third element. You now have a companionable, stimulating, arresting entity; that is, if you buy the idea that TV can be any or all of those things.

CP: A writer, Seymour Krim, maintains that the secret of the talk show's appeal is that it seems to humanize those almost mythical beings, celebrities, making them as easy to identify with as the viewer's own family and friends. By the same token, Krim says, the talk show feeds the viewer's fantasy that he himself could enter into the celebrity mythology, having his own overlooked virtues discovered in front of millions of people. Krim stresses that all this is an illusion. The reality, he says, is plugola and insincerity, "a calculated format that makes a sideshow out of truth." Your witness, Mr. Mason.

DC: He's right about a lot of it. As I too have said, a vast part of what passes for sincerity, piety, and good old-fashioned folksiness on these shows is about as authentic as a three-dollar bill, a dancer's smile, or Danny Thomas's humility. Also, the real people discussing matters vital to the heart and soul are there by the grace of manufacturers of hosiery and gargles. If there's a choice of what gets sacrificed, it's always the matters of the heart and soul. I have a dream in which I say to the Messiah, who has appeared and consented to an interview, "I'm sorry to interrupt, Jesus, but we must pause for this last commercial"; or "Perhaps you can come *back* and tell us about the road to salvation. It sounds interesting, but, well, you know, the old clock on the wall . . . (*theme sneaks in, camera already pulling back*). Good night, everybody! Have a nice weekend!"

However, by making such a sweeping generalization Krim

not only risks being full of crap, but succeeds. That is, if he is saying that sincerity is impossible in this format. I have seen moments of devastating sincerity. And, since I recall Krim's article, let me reply to something else in it, which you didn't mention. Krim complains that too many talk-show guests are from the world of show business, even on my show. He asks, "where are . . ." and lists a roster of names from literature, psychiatry, music, art, and so forth. Well, a goodly number of them *had* been on my show at the time Krim's article appeared: Lillian Hellman, Joseph Heller, Jerry Rubin, James Dickey, B. F. Skinner, R. D. Laing, and, to quote Krim, "McLuhan himself." Where, one might ask, was Krim? The defense rests.

CP: Earlier, you mentioned your, shall we say, strained relations with ABC at the start of your morning show's run. I wonder, especially in view of the number of times the network has actually or very nearly bumped you off the air in the years since, how you feel about ABC now.

DC: In an interview I gave once, back in the most frustrating early days, I said, "They haven't been very helpful. No one at the network really knows how to help the show. It's extremely difficult to find anyone at the network who regularly *watches*. Oh, they sometimes know who's been on, but that's usually because they've read about it somewhere. They're always telling me they don't stay up that late."

In those turbulent early days, I remember going to a meeting with a network exec to discuss some problem with the show, and he opened the conversation by announcing how much he had enjoyed the late movie that had been on opposite me the night before. This, plus the fact that on the wall was a picture of him disporting himself with Monty Hall, host of *Let's Make a Deal*, at a company blast on some tropic isle, gave me a sneaking suspicion that perhaps I wasn't his type of guy. A series of such experiences at high levels, and you begin to get a faint whiff of goose cooking.

During this same meeting a call came in. Hanging up, he announced that a station in some city had dropped the show. "Why?" I asked, somewhat stricken, knowing that on ABC's short station line-up every hamlet counted. "Because somebody said 'ass' on last night's show." (This was said during my colloquy with Jerry Rubin about politics.) I asked what is done in such a case, and he said he would call the station in a few minutes and straighten it out. A few hours later, near air time, I called the station management myself. They had not heard from New York, and said that if only someone at ABC would call them with certain simple assurances that the network would be more vigilant about such matters in the future, they would put the show right back on.

I resented the fact that, in the migraine-producing agony of clinging to a cliff with my fingernails, *I* had to make the call to get the show put back on in an important city.

I also quickly learned that I could bring conversations with network executives to an embarrassed halt by innocently referring to something that had happened on my show, naïvely assuming that because it was on their network they might have caught it. This was a bitter pill I didn't know whether to chew or spit out. "Perhaps if you watched the show you might know what to do with it" seemed too obvious a statement to waste good breath on.

CP: In the spring of 1972, during one of your show's periodic teeterings on the brink of extinction, you made a statement on the air about ABC's support—or lack of it—in the areas of advertising, promotion, and publicity. You said, "Has some of the performance of some of the help I'm supposed to get from the network been effective? Yes. And to that I would add, sometimes lazy, inept, and incompetent." Could you amplify on how it has sometimes been lazy, inept, et cetera?

DC: My opinion was that, instead of the network's doing things themselves that would help, they would ask me to do things that were time consuming and robbed me of the energy needed to do the show itself, like asking me to go out and appear at some far-flung station, in order to shake hands with local people in some way that's supposed to help the show. I almost always refused to do it, partly because it seemed to me not *my* job. On the few occasions when I have done these trips, I've gotten so irritated at myself for going that I've been dangerously close to doing or saying something that would make them sorry they asked me. Once I went to Washington, D.C., for the excellent ABC affiliate there, and rode in my first and last parade. I can't tell you how stupid you feel sitting in a convertible, with people snapping you with Instamatics and yelling, "Hey, Dickie," especially when the parade comes to an inexplicable halt, and you sit in one place while the same guy yells, "Hey Dickie," fourteen times in a row, and you have exhausted your repertoire of waves and forced smiles, and a wide-assed lady in Bermuda shorts and curlers holds her runny-nosed little daughter up to kiss your cheek and then musses your hair and says, "What makes you so cute? Go on, autograph my daughter's arm!" Only by muttering, in a W. C. Fieldsian undertone, "I'd be delighted to endorse the little homunculus, and could I entice you, perchance, into fucking yourself?" can you survive such soul-maiming encounters.

At one point in the Washington parade I was deposited on the reviewing stand to take over the announcing chores, reporting on the floats as they went by. Because I made some slighting remarks about a wealthy local who wore a bush jacket and sported a double-barreled shotgun, on a float bedecked with the heads of most of the endangered species he had slaughtered—when he passed I opined as how a ripe tomato would be in order as the proper comment on his offering—I was rather suddenly relieved of my turn at the microphone. By reacting as myself and mouthing a heartfelt opinion, I was not playing the game.

cp: There goes your political future. You've just flunked all the known aptitude tests for campaigning.

DC: I don't want to be mayor of New York anyway, no matter how they try to force the job on me.

CP: Surely some of ABC's efforts have involved promoting the show itself and not just exploiting your personality on a piecemeal local basis.

DC: Surely. Or, rather, not very surely. Once it was agreed that as a gimmick to get some extra promotion money out of the network I would make an effort to do a week or two of extraordinary one-guest shows and air them all in a row. Because promotion machinery involves at times a press conference, a press conference was called. Since a press conference suggests something momentous, there were expectant looks on the faces of the press who were summoned to the Hunt Room of "21" and seated before a table that looked like High Mass was about to be celebrated on it. Was I going to quit with a blast at the network? Was the network going to cancel the show with a blast at me? Was I going to announce that Garbo had agreed to cohost the show for a week? Was the show going to be the first live broadcast from the moon? Had I found Martin Bormann? Was there balm in Gilead?

Behind the table sat an ABC vice-president, an ABC press man, and me. I had traveled several hundred miles for this event, since it fell, as such things invariably will, on my vacation. By some slip-up, the press had been told *as they came in* that I was going to do a series of one-man shows, and therefore wondered what else, besides that, they had been summoned to hear. When it became clear that that was all there was, they became understandably hostile, and I remember bumbling and funfering and trying to make up something while flop sweat formed on my forehead. I don't know why, but for some reason I didn't just say, "Look, fellas and gals, I didn't want to be here today, this so-called press conference wasn't my idea, I'm as mystified as you are as to why the phrase used to describe a meeting of the president and the fourth estate was applied to this pointless little *Kaffeeklatsch*, but apparently someone thought it was appropriate. I'm going to do some one-man shows. It is not a new idea, I have done it before, and I will do it again. That, in a nut's outer covering, is the nugget you were summoned here to marvel at. Why this information was not conveyed to you on the border of a Liechtenstein air-mail stamp, I do not know. I suggest that in order to save what's left of an otherwise stultifying experience we now turn on Mr. ——, the ABC vice-president on my right, and remove his clothing and chase him into the street, for the amusement of ourselves and any passers-by who find themselves stuck, as we are, in the city on this beautiful day."

CP: Does the ABC censor on the premises when you tape a show give you much trouble?

DC: I've usually found him a decent chap. The only trouble is that he occasionally has to act as the spearhead for the network's ridiculous recurrent corporate fear of candid adult conversation. A foolish and therefore appropriate example was the time I did a two-part show on pornography. Both parts were taped the same evening, the first part to be broadcast later that night, the second part to be broadcast the following night. During the first part we got into a discussion of the depiction of oral sex in movies. I asked the guests if they thought oral-genital sex was dirty. In using the phrase "oral-genital sex" I added, parenthetically, "mouth on sex organs." After the taping was over, and five minutes before the taping of the second part was to begin, word came down that the fan had been hit and that "mouth on sex organs" had to go or else the network would not air the show that night. They would substitute something else—presumably an organ interlude. Small joke.

CP: Yes.

DC: Sorry. Anyway, I hit the ceiling. "How the hell am I supposed to even attempt to do an intelligent show every now and then, with this kind of stupidity to wade through?" I screamed at my producer, to no avail, since he was already on my side. I was told the decision was irrevocable. It had already gone to higher authority. Higher on what? I wondered.

I opened the taping of the second part by saying into the camera, "I'm furious . . . ," and telling the whole story, taking care to use the forbidden phrase and thus complicating the matter for the network at least a hundredfold. When the taping was over, I assumed, they would have come to their senses. But no. I was ushered into the censor's presence. He was chain-smoking and perspiring a great deal, as who would not in his position? A sample of the conversation follows.

ME: Why are you taking it out?

CENSOR: Because it was unnecessary. You had already said "oral-genital sex," and there was no reason to add "mouth on sex organs." You had said it once, and there was no reason to say it again.

ME: I said it because the phrase "oral-genital" is not clear to the ear if people are not familiar with it. It sounds like "aural jettable" or "otto general" or something.

CENSOR: Well, it wasn't necessary.

ME: So the new criterion for censorship is not that a thing is dirty, but that it is unnecessary. It wasn't necessary to mention Shirley Temple's name on Monday's show. Why didn't you take that out?

CENSOR: You know what I mean.

ME: If I do, I'd like to hear you say what you mean, because what you said isn't a good enough reason.

CENSOR: It was not necessary to say both "oral-genital" and "mouth on sex organs." One would have been enough.

ME: Then take out "oral-genital" and leave in "mouth on sex organs."

CENSOR: Come on!

ME: Why not? What part is dirty—mouth? Sex organs? On? They mean the same thing. There is no other conceivable interpretation or meaning of "oral" except mouth or of "genital" except sex organs. I merel wanted to make it clear. Is it all right for some viewers to know what we're talking about and not others? Is this discrimination against the less educated?

This went round and round, getting nowhere, until he finally admitted the decision had gone over his head. I asked why we were wasting our time and who was the higher personage. They got him on the phone, and I explained the whole thing and said it was foolish to cut the phrase, that cutting always looks bad and makes it appear that you said something truly foul. I said he could grasp the chance to one-up me by showing that I had misjudged the network; that when my second-part outburst was aired the following night the audience would know that nothing had been cut from the previous night's show.

He said he had already decided. When I tried to get a reason out of him I got double-talk. He said they would make the blip cutting m.o.s.o. out of the first show, but would leave the second show intact. I asked why it was all right to say m.o.s.o. on Wednesdays but not on Tuesdays.

Eventually the reason stated originally was changed to the opinion that m.o.s.o. was in poor taste. I asked why he had switched reasons and opined that because they were scared of the show in general, they tried to demonstrate to the affiliates they had cut *something*. He denied this. He went on to switch reasons two more times and ended by conceding that he simply didn't want to reverse himself. After slamming down the phone with some Shavian parting shot like "Fuck off!" I realized that they were in fact scared, that the man on the other end of the phone had a job in which he was constantly forced to justify unjustifiable behavior in order to satisfy capricious masters.

Incidentally, during the second part of the taping I had asked one of the guests, the legal scholar Alexander Bickel, who happened to be in favor of the Supreme Court's limitations on pornography, what he thought of the network's proposed excision. He said, on the air, that it was foolish, misjudged the issue, misjudged the audience, and was indefensible. I enjoyed getting that into the show. Afterward I overheard that comment being relayed to the higher personage at the other end of the phone. He evidently asked who had said it, for the guy doing the relaying said, "Yes, the *conservative*."

In the end, they did blip the first show and leave the second intact, and another silly censorship flap had wasted a few dozen expensive man-hours as lawyers, tape editors, engineers, producers, censors, higher-ups, and the theater custodian were kept on overtime while it was decided if America could survive hearing the phrase "mouth on sex organs" around midnight. As far as I know, the star-spangled banner still waves.

CP: Even though viewers probably have no idea that so much infighting can lie behind a short little blip, they at least hear the blip; they at least know that some censorship has taken place. But how much censorship is there of the kind that viewers can't see? The kind, in other words, where the network tells you who you must or must not have on the show, or what you can or cannot talk about?

DC: Less than you might suspect. The network has been good about this in the main, with some ludicrous exceptions. I can always guess which things they would rather not have on, but they don't exert pressure, that I'm aware of, in a precensorship way, with the single exception of vetoing in no uncertain terms the appearance of Angela Davis. They were adamant about that and did not care who knew it, and I don't know to this day exactly what mechanism was called into action.

CP: Can you guess?

DC: I tried to find out just who was saying no, and I got one of those bewildering conversations: "Are you personally saying she can't be on?" "No." "Well, then, who is?" "Dick, let's look at this from another angle . . ." Knowing what we have learned from Watergate, I expect the answer was not far to seek. I expect it was someone in Washington, who picked up a phone and said to someone at the network in New York, "We do not want that woman on television in what might be a sympathetic light. Keep her off without implicating us." So it was decided that she must appear with someone guaranteed to oppose her every utterance—an arrangement that she would of course find unacceptable. She canceled, the network was not forced to say flat out that it would not allow her to appear, and everybody was happy. I wish she had consented to appear even under the proposed restriction, but I think that probably fear was involved in her cancellation, since she was daily receiving threats from some people who felt that they should make up for a system of justice that had failed by acquitting her.

CP: The same mechanism—a phone call from Washington —was used when you were forced to have an administration spokesman on the show during the SST debate in 1971, wasn't it?

DC: That was a simple case of the network buckling to White House pressure. In the light of Watergate, I don't think that it would happen again. I had had a number of guests who had spoken against the development of the SST. The most effective was Arthur Godfrey, due to his long-time association with the military and with aviation. He said the plane would be a financial, scientific, and ecological disaster and should go down in flames, which an actual SST did later at a Paris air show.

The White House called someone high at ABC and said, "You will put Mr. William Magruder, director of SST development at the Department of Transportation, on the Cavett show to defend the SST." The White House caller then read an inaccurate list of the SST opponents who had been on the show. I submitted that our record was not *that* unbalanced and came up with two names that the White House listkeeper had forgotten who had spoken in favor of the plane, including one astronaut.

Nevertheless, Magruder appeared. He and I tangled, but he got more time than all the other pro-and-con spokesmen put together. The voluminous mail said that I was too mean to him, that I was too nice to him—the usual bewildering range of opinion. The ironic thing was that a large segment of letter writers said they had been indifferent to the SST issue before, but one look at Magruder had made them sworn enemies of it. There is a lesson here for past and future White Houses.

The episode renewed for me the question of the opinionated host. I have asked in vain to be shown where it states that a TV host should not, must not, and cannot be allowed to give his opinion. I agree in the main that his role is that of conductor of conversation and also arbitrator if necessary, and that it would be better if he kept his nose out. But never?

An example of how perceptive viewers can be. I said, at the conclusion of Magruder's arguments, "Well, I certainly hope the SST bill *is* defeated in Congress." Several hundred viewers wrote in, "It was easy to see which side you were on!" I wonder if I could have made it any easier. Incidentally, when the SST bill was defeated there were stories in the papers headed "White House Blames Cavett Show for Defeat of SST." That can have a decidedly unsettling effect on you when it leaps out at you from your breakfast tray.

CP: Have you ever deliberately used your access to the airwaves to support a pet project or bill or such?

DC: I guess the only cause I've pleaded in that sense has been that of endangered species. There are still women who don't have nimble enough minds to see what's wrong with buying a spotted-fur coat made from some endangered animal, either here or in Europe, "because the animal is already dead anyway." You wouldn't think it would take a trained logician to perceive that this coat, made of maybe eight skins, when removed from the window and sold, is an automatic order for eight more animal skins. One time nine additional animals were placed on the endangered list as a direct result of my confronting Secretary of the Interior Rogers Morton about them on the show. I'm proud of that.

CP: Are hunting and hunters your main targets, so to speak?

DC: Not entirely. Sad to say, certain animals do have to be killed in order for the rest to survive. Many hunters are conscientious and responsible, although how anyone can enjoy seeing a magnificent animal drop and its eyes go dim, in order that he can hang on his den wall the gruesome evidence that he killed it, is beyond me.

The idea that hunting is one against one is ludicrous. It's one animal versus the hunter, the manufacturer of the rifle, the bullet maker, the designer and manufacturer of the telescopic sight, the auto manufacturer who made the car the hunter got to the edge of the wild in, the maker of his waterproof shoes, the various manufacturers of his mittens, glasses, overcoat— and that's only the beginning of the list. The "sportsman" who shoots an animal should then make a speech, like the actor who wins an Oscar does, thanking the multitudes behind the scenes who made this "victory" possible.

Some psychologists say hunting is the sport of the impotent. You can always get your gun up. For some people I'm sure it is, but since the odds in hunting are so unbalanced, I fail to see how it can be considered a manly exercise. The man who bravely faces the ferocious deer, or duck, or even bear, considering the odds, is about as manly and brave as Hitler was in invading Poland.

CP: What if this manly, brave man didn't have a gun to get up?

DC: Just so. Perhaps the single most deplorable abiding scandal in this country is its lack of gun-control laws. Any yahoo who wants to can get a gun and shoot anybody he wants to, as we see daily. The cretinous gun magazines have fought effectively for years, using the argument that gun laws are Communist plots. And they are without pity. In 1973, they tried to bring the *YWCA* to financial ruin because the Y dared to advocate gun laws of the sort every other civilized country in the world has. Ours are those of Dodge City. The gun magazines urged their members to boycott not only the YWCA, but also any lump-sum charity that *included* them. (Kill everybody in sight, while you're at it.) Them are he-men, buddy.

The funniest part, to me, is that the gun organizations, in consistently misinforming their members over the years, have helped convince the less thoughtful among them that if guns were registered, an enemy taking over America would have only to get hold of the registration records in order to locate the armed citizens and annihilate them. It seems never to have occurred to them that those records would be scattered all over the country, whereas the records of the National Rifle Association are all in one convenient place in Washington, D.C. Perhaps the building is mined with a Commie-detecting device.

Say, it's getting windy up here on the soapbox.

cp: Getting back to precensorship for a moment, wasn't there also a case in which the network tried to prevent John and Yoko Lennon from singing a song on the show called "Woman Is the Nigger of the World"?

dc: The show with that song had already been taped, so it was precensorship in the sense that the network wanted to delete it before the tape could be aired the following week. Here the dialogue of the high-level meetings could, with a little rewriting, go right into a satirical revue. Given the vehemence with which this battle was waged, it was apparent that the Department of Measuring Probable Human Behavior at the network had concluded, after some overnight pulse taking of the nation's blacks, that they would march on the network as a body and that Elton Rule, the president, and Leonard Goldenson, the chairman of the board, would look undignified riding out of town on a rail sporting tar and feathers.

The meeting began, as they always do, with a network fellow stating that this was an irrevocable, nonnegotiable decision on their part and with our announcing the same position. Then, while sandwiches were ordered, through tense smiles and through assurances on both sides that everybody could see everybody else's point of view, some sort of soul-mortgaging compromise was sought.

I cannot master the art of not becoming angry in argument, and consequently I come off badly in these things and generally damage my case. I asked why the network anticipated a bad reaction, and an ABC man said, "We talked to eight black employees of ABC, and all of them said they were offended." I replied that the sort of black who would take a network job in which his main duty was to say he was offended at times like this was not a reliable barometer. I asked whether, if I could produce eight blacks who would say they were not offended, this would cancel out his eight network blacks. Would nine? Sixteen mulattoes? This kind of impertinent retort on my part always leads to an impasse during which I am told my argument is not the crux of the matter, and then there is a pause while people try to decide what the crux of the matter is. During this pause, I said that if I were a black I would resent being considered so predictable that a network knows ahead of time what will offend me; that this kind of prediction is reduction to stereotypes.

One of the network men said that his teen-age son was offended by the song (he must have meant the title, since the son couldn't have heard the song yet), and that he was no square. When I asked if he was black there was poorly feigned amusement.

My argument was that a mountain was being anticipated from a molehill, that this was not the last show I would do, that if there was unprecedented negative reaction we had the

machinery to deal with it—the use of later shows, for example—
and why were the people who presumably would be offended
more important than the vast number who might be offended
by deletion of the song? When asked how they would know it
had been deleted, I said that I assumed word would leak out,
and that if it didn't I would help it to.

CP: History records that the song was left in. What happened?

DC: What always happens. A compromise was reached that
made it possible to retain the song and impossible ever to know
what the reaction would have been. I taped a little statement
that was inserted into the show saying that the song was being
included over the objections of some, but, rather than censor it,
we felt that people should get a chance to make up their own
minds, and so on. It was a way out, and a solution I was not
content with, but I agreed to it, because you get to the point
where you just can't spend any more time standing on your
principles when you have other shows to do.

The song played; some were offended by it; most were not.
Many were offended by the imposed disclaimer, presumably
some were not; but after a couple of days there was calm
weather in the network's teapot again, and the heads of ABC
escaped tar-free.

CP: There's no end to it, is there? After hacking your way
through ratings, ABC, and censorship, I suppose the next
tangled thicket you face is the special-interest groups who want
to use your show as a forum, like—well, the National Rifle
Association, or the Indian activists, or Cesar Chavez's grape
pickers.

DC: In a sense, every guest on my show represents a special-
interest group, even the performers.

CP: How so?

DC: One of the quietly accepted immoralities of talk shows

is that in exchange for an appearance by a big-name guest, who will attract viewers and strengthen your ratings, the guest gets to plug his latest project. The moral discomfort experienced by the host varies in proportion to the quality of the project.

Before a Navajo Indian can ask on the air that people so inclined send money to the Navajo Scholarship Fund for the Blind, the network must first check out the charity. I once suggested flippantly that before someone is allowed to plug his movie it should be checked out to see if *it* is a public service or a crime against humanity. The same would be true of comedy record albums, specials, and openings in Las Vegas and the Westbury Music Tent. If, by prevailing community standards, the act, record, or film stank, the plug would be blipped or disallowed.

CP: I'm sure you're not volunteering to do the checking.

DC: Heaven forfend. I think I am the only talk-show host in history who has been sap enough to let himself in for the alleged demand by the star guest that I see his movie. This demand is presented by a PR person as a requisite of the star's appearance, and the demand is usually presented within twenty-four hours of the show. On many occasions I foolishly accepted this, went to a film I didn't really have time to see, usually in a screening room, along with a sandwich and a stale pickle, and, more often than not, later found myself faced with the task of finding *something* nice to say about it.

CP: If it stinks, do you really have to say something nice about it?

DC: I still haven't found a satisfactory answer to that one. Once I tried to be honest, when Lee Marvin came on to plug his latest release. The studio had schlepped the offending spools of celluloid out to where I was spending the weekend prior to the show and actually rented a theater to show it to me. Not only did it spoil the middle of a beautiful day that I wanted to spend horseback riding, but I also had invited eight innocent

people to the screening. In about the first eight minutes, the
film began to exude an odor of dead mackerel. Paul Newman
was up on the screen too, and, as much as I like both Marvin
and Newman, I knew that if I said anything good about the
movie I might lead some poor stiff to lay out hard-earned
pumpernickel to see it. The dialogue on the air went something
like this:

MARVIN: I guess we better talk about *Pocket Money*.

ME: I hear some interesting things about it.

MARVIN: Hear? Didn't you see it?

ME: Was I supposed to?

MARVIN (*shaking head*): They told me you saw it.

ME: Well . . . I did see it.

MARVIN: You didn't like it.

ME: Something like that.

MARVIN: Wonderful.

ME: Does that irritate you?

MARVIN (*convincingly*): Hell, no. That's your privilege. One person likes it, somebody else doesn't. That's what democracy's all
about. (*Laughs*)

Feeling sorry for Marvin, I took refuge in the possibility
that I had seen a bad print, which I based on the fact that the
light had been weird. But Marvin revealed during the commercial that that was the director's notion of how light in the
American Southwest looks. As I say, I have never solved this
problem.

CP: How about the really organized activists and crusaders?

DC: Like the gay libbers? I once got my picture on the
front page of *Gay*, the homosexual newspaper. It was part of a
headline article on how I was the only talk-show host with the

courage to have them on. I wasn't aware it took any. Their first appearance, two men, was dramatic in that one of the guys, a hard-hat, was announcing his gayitude for the first time, wondering aloud if his family was watching. I was more concerned about his colleagues at work and the reception he would get on the morrow. They were quite effective as guests, I thought, reasoned and self-possessed, considering the pressures they must have been under. I did think that they and their companions made a rather excessive show backstage of kissing each other on the mouth.

The usual number of people wrote in saying they had always been fans of the show but that putting these sick, disgusting creatures on had turned them off forever. Many of the letters ended, "Now we know what *you* are, Mr. Cavett, and we are leaving you forever." To borrow from Peter Cook, I thought that "Glad to see the back of you" would have been an appropriate response on my part, but they probably wouldn't have got it.

I must say that "gay" is about the silliest choice of a word for homosexual. How was it picked? The word means "joyous" or "exuberant," and what that has to do with homosexuality is anybody's guess. What are "straight" people to be called then? The "glums"? It follows that the proper word for a bisexual would be something akin to manic-depressive. "Gay" was such a good word before it was appropriated; when read aloud today from literature of the eighteenth and nineteenth century, it gets a laugh.

CP: Didn't you once tell me you had come across references to homosexuality among American Indians?

DC: Yes, and, judging from those few references, the Indians were not uptight about it. They accepted the idea that there was what the Sioux called a woman-man, and, if anything, he was exalted rather than persecuted. At the Fetterman fight, a well-known Sioux transvestite was taken along to the fight, and played an active role in it, because the Sioux felt transvestites brought luck and had a supernatural power of divination. It's believed that some Plains tribes felt that the moon appeared to an adolescent male in a dream and offered him a man's bow or a woman's bridle strap, and would sometimes blur his vision in such a way that he chose the wrong one. Whether or not homosexual acts among warriors were discouraged, I don't know. It may be a neglected area of Indian scholarship.

CP: I don't want to sound like some of those letter writers, but does this fascination of yours stem from, ahem, something in your background?

DC: I grew up in an atmosphere of "If any guy tried to lay a hand on me he'd get a mouthful of bloody teeth," and it was not until later in life that I questioned this. I don't mean this was my parents' attitude—the subject never came up with them —but it was that of my friends, striking a blow for red-blooded manhood and all that. I can think of times in my youth when I reacted in this bravado way toward unexpected advances from another male, and I blush when I think of it. I remember leading one of my mouthful-of-teeth friends through the now usual steps of showing that slugging a homosexual can itself be a homosexual act. He agreed to all of them, yet had to admit, "I can't explain, but I'd just have to hit the guy." I suppose in some cases this might be an admission of somebody's own repressed homosexuality, and although I tend to favor that psychological theory, I also think it is possible that, for some people, it is just fun to hit other people and this is as good an excuse as any.

CP: Don't you think there's a sort of corresponding form of bullying on the part of some militant gay libbers?

DC: In a sense. I think their urging of homosexuals to proclaim their homosexuality loudly from the roof tops not only is a little silly, but also becomes a form of persecution. A great deal of skill and effort may have gone into fooling the public, in certain cases, and the individual may even enjoy wearing the mask of normality, simply for the fun of having a secret or the sheer pleasure of acting. Or maybe he or she simply wants to spare certain friends and relatives the anguish it might cause them to know they have somehow been deceived for years. Why should these people be dragged out of the closet by someone who formerly occupied it with them?

Some homosexuals think that the best thing that could happen would be for a number of people the public thinks are straight to reveal that they are not. I don't think it would have much effect. For example, if either of the pro football players who propositioned me on my show during commercial breaks (I hope Richard Nixon doesn't hear about this) was to confess his secret on the air, in the minds of the bigoted it would merely make him a "fag," rather than make fags more like football players, if you follow me.

Most people don't want to admit that the line between normality and deviation is not readily perceptible. It is somehow important for them to draw the line themselves, somewhat as white liberals draw the line at their daughters marrying a you-know-what.

CP: I suppose it will be the eve of the millennium when every father can say he doesn't care if his daughter marries a black faggot.

DC: No, that will be two days before the millennium. The day before, every father will be able to say he doesn't care if his *son* marries a black faggot.

CP: At several points, you've mentioned the letters that come in from viewers. Could we talk some more about your mail, or have I already heard the best of it?

DC: You haven't even heard the worst of it.

CP: Which is?

DC: Oh, the stuff that seems totally out of touch with the reality of the show, or of me, or, indeed, of anything. You really wonder what could have gone on in the minds of the writers when they were concocting the letters. When my staff sits down to answer the mail much of their time is spent devising replies like the following. I have invented a little, but, believe me, I am not exaggerating.

*Dear Sir, Madame, or Whatever:*
 *Mr. Cavett has asked me to inform you that:*
 *No, he will not be able to fly to Corpus Christi to appear at your daughter's 14th birthday party. Ditto her 15th, 16th, etc.*
 *No, Mr. Cavett will not have his picture taken wearing*

*the T-shirt you enclosed bearing the words "Hiya, Roy & May!"*
*nor will he return it to you at his expense.*

*No, Mr. Cavett does not know what the meaning of life is.*
*Should he suddenly come into possession of this information,*
*he will start a religion at Gardena, California.*

*No, Mr. Cavett will not be able to attend the "Fritter Fes-*
*tival" in your city, nor be crowned "King Fritter" at the outdoor*
*Fritter Fry. He once had an upsetting experience at a fritter*
*festival and would rather forget the entire subject.*

*No, Mr. Cavett does not wish to purchase 1,000 additional*
*copies of your poem, "Step Up and Say Howdy to Jesus," on*
*simulated birch bark.*

*No, Mr. Cavett has not had the time to listen to the two*
*twelve-inch reels of audio tape you sent containing your orig-*
*inal opera on the life of Thomas Edison. Nor does he foresee*
*such a time.*

*No, Mr. Cavett would not desire any further nude photo-*
*graphs of yourself. He is satisfied.*

*No, Mr. Cavett cannot tell you what the answer is to the*
*question "Is there a life after death?" He informs me that he*
*once knew the answer, but forgot it.*

*No, Mr. Cavett does not think your song, "The Jivey*
*Canal," is destined for great success, and suggests you not give*
*up the job at Safeway and come to New York just yet.*

*No, Mr. Cavett has not, as you put it, "humped every chick*
*who appears on the show." Neither will he be able to meet you*
*and your "buddies" when you are in town in November. Mr.*
*Cavett regrets all of this.*

CP: As a couple of those replies suggest, you get a certain
amount of mail from viewers who want to do far more than
meet you.

DC: I do. Sometimes there will be a fairly straight, ordinary,
complimentary letter, which suddenly, in the last paragraph,
says, "Incidentally, I have auburn hair (shoulder-length), jade-

green eyes, and am considered by my husband (and some of his friends, I might add) rather attractive. If you are ever in Peoria (God knows why you would want to come to this god-forsaken place!!) my husband is often off on trips for International Harvester and my number is 774–0876. If a woman answers, don't hang up, it's me. [Here a smiling circle face is drawn.] Well, Dick, I guess I'm only dreaming. But it is some dream. Well, so long and don't lose the phone number. You see, I can't get off this subject. Well, bye."

CP: What was that phone number again?

DC: Hypothetical, is what it was. The real ones are locked away in my safe.

In all this time, I have received only one nude photograph. Perhaps someone on my staff is swiping them. I know other performers get them, and I'm curious to know why I'm not considered the sort to use that particular approach on. I did once get a rather wistful letter from a fellow in a small midwestern town who wanted one of my shoes.

All the proposition mail is sort of touching, actually. It points up the pressure of living in a small town, where frustrations are not easily satisfied and the consequences can be serious, because of gossip. How is the fellow who wanted my footgear going to find another shoe freak in Ottumwa?

CP: Are you ever tempted to answer in kind?

DC: And break up a good pair of shoes?

CP: I mean to the conventional propositions.

DC: Not seriously, but I have had a fantasy about this. Someone could do an amusing comedy about a guy who is on TV who actually looks up the people who write these letters—actually goes to the door in Peoria and says, when the startled housewife answers the bell, "Well, I'm ready." He would take an unannounced journey across the country in an unmarked car, dropping in on people who have written him, not only sex come-ons, but also fan mail, hate mail, long private confessions, and all the rest. It could be called *Guess Who's Coming to Dinner*—or has that title been used? In any case, I do indeed think there is subject matter here for a picaresque novel or movie.

CP: Anybody special in mind as the star or central character?

DC: Modesty forbids. I should stress, though, that this is sheer fantasy. A singer once told me that he gets turned on by the thought of thousands of women writhing on their beds and caressing themselves and pretending the bloke in the sack is really him while he is singing on the bedside TV. I'm happy to report that I have never had this thought in regard to myself. It would be a bit distracting to sit there imagining thousands of women knotting themselves into contortions of lust on their satin sheets while you're saying, "Tell me, Mr. Secretary of Agriculture . . ."

CP: Does hate mail get under your skin?

DC: The real hate mail is merely amusing, because it lays it on so thick, the "You-Commie-nigger-fag-bastard-Jew-kisser!" type; whereas a letter from someone you might like and who is a little disappointed in something you did or said can hurt for days.

It does gripe me when they use the ploy "I wrote the network when they were trying to cancel you, but after last night I am sorry I did." You only get one mistake with these people. Serves them right for thinking I was perfect.

The savagery with which former professed devotees can turn on you is monumental. "I never missed your show for two years, but after *last night* [the use of "last night" always sounds as if I had tried some sexual bestiality on them after a drunken party] I am going to write to every one of your sponsors and, believe me, Mr. Cavit, I have a lot of friends and members of my church group who are going to write too. I don't know if I can swing enough wait [*sic*], but you might just find yourself out of a job." The thought of the ladies' auxiliary sitting around after Bible class penning poisonous notes to the president of Quaker Oats because of me gives me the giggles.

CP: Many of the letters profess a kind of apple piety, don't they? If not religious, then patriotic?

DC: Yes. My favorites are the ones that arrive in envelopes carefully stamped with postage bearing the American flag, whose margins contain handwritten or rubber-stamped slogans like "Register Commies, Not Guns," "We Support the President and Our Boys," "Stamp Out Welfare Chiselers," and such, and which are invariably signed "A Courageous American." No signature. The courageous American does not want to get himself into any trouble.

CP: What about the professionals, who are paid for printing their particular versions of fan letters, hate mail, and so on?

DC: The press?

CP: If you must use that term.

DC: I agree that it's practically meaningless. Any term that applies equally to James Reston, Earl Wilson, Nick Von Hoffman, Bob Considine, Rex Reed, and the TV columnist from Keokuk, Iowa, has to be meaningless. I don't mean that the Keokuk columnist necessarily is the least qualified either. Far from it. Some of the best writing—what you could actually call criticism—has come in from some papers in small towns. Really small towns. By the same token, there are some unbelievable dolts on big-city papers. What I mean is that the press should be knocked only on an individual basis.

CP: Before you begin perpetrating any libel, could you explain what it is about certain journalists that makes you want to knock them? Is it that they give you bad reviews?

CAVETT

DC: No, I'm really not annoyed by bad reviews, unless they're wrong. Factually wrong, or based on wrong criteria or expectations.

One recurrent petty annoyance is when critics don't get something that was meant to be funny and was taken as funny by the audience, and then chastise you for it. For example, "Cavett urged Brando to do the eye-shadow commercial, but the actor refused. 'See, the man has integrity,' cooed Cavett admiringly." No he didn't. He said it jokingly, dumb-ass.

I suppose witlessness on the part of the reviewer is among the most unforgivable sins, from my point of view. The late Dorothy Kilgallen (who, incidentally, got tired of people telling her how funny W. C. Fields was, so she went to see one of his movies and announced in her column, "I was right. He is not funny") once arbitrarily took Johnny Carson and Woody Allen over the coals in a front-page blast for their supposed "bad taste" at a White House function at which they had entertained. Woody was accused of "making heavy racial points" (I think he had used the word "bagel"), and Carson, you would have thought, had at the very least exposed himself to the First Lady. I was furious *for* them, and got at least a vicarious revenge. I wrote a line for Carson that he used on the air: "Having your taste criticized by Dorothy Kilgallen is like having your clothes criticized by Emmett Kelly."

CP: You've even told me that some writers are so petty as to praise your competition in transparent fashion when they're sore that you didn't return their calls.

DC: Yes, and nowhere does that sort of thing happen more than with certain columnist types. These are people who are nice to the last person who fed them. If someone else snubs them, they go out of their way to say something nice about you—and it's all too silly.

CP: Most of the time you get good reviews anyway, sometimes embarrassingly good ones. Does it bother you almost as much to get a fulsome review as a stupid or misinformed one?

To be praised as the moderator of a nightly moral witness, a savior of the Republic, and all that?

DC: No, I love it.

CP: You once went against tradition, the lessons of experience, and the advice of friends and colleagues by writing—for publication—a lengthy and spirited rebuttal to a critic. That was your letter to the New York *Times* replying to a column by John J. O'Connor. I don't want to stir up old arguments, but it seems to me that the exchange between O'Connor and you had enough general import to be worth recapping here.

DC: O'Connor's piece certainly expressed some complaints about me that have been made more than once, by others as well as by him. And in my letter I tried not only to reply to his specific points, but also to sum up some of my basic feelings about critics and criticism. First, here is most of what O'Connor wrote, in the *Times* of January 30, 1973.

*Frequently touted as a prominent yardstick for the "intellectual" content of television, "The Dick Cavett Show" has an almost startling capacity to be depressing. Perhaps 10 commercial breaks in the course of 90 minutes would annihilate any show's pretensions to seriousness. But the problem only begins there. . . .*

*While other TV entertainers are always "on," we have been solemnly told, Mr. Cavett's secret is that he is always "off," always natural and self-effacing, always jes' folks, so to speak. That is nonsense. Mr. Cavett's ingratiating juvenile image is the most adept of its kind since Jackie Coogan tugged national heartstrings as The Kid.*

*Two of the Cavett shows last week featured solo guest turns. One had Laurence Olivier, the other Orson Welles. Both were recorded in London, and both provided fairly typical illustrations of the weaknesses in the Cavett technique.*

*For the Olivier interview, the host was appropriately attired in a dark, formal looking suit. After noting that the British actor had been elevated from Sir to Lord, Mr. Cavett began a running gag on the form of address that might be proper. The actor noted, reasonably enough, that most acquaintances simply called him Larry. But the host remained adamantly awestruck.*

*"We're talking with . . . Larry Olivier," he explained after one commercial break, adding that "if you say it very fast like that it sounds all right." The entire routine was, to use a favorite Cavett adjective, silly. . . .*

*Near the end of the program, Mr. Cavett made a request that came out sounding like "would you lay a liddle Mildon on us?" The actor leaned out of his chair, gazed with puzzlement into the face of his host, and after a slight pause deciphered the message. "A little Milton," he said with undisguised relief. "Oh, yes!"*

*For Mr. Welles, the host returned to a light-colored suit and assured his audience that I "think of him as a sort of bottomless pit of conversation." Mr. Welles meandered about a broad range of subjects, the basic forms consisting less of anecdotes than of yarns, several of them just slightly too tall to be completely believable.*

*He told of the psychic-physical dangers of jet lag, the genius of Houdini, the annoyance of saving acquaintances from suicide, the adventure of living with his father in Peking ("I used to speak a little Mandarin"). Mr. Cavett was predictably awestruck.*

*It was interesting to discover that Mr. Cavett is sticking to those dreary opening monologues, still dotted with numerous, and necessary apologies. He really doesn't like doing them, we have been told, but an entertainment format is an entertainment format.*

*Relatively speaking, of course, Mr. Cavett may be the best of a mediocre lot. In absolute terms, though, his show is depressing.*

Now here, also somewhat abridged, is my letter, which appeared in the Sunday *Times* of February 11, 1973.

*To the Editor:*

*I often ask, and am asked, when should you respond to a critic? The answer is: virtually never. For several reasons. It makes you look like a poor sport, thin-skinned, and one who can't take it. It also calls attention to something that people have either missed or forgotten. Besides, he is a professional critic and writer and you are not. These are all good reasons, as I am undoubtedly about to prove.*

*I refer to a piece by your John J. O'Connor on Jan. 30, which was a belittling review of two programs I did with Laurence Olivier and Orson Welles. I think these were two unusually fine shows, and an avalanche of viewer-response seems to confirm this. (Lest anyone think I feel all my shows are good, I will submit on request a list of my lousy ones.)*

*. . . O'Connor's complaints centered on my clothing on the two shows (a dark suit for Olivier, a light suit for Welles) with no mention of why he felt this information was worth reporting; the number of commercials (after 14 years of commercial-ridden late-night shows, he has noticed this); some byplay he found objectionable about Olivier's many titles (a small attempt on my part to lighten the heavy prestigiousness of the occasion, which Olivier had requested); my seeming "awestruck" at Olivier (which I am) and my saying to him, "Would you lay a little Milton on us?" (a mild levity; see above, re: prestigiousness) which I guess O'Connor felt was not awestruck enough. (I am at a loss to explain his impression that I said "a liddle Mildon," so let that pass. I have applied every test of humor that I know to it, and it comes up negative.) . . .*

*. . . Why pick at nits like these when there is so much more interesting material at hand? It is this sort of pettiness which gives the review the tone of a kind of inept crank letter everyone in TV is familiar with. ("Caught your show about the Nuremberg Trials and you looked silly, and your hair looked funny, and your crack about the Germans fell flat, and . . .") And he complains that my innocent act (didn't know I had one) is the most adept since Jackie Coogan. (A new experience, to be knocked for being adept.)*

*He adds some remarks about my "intellectual" image (a label I have never claimed, wanted, or deserved) and someone's assertion that I am "jes folks" (ditto). He ends up with the pseudo-compliment that I am probably the best of the talk show hosts, but adds that my program profoundly depresses him; an intriguing thought thrown into the last sentence but not elaborated on. . . .*

*I humbly consider a full-length interview with Lord Olivier, the first ever seen in America, a coup. When during that interview Olivier reveals his thoughts about his art, discusses the importance of theater to mankind, gives opinions of living actors, compares the techniques of stage and screen acting as he practices them, reveals*

*his fears and feelings about his own work, his reactions to his bout
with cancer, and throws in an uncanny imitation of Sam Goldwyn,
I feel that all or at least some of that is more worthy of comment
by a critic than what I was wearing. Olivier deserves better. And
future (and present) readers of The Newspaper of Record might
have some curiosity as to what he actually said.*

*As for Welles, if O'Connor knows people who talk more in-
terestingly or entertainingly I would be glad to have a list of them.
His complaint that a flamboyantly entertaining raconteur like
Welles tells what occasionally sound like "tall tales" is a howler.
It's like saying that Niagara Falls seems a little large from certain
angles. . . .*

*Since O'Connor appeared at times to be reviewing my week
. . . I found it odd that he did not mention a lively and gripping
show on Tuesday (on which Barry Goldwater had the novel experience of hearing himself called an ass on television by Lieut. Col.
Anthony B. Herbert) which contained some revelations involving
well-known military figures and which made news on a week already full of it. But that has no place here because I am used to
the show making the news columns of the* Times *(on political news,
drugs, Attica, Kent State, retarded children, war crimes) with no
mention from O'Connor. It is so bloody hard to get anything news-
worthy on TV with the constant pressure to be escapist and show-
biz, that it seems part of a critic's contribution might be to give
credit when it is done. Or at least indicate that he is aware of it.
It would help. . . .*

*A final danger in answering a critic is the tendency to say
something nasty about him to get even. I will not. Suppose for a
moment that I think his prose has all the sparkle of a second mort-
gage. I would be foolish to say so here, because it would not be
relevant.*

*Besides, we performers are vulnerable and sensitive creatures,
wanting affection. I want O'Connor to like me. In hopes that he
will, I am going to send him a list of what I plan to wear in the
upcoming weeks, so he can continue his fashion reporting without
actually tuning in and risking depression.*

CP: Have you ever felt the urge to be a critic yourself?

DC: No, but there are times when I see that the great satisfaction of being an influential one would be the ability to warn the innocent. Only once have I been so offended artistically and every other way by something that I wanted to take pen in hand, if not a blowtorch or a machine gun.

CP: Can you bring yourself to dredge up the loathsome memory and name it?

DC: I can *just* bring myself. The last world premiere of a film I went to—and, if I have anything to say about it, ever will go to—was the black-tie unveiling of *Candy*, a film so egregiously witless, so laboriously atrocious in its attempts at "wild" humor, that I began to ask those near me for a hara-kiri knife, first to slash the screen with, and then anyone connected with it, and ultimately myself, for having remained in my seat to the end. And it was a confirmation of my rule that things you have to wear a tuxedo to are never any fun.

A lot of people walked out, but those who remained infuriated me further by privately mumbling how rotten the picture was while gushing praises to the people connected with it. I was dying for one of these to ask my opinion, but I am unobtrusive, and they apparently failed to see me through the glare from their fixed smiles.

Afterward there was a big freeloading party at the Americana Hotel. The reason I went was my hope that I could somehow find a release from the pressure of wanting to savage the film. The opportunity came when a television interviewer took a mike from table to table; it was assumed that you would beam into the TV camera and say just how much you had adored the flick, returning gratefully to your free Châteaubriand and champagne. I was so excited with anticipation I couldn't eat. When the interviewer, Pat Paulsen, got to me, he asked what I thought the critics would say about *Candy*. I said I didn't think it would be reviewed by the regular critics, that they would have to reconvene the Nuremberg jury to do it justice. He laughed and asked what I *had* liked, and I said I liked the lady who showed me the nearest exit so that I would not be forced to vomit *indoors.*

Over near the TV camera I could see a formerly smiling man, whose face had turned an orchid hue, gesturing violently to Pat with the finger-across-the-throat gesture. Pat moved on chuckling, and I felt a whole lot better. Later I learned I had been cut from the tape.

CP: It's the power of the critic's position, then, that would appeal to you about it?

DC: See here, Smedley, what are you getting at?

CP: Just our old parlor game from Yale days. The one that started from the premise—dubiously attributed to Freud—that all men are driven by a desire for power, fame, wealth, or the love of women. Twenty years ago, we used to choose one or two of the four for ourselves. Now, as a highly paid, well-known, and influential TV performer who gets propositions in the mail every week, would you say that you have the whole package?

DC: If I do, I haven't opened it. I suppose I have some of each, but I am not, as a result, remarkably happier now than I was at any other time in my life. Since I've never found the roots of my ambition, I can't identify my goals with any exactness. When I'm not hungry and don't have a headache and neither of my shoelaces is broken, I'm pretty content.

CP: For the benefit of those of us whose appetite for all four remains unappeased, which would you say is best?

DC: The love of a wealthy, famous, powerful woman.

CP: Have you, in the days of your supposed glory, felt the sting of the saying "Beware of the things you want, for you shall have them"?

DC: Who said that?

CP: I'm not sure. It's been variously attributed to Emerson, Goethe, and Dr. Joyce Brothers. Well?

DC: The answer is yes. When you feel that your hard-bought leisure is used in indulging your worst habits instead of developing the good ones, that you generally waste the opportunities that come with success, and that you squander your talents for momentary gratifications, rather than meaningful long-term satisfactions, yes. When you find that you are dissipating yourself in gluttonous excesses of the flesh, awakening in unfamiliar, cheap water-front hotels wearing a sinister leather-and-plastic garment whose precise function is unknown to you, you wonder if you are being a mature, good citizen. I am speaking, of course, of others.

CP: Do you enjoy the star bit?

DC: I think I like to be treated as a star only in that I insist that the people who work for me do their jobs competently.

CP: But you also feel that talent, whether yours or somebody else's, should get its own way up to the breaking point, don't you? That it's such a valuable and fragile thing that every possible allowance and concession should be made for it?

DC: Yes. Performers are insecure. An incredible amount of coddling, patience, bending over backward, and indulgence to the breaking point is often necessary to get them to deliver that golden egg that only they know how to lay. After a point, if it is a choice of running out of money from employing them or of firing them, then you have to fire them. But they should be the last to go. Directors, agents, producers are a dime a dozen. Well, agents anyway.

CP: Do you like getting special consideration from restaurants, airlines, stores, and so on?

DC: It makes things easier. Whenever I feel momentary

guilt over getting in somewhere ahead of someone who isn't well known, I assuage the feeling by reminding myself that, because of that same fame, I suffer any number of petty annoyances and inconveniences that other people don't have to put up with. Often both elements, good and bad, are there at once. The waiter who gives you extra attention can also become a bore by talking to you longer and more predictably than he would to someone to whom he awards the minimum businesslike service. The salesperson who waits on you before three other people competing for his attention also asks for tickets to your show or for advice on how to get his nephew's rock group an audition. Of course, when an accountant and his wife stand in line for a movie, and then don't get in because a limousine pulls up just before the movie starts and disgorges a celebrity and his party of four, who are let in first, free, it's hard to ask this guy and his wife to reflect on how lucky they are that they don't have to give an interview the following morning to an irritating journalist, or have their picture taken at the opening of a supermarket.

I once asked Jack Benny, on the air, if he liked being famous. He instantly said he did. He likes being taken care of at airports, having his luggage given special attention, and getting a table when officially there aren't any. On the other hand, the critic Diana Trilling wrote, about Marilyn Monroe, that fame has a way of dealing a bad hand to the stars sooner or later—a hand that outweighs the glamour and luxury of their lives. She called it a law of negative compensation.

CP: Whenever I'm with you in public, you seem to have two reactions to being recognized. You love it and you hate it. Does that about sum it up?

DC: About. When I was younger, I was forever saying to celebrities, "It must be irritating to walk into a hotel lobby and hear your name whispered on all sides." I said that because I wished it would happen to me, and I was jealous and eager to hear that it was a big pain. Well, it is and it isn't, depending on the circumstances and style of the recognizer. The good side is that it shows that your work has had an effect, that whatever you have broadcast (in the literal sense of the word) has landed somewhere and taken root.

The worst of it is when someone bullies you for not being totally charming and accessible to him, when you don't know him from Adam and can see no reason to begin a relationship. I mean the person in the restaurant who begins with "I really don't mean to interrupt your dinner, but . . ." At which you want to say, "On the contrary, you obviously *do* want to." Then he finishes his compliment, gets his autograph, grabs your sleeve, and says, "Come on over and join us for a drink." When your excuse is not accepted, he says, "Whatsamatter, are you too good to meet some plain, ordinary people?"

People who work with Bob Hope say that it made him antsy to be in Russia, where he got blank looks from everyone on the street. You never completely lose the desire for recognition, but you feel ashamed when you catch yourself enjoying it.

CP: You once told me that, as a boy in Nebraska, you used to say to yourself, "If I ever become famous, I'll talk to everybody who wants to talk to me. I'll be nice to people; I'll drop in at little houses on side streets, where they don't expect me, and dazzle and thrill them, and that'll be the fun of being famous. I'll stop in at drugstores and sit at counters and give the people a look at me and a little something to talk about." Nobody's childhood visions should be held against him; but the fact is, now that you are famous you don't behave that way, do you? Why not?

DC: I do sometimes, but it is almost always very costly of time and privacy. People want to prolong the relationship beyond practicality, want to call you and write you and visit you and bring their relatives, and then they feel hurt when you have to terminate what seems to them at that moment a richly promising experience. Or they want you to read their play about the childhood of William Dean Howells or an imaginary romance of Rosa Luxemburg's.

There are celebrities (no names, please) who get their kicks in a sick sort of way, inviting the hardware-department clerk home to dinner in Bel Air, going fishing with strangers and dropping in at their humble abodes to boggle the minds of the unsuspecting family ("Hey, guess who I brought home!"), and carrying on rather lengthy relationships with people who are raised to suddenly dizzying heights of vicarious celebrity, only to drop them suddenly, change phone numbers, and then move on to some other unsuspecting person they can befriend, in order to see if their magic effect can work all over again. I suppose this is the *reductio ad absurdum* of the idea of the guy following up on his fan mail. It is a kind of Cinderella-making complex that is sometimes purely sexual, bestowing undreamed-of physical luster on someone who will, rather pathetically, talk about it the rest of his or her life.

It is a curious psychopathology available only to the famous. I suppose the perpetrator tells himself (or herself, as in the case of the famous film actress who has a ding with the meter man) that he owes it to himself to meet some Real People and get in touch with Life As It Is Lived. But there is more condescending narcissism here than charity.

I don't even know if it is always entirely bad for the victim. America is probably full of aging hashhouse waitresses who can tell (or conceal from) their grandchildren that they were screwed by John Barrymore and not only are no worse for the experience, but have gotten a lifelong kick from the memory. But I would guess that in the type of thing I'm talking about there is mainly a cruel letdown.

I know a well-known actor who awards himself intermittently to fat girls who can't get dates easily. I suppose in a way it is unkind, but maybe it isn't. Maybe there are fat girls who exploit movie stars by pretending they can't get dates and take advantage thereby of the star's charitable instincts. I seem to have lost the thread of this.

CP: Let's pick up a new thread—a golden one. Remember the rich friend of ours who dabbled in tap dancing and was so struck by the other people in his dancing class? He was dancing for fun, but they were dancing, as he put it with naïve wonder, in order to get jobs that would pay them money, so they could buy food to put into their mouths. Do you find that you have to remind yourself nowadays that other people can't take money for granted, as you can, that what they do or can't do in their daily lives is conditioned by money? Also, can you let me have ten dollars till next week?

DC: Leaving aside the assumption that anyone can afford to take money for granted, forgetting for the moment the headliners at Vegas, and the major movie stars who have to outfumble you in a cab when it comes time to pay, because they are barely keeping nose above water thanks to a combination of alimony, bad tax problems, and an expensive drug habit—yes, I do find it hard to remember that people have to lead their lives hour by hour with an eye on their pocketbooks. But then, I found it hard to remember that when I *didn't* have any money, too. I would have fifty dollars to live on for two weeks, and buy something that cost forty-eight, and then realize, through slow calculation, that I had only two dollars left. In short, I can't let you have ten dollars. In fact, I was wondering if, maybe . . .

CP: A friend of ours, TV producer Carey Winfrey, has come up with a quotation that he believes is the best one-sentence description of you that anybody could devise. It's from something Malcolm Cowley once wrote about F. Scott Fitzgerald: "It was as if all his novels described a big dance to which he had taken . . . the prettiest girl . . . and as if at the same time he stood outside the ballroom, a little Midwestern boy with his nose to the glass, wondering how much the tickets cost and who paid for the music." Can you see yourself in that?

DC: Yes. As the girl.

CP: Do you want to come around again on that one?

DC: Okay, score one for Winfrey—and for Fitzgerald. I once got into a limousine with Groucho, and as it pulled away from the adoring, envious throng on the sidewalk I thought, "I'm here in the limousine, but I'm also back there on the sidewalk watching the car pull away and wondering what Groucho and Cavett are saying to each other."

CP: Are you basically insecure?

DC: I'll look.

CP: Are you incapable of planning ahead, or just unwilling?

DC: Incapable. I keep having this fantasy that someday I'm going to get up and plan every minute of an entire day. The way I used to outline a study plan at college (8:00–8:25, breakfast; 8:25–8:30, walk to library; 8:30–9:45, study German, and so on). Like the day I plan to spend reading *Dombey and Son* from cover to cover before a fireplace, it never comes. I get partway into making up the schedule, drop the pencil, crawl under the desk to retrieve it, find an old *New Yorker*, which I start reading, and the next thing I know another day has slipped away.

CP: That may be what Woody Allen is talking about when he says the image he gets from you is one of personal serenity. I would say it's a rather ruffled serenity, but I'd agree that it is serenity. Would you?

DC: Sort of. Woody is a work junkie. I envy that in him, and I don't have it at all. Whatever drives him to work, I don't have. I am generally content. Marlon Brando said to me once, when we were talking about how easily people's lives get screwed up, "You don't seem to have anything chasing you." I guess that's right. But tell me that I have a month in which to do nothing, and I can think of a hundred unambitious things that will interest, amuse, and absorb me.

CP: But what do you want to be when you grow up?

DC: A giant Ace bandage. Any more questions?

CP: Just one. Would you buy a copy of this book if you didn't know one or both of the authors?

DC: I think I'd wait for the movie.

DATE DUE